VOICES OF AMERICA

TAHLEQUAH

AND THE CHEROKEE NATION

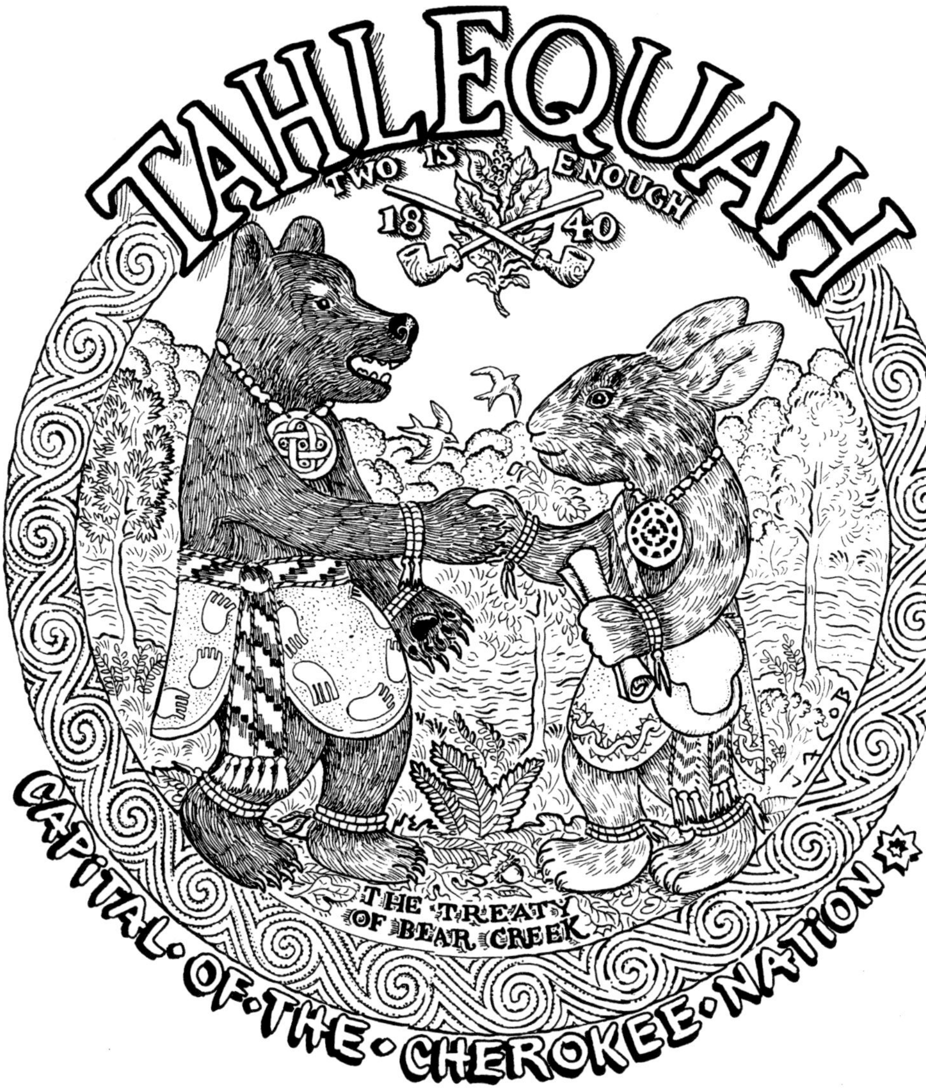

Artwork by Murv Jacob.

VOICES OF AMERICA

TAHLEQUAH

AND THE CHEROKEE NATION

Deborah L. Duvall

ARCADIA PUBLISHING

ISBN 978-0-7385-0782-8

Published by Arcadia Publishing
Charleston, South Carolina

Printed in the United States of America

Library of Congress Catalog Card Number: 00106467

For all general information contact Arcadia Publishing at:
Telephone 843-853-2070
Fax 843-853-0044
E-mail sales@arcadiapublishing.com
For customer service and orders:
Toll-Free 1-888-313-2665

Visit us on the Internet at www.arcadiapublishing.com

DEDICATION

For Nick and Roxanne

Contents

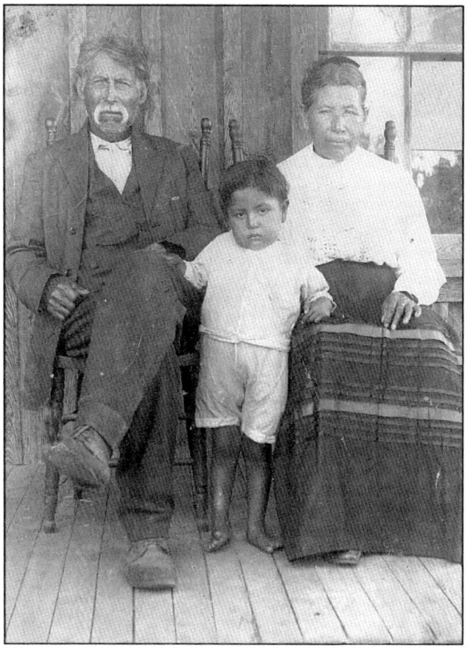

Traditional Cherokees, late 1800s. (Courtesy Cherokee National Archives.)

Acknowledgments

For their generous contributions to this book, I wish to thank the Cherokee National Historical Society, the Cherokee Studies Institute, Rogers State College, Greg Blish, Robert J. Conley, Murv Jacob, Pat Moss, Perry VanBuskirk, Kathy VanBuskirk, Gayle Ross, Marion Hagerstrand, Sioux Nell Smith Vann, Sally Sanders Finch, Roger Dunham, Virginia Vann Perry, Garland Eagle, Brian Corntassel, David L. Vann, Sequoyah Rogers, Paul Ridenour, Leon Corntassel, Larry McAlister, Jr., Barbara McAlister, Talmadge Davis, Loretta Dunham, Carl Barnes, Wayne Mitchell, Ralph Dunham, Neicey Dunham, Nick Duvall, Joel Mayes Finch, Charlotte Carstens, John D. Loudermilk, Bob Rucker, and the Cherokee Honor Society.

D.L. Duvall

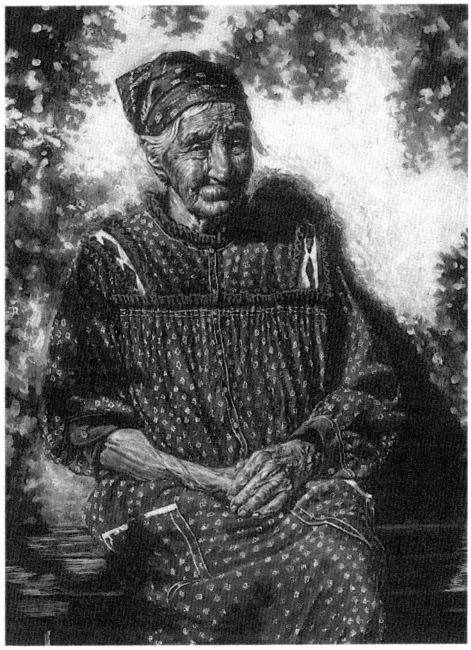

"Quiet Dignity—My Grandma."
(Artwork by Talmadge Davis.)

INTRODUCTION

Within these pages are stories, some handed down for centuries, that capture a part of the history, color, and humor of the great Cherokee Nation, from the days of legend to modern times. Some contain historic facts and detail dramatic events of the past, while others awaken memories of carefree childhood days. Some reveal wonderful secrets, which even the skeptics among us will want to believe.

Those who contributed these stories and memories reflect a broad cross section of the people who have lived and worked here for decades. They range in age from 20 to nearly 90, and come from a variety of backgrounds. Their lifestyles and views may differ, but one thing they all have in common is a deep love of their homeland, the Cherokee Nation.

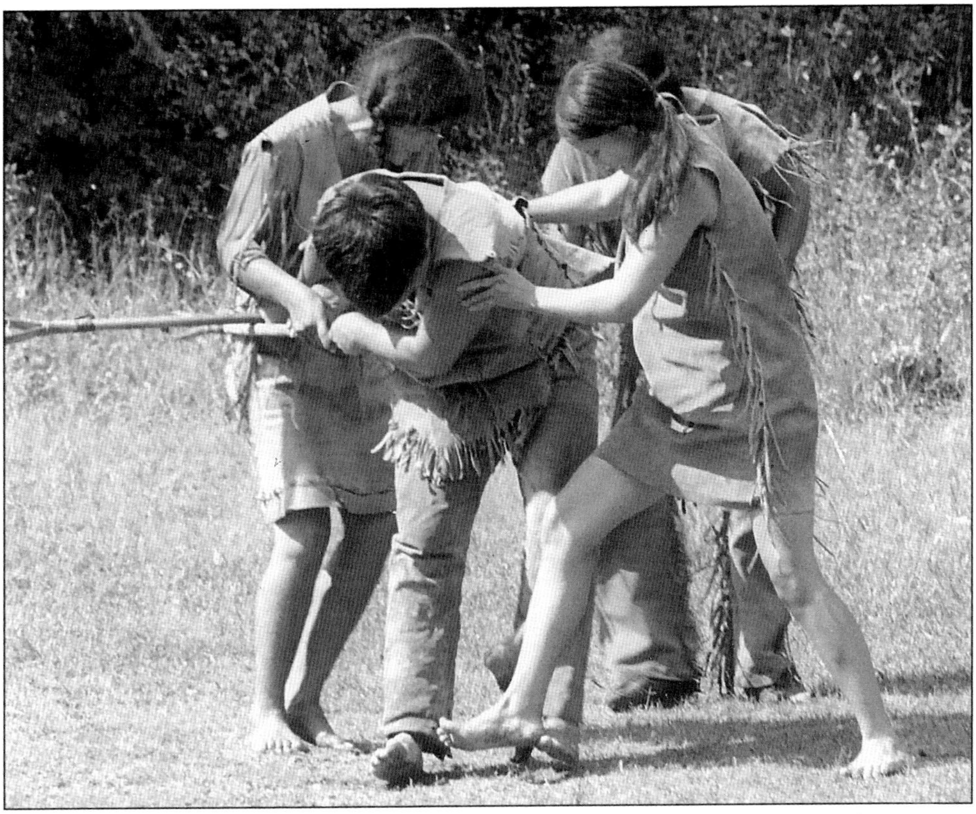

The Ancient Game of Stickball, c. 1970. (Courtesy Cherokee National Archives.)

CHAPTER 1

THE CHEROKEES

Cherokees live and prosper in every corner of the world. Their achievements in business, science, and the arts are testaments to the resilience and courage of their ancestors. Since the days of Jefferson and Jackson, the tribe has endured atrocities that would never be tolerated in today's society. But the Cherokees did not disappear. Counting only enrolled members, theirs is now the second largest tribe of Indians in the United States.

The Cherokee Nation is made up of 14 counties in the lush hills, valleys, and prairie lands of northeastern Oklahoma. The capital city of Tahlequah is centrally located in Cherokee County. Here officials of the tribe direct the executive, legislative, and judicial branches of Cherokee government in modern, efficient facilities.

The years spanning Indian territory days and the coming of statehood are but a brief episode in the colorful history of the Cherokees. Theirs is a rich tradition of remembrance, preserved and passed down through centuries to each new generation since the days of legend.

The Mother Town

Recently, Cherokees reacquired the land believed to be the site of the original mother town. All future Cherokee villages and settlements in the southeast sprang from this town called Keetoowah.

Before the tribe bought it back, the land had been farmed for years. One day the owner said to her husband, "We're not going to plant here anymore. This should belong to the Cherokees."

Once Tommy Belt took Robert Conley out to visit the site. Even after being subjected to years of plowing, the temple mound was still visible. Robert says it was an unforgettable and powerful experience to stand there. "This is it," Tommy told him. "Where we all came from."

Robert J. Conley

Ancient Cherokee Warriors

Since their history began, the early Cherokees were continuously at war with one neighboring tribe or another, particularly the Senecas, Catawbas, Delawares, and Creeks. Likewise, they had allies among their neighbors. The act of war was one of ritual, with established ceremonies and rules of conduct. A favorite pastime for young men in those days was to abduct young women from a neighboring village. Such behavior was almost always answered with a battle, another favorite pastime.

A delegation would be sent to the offending village to issue a challenge of war. A location for the match was selected, and a date and time were set for the meeting. Fighting took place in a clearing fairly close to town so that the wounded could be carried home easily. Villages were not attacked, assuring the safety of the women, children, elders, and their homes.

Those who fought in wars relished the experience. Men had a choice of whether to fight or not, and those who did could gain honor and prestige within the tribe. An additional honor was given to the warrior chosen to be the War Dance Leader. Carved into the forehead of the red mask he wore was the emblem of a rattlesnake. He began his dance alone, shaking his rattle around the fire, and those warriors who wished to participate in the fighting joined in.

When the day arrived, the warriors carried their weapons of war, knives and lances made of wood and stone, to the battle ground. Their hunting bows and arrows were of no use to them in hand-to-hand combat. The fighting lasted for a set amount of time, and then it would simply stop. Those killed or wounded were carried home and the battle was over, sometimes with no decisive winner. Victorious or not, the returning warriors celebrated the battle with another big dance and a huge feast. A similar celebration took place in the opposing camp.

Delaware artist and historic researcher Don Secondine states that ancient warriors of his tribe became totally obsessed with the excitement of war. They were constantly going off to fight one tribe or another, until finally the Delaware women decided to put a stop to their antics. The women would find out the location for a proposed battle. When the warriors arrived at the field, they found all their women there, sitting right in the middle of it. After several such protests, the men settled down for a time.

The Cherokees were known throughout the southeast as fierce fighters, and ritualized combat was an essential element of their culture. They continued to perform the Scalp Dance until the early 1800s.

Murv Jacob

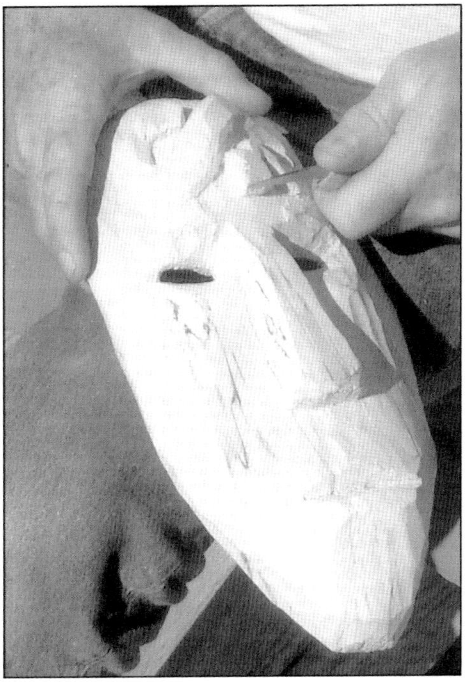

War Dance Mask. (Carving by Murv Jacob. Photo by Edison Stinson.)

The Little Mountain People

In his "Legends and Folklore of the Cherokees," Dub West includes a story of giants who once visited the Cherokees in their southeastern homeland. They came from far away in the direction of the setting sun. The giants were twice as tall as normal people, and their eyes were set in a slant. Cherokees called them the "slant-eyed people." They stayed for a time with the Cherokees, where they were treated as friends. Then the giants returned to their home in the West.

There was another story of a race of people who were living in the Smokey Mountains when the Cherokees first arrived there. These people were very small, frail, and meek, with pale skin. Migrating birds of a certain kind would come to the mountains once every year and attack the little people. The tribe would see the bird feathers blowing in the wind, and know that they were coming. They would hide from the birds in caves until they went away. The Cherokees felt sorry for the pale people, but were unable to do anything about the birds, which came by the thousands.

After the Cherokees had lived in the area for a few years, the pale people moved away, never to return. The story has come down through many generations that the little people left because they were somehow offended by the Cherokees.

Pat Moss

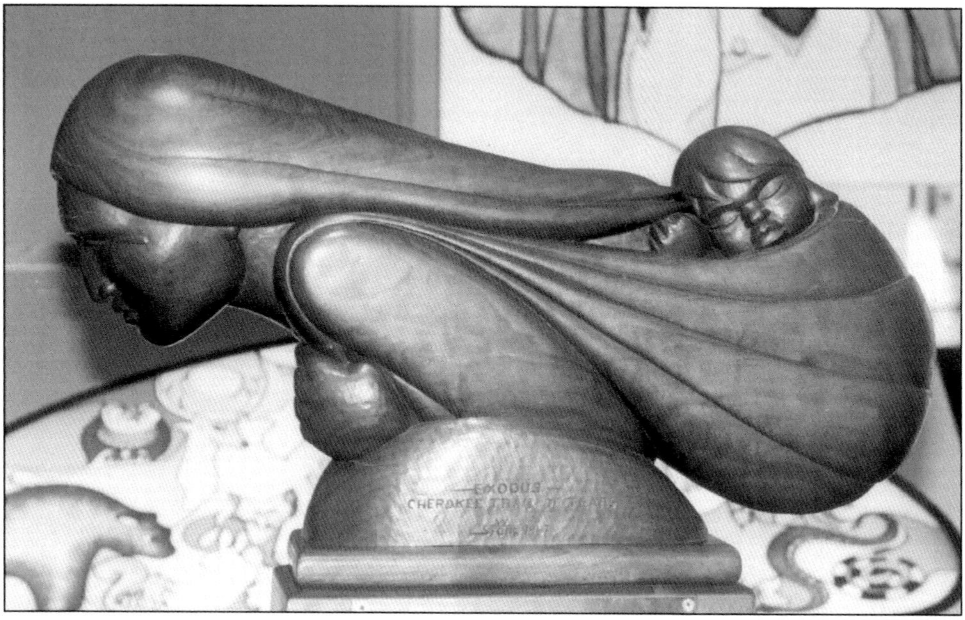

Willard Stone's "Exodus," Tribute to the Trail of Tears. (Courtesy Cherokee National Archives.)

When Women Sing

The following are two examples of the few times when women joined in the ceremonial singing of songs and prayers.

In the southeast, when the autumn stickball games took place, the Cherokees had a dance that lasted until sunrise. All the people involved in the dance performed certain ceremonies through the night. The players' ball sticks were placed up on a rack, held up by four poles. At least four times before daylight, the Cherokee women would stand by the ball sticks and sing the ball stick song. The Cherokees stopped the practice of the ball dance after the Trail of Tears. The Creek Indians still perform the full stickball ceremony, and often they will include the old Cherokee ball dance songs in their preparations.

At one point in the Cherokee stomp dance, the line of dancers leaves the Fire and forms a tight circle around the stickball pole. The dancing ceases, and all the people, including the women, sing a most sacred song. It sounds almost like gospel music. This is supposed to be the first prayer ever sung, the "primordial prayer." The meaning of its words have been lost in antiquity.

Pat Moss

Women and Song

In the traditional Cherokee religion, a stomp dance leader sings phrases of the sacred songs, which are then echoed by other men as they dance around the Fire. The women wear turtle shell shackles and keep rhythm for the dancers. Many of these women know the words to the old songs, but tradition does not allow them to sing. However, there is some mention in very ancient history of prayers being sung by women.

Those who have participated in the stomp dance can understand how all people might have the urge to join in the song. Perhaps part of the attraction to Christianity of the early Cherokees was the opportunity for women to join in the singing of hymns, as they so joyfully do today.

Murv Jacob

Living Sacrifice

Cecil Dick spent his life studying and painting the ancient Cherokee culture. One day Cecil and Robert Conley were standing on the back steps of the old Cherokee Capitol. Leaning against the porch rails and looking off in the distance, Cecil said, "A long time ago, the Cherokees used to practice human sacrifice. Then they went to chickens. They don't even do that today."

Cecil told his student Murv Jacob that in ancient times the people gave human blood to the Sacred Fire. Then the Christians came along, telling them that this was wrong, so they began to sacrifice dogs, and then chickens. The practice continued into the 1900s, and Conley said that photographs still exist showing the people on the ceremonial grounds holding sacrificial chickens.

Robert J. Conley

Cherokee Flute Players

Contemporary Cherokee flute players originated when Dick West and Woody Crumbo were teaching art at Bacone College in Muskogee. They were initiated into the Kiowa Flute Society. They taught their art students, some of whom were Cherokee, to make and play the Kiowa style flute. Years later, Cherokee musicians like Tommy Wildcat and Choogie Kingfisher continue to revive this ancient art form.

In ancient Cherokee tradition, the flute was used as a formal instrument on special occasions. In those days, Cherokees traveled only by foot or in canoes, some being huge crafts that held up to 50 people. When dignitaries went to call on neighboring villages to make offers of peace, challenge them to a game of stickball, or for any important reason, they marched into the village on foot. Leading the procession were the flute players. Imagine what a sight that was, with the Indians dressed in their finery, being heralded into town with the music of Cherokee flutes.

Murv Jacob

Music of Love

Traditionalist Perry VanBuskirk says that the ancient Cherokees had a high regard for musical talent. A young man who could play the flute well was considered a good match for a daughter. The best flute players would likely be good providers as well.

When a Cherokee girl came of age, the young men of the village would hide in the woods and play their flutes. She walked among them until she heard the flute song she liked best. The player of that song became her mate.

Perry VanBuskirk

Pluck it Out

When white men first laid eyes on the ancient Cherokees, they thought them almost hairless. The Indian men and women considered hair growing on their skin to be most unsightly. They used clam shells with both halves intact like tweezers to pull out all their body hair.

Cherokee men plucked the hair from the sides and front of their heads. The top crown was left to grow long, and it was tied in an actual knot, forming their "topknot." It was much more expedient for the sides of the head to be smooth when a man ran through tree branches and undergrowth hunting game. Hair on the head also interfered with the drawing of the bow. When the Shawnees captured Daniel Boone, they plucked out most of his hair, and it never grew right again.

The Cherokees tattooed both the sides of the head and the body with geometric designs. Tattoos helped to camouflage the hunters in the woods. Ink was made from very black charcoal mixed with water and was forced into the skin with sharp fish bones.

Maidens wore their hair down, long and straight, but the married women drew theirs into a knot or bun at the back of the neck. This practice kept their long tresses from interfering with their work.

Murv Jacob

Adoption of Whites

Before Europeans made their way to the New World, there was not any knowledge of being "Indian." Prisoners of war were often taken into tribes and either kept as slaves or adopted as part of the clan, or family. The same held true when the Native Americans began to capture white prisoners. Cherokee law allowed a person to claim whatever captive they might choose as either slave or family member.

Captors might offer their "slave" to a family in mourning as a replacement for the lost loved one. Payment for the individual was collected from all the family and relatives. According to ritual, the seller would have to carry all the items taken as payment for the slave until the collection was complete. If the seller were to lay the merchandise down, then the first person to touch it had claim to it.

Once adopted, the new family member had all the rights and privileges of the Cherokees, and essentially became one of them. This included protection and blood vengeance from the entire clan. Thus, if an adopted white man were murdered, his killer was at the mercy of his clan. But a slave not fortunate enough to be adopted could be killed by anyone with no recourse.

A white man was sometimes adopted as a brother, often to replace one lost to war. This was a powerful relationship to obtain in a clan, as all members of about the same age were considered brothers.

The Nighthawk Society of Keetoowahs

An old interpretation describes "Keetoowah" as a traditional, full-blooded Cherokee. According to oral history, Keetoowahs were organized in pre-Columbian times, and may even be traced to the Ani-Kutani, or the Medicine Society. The White Path Rebellion of 1828 was thought to be a Keetoowah movement. Those individuals wanted to abolish the new Cherokee constitution and return to the old, traditional ways. In 1859, and later during the Civil War, the Reverend Evan Jones reestablished the Keetoowahs to fight for the Union's cause as abolitionists.

On July 19, 1850, Pig Smith, a full-blood and his wife, a half-German of the Wolf Clan, were traveling from their old settler home in Arkansas to the Cherokee Nation. Just as they crossed the Arkansas River into Indian Territory, Redbird Smith was born. He was to become the beloved leader of the Nighthawk Keetoowahs.

Redbird obtained his training near Notchee Town in the Illinois District of the Cherokee Nation. There the Cherokees, Natchez, and Creeks practiced their traditional beliefs. After the Civil War, the Keetoowahs held a meeting in the Saline District. Elders with

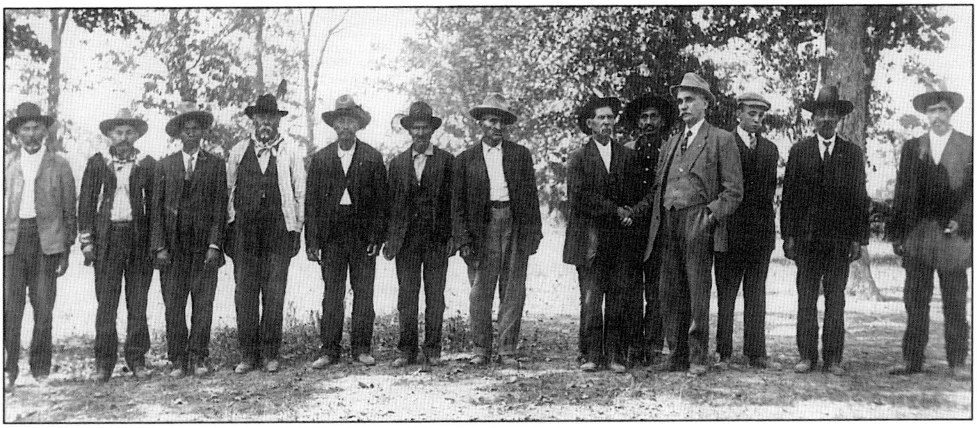

Nighthawk Keetoowahs, Early 1900s. (Courtesy Cherokee National Archives.)

the gift of vision foresaw that Redbird would one day lead the Keetoowahs. His father, Pig Smith, chose the Natchez traditionalist Creek Sam to guide and teach his young son.

The Natchez Indians were nearly destroyed by the French over 100 years before the Trail of Tears. They were considered the most authentic temple mound culture to have survived, and many of the Natchez refugees lived with the Cherokees since that time. It is said that the Sacred Fire now tended by Keetoowahs came from a Natchez/Cherokee settlement in North Carolina. The Fire was ceremoniously brought west by Creek Sam's family during the move to Indian Territory.

Following the Civil War's devastation, the Keetoowahs were reorganized again in 1874 by Bud Gritts, a Baptist minister. The constitution was amended in 1879 to allow the organization to be both religious and political. The Keetoowahs continued to meet in a secluded part of the Illinois district, and Redbird Smith went there as a young man. He married Lucie Fields, daughter of Cherokee Attorney General Richard Fields. Lucie gave birth to eight sons and two daughters. The Smith family settled on Blackgum Mountain and in 1890, Redbird Smith was elected to lead the Keetoowahs. In 1896, the first stomp dance was held at the Redbird Smith grounds.

According to legend, seven of the wisest men of the tribe fasted and prayed for seven days and nights on the highest mountain top, asking for guidance. On the seventh night, they were shown the pathway to righteousness, and were told by Spirit, "You shall be Keetoowah."

Stoke's Stomp Grounds

Participants in modern Cherokee festivals and stomp dances will likely travel to the Stoke's grounds in the southern Cherokee Nation. The establishment of this sacred spot was not done without controversy.

Stoke Smith, son of Redbird, is said to have sold his portion of Redbird's 360-acre allotment to his siblings, moving 18 miles away to his wife's land. He took along a portion of the Sacred Fire and started another Fire at his new home. Some in the Nighthawk Society said that the move violated the Keetoowah constitution, and that moving a part of the Fire was illegal since it could only be moved in its entirety. The stickball pole was also taken to the new site, along with precious wampum belts, which were sacred ceremonial objects.

The wampum belts and other sacred items are brought out to be viewed each year on July 19, Redbird Smith's birthday. Tradition says that Redbird interpreted the meaning of patterns and symbols woven into the belts. This information was used to set guidelines and policies for the Keetoowahs.

Some say that Redbird Smith envisioned a time when the Christian Cherokees and the traditionalists would have a meeting of the minds and come together again. However, his son Stoke hoped never to taint the old religion in any way.

The Wampum Belts

Gayle Ross, a direct descendant of Principal Chief John Ross, says that the wampum belts were brought to the Cherokees in the 1760s by the Senecas. The two tribes had gone up and down the War Trail fighting each other for centuries. The belts were an offering of eternal peace, and were carried by the Senecas to the only Cherokee village they could safely enter. Tradition has it that the peace party was mistakenly heading for a hostile village, where they would have surely been killed. A Cherokee woman intercepted them first and sent the party in the right direction. The symbols woven into the belts are said to contain the terms of the peace agreement decreed by the Senecas.

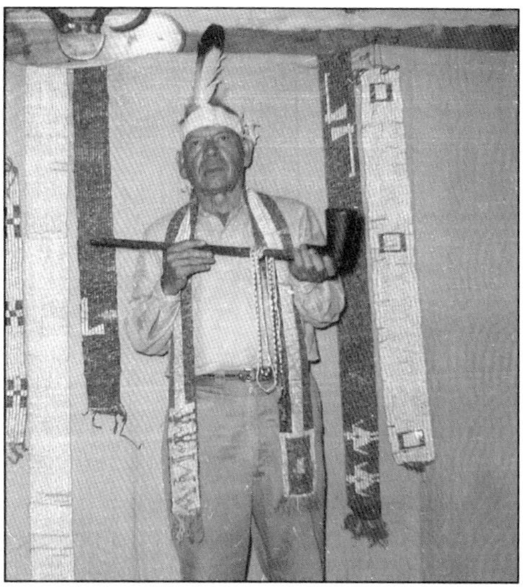

Sacred Wampum Belts, 1959. (Courtesy Cherokee National Archives.)

The belts were handed down through Cherokee chiefs to Principal Chief John Ross. Upon his death, they went to his son, Allen Ross, who passed them on to Robert Bruce Ross, who eventually transferred them to Redbird Smith. There are seven belts now in the custody of Stoke Smith's family, although originally there were eight. The eighth one was stolen and possibly sold to the Smithsonian Institute.

Gayle Ross

About Bows

Scott Rackliff was a special man who mastered the traditional art of bow making. He passed the skill on to his nephew, Perry VanBuskirk, who spent hours with Scott just watching him work.

The section of wood used to make a bow must be straight, strong, and pliable. When cutting, Perry selects one growth ring and follows it, never getting off that ring, even if it bends and goes around knots in the wood. This method insures that the bow will not break when bent.

The wood must also be straightened. Perry uses steam to soften the wood, then his hands to straighten it. He was surprised when he asked Scott to show him his straightening methods. Scott took the section of wood and placed it in the fork of a tree. With his powerful arms and shoulders he twisted and pulled at the wood until it was perfectly straight and ready to be made into a traditional bow.

Perry VanBuskirk

Gifts from the Little People

Sioux Smith Vann was sitting on the porch steps talking with her dad, Julius Smith, who told her this story. Julius always taught his children that whenever they find a feather on the ground they should keep it. When Julius was a child, he was not able to go to school very often because he was needed at home. On the days when he did go, he was instructed to bring along something (an object, paper, or a story) to share with the class.

One morning he started to the school, but could not find a single thing of interest to take with him. He was walking down the drive from his house to the road when something caught his eye. There before him, lying in the wagon tracks of the drive, he found an arrowhead and an eagle feather. He said the "little people" had brought him the two gifts to share with his friends.

Sioux Nell Smith Vann

The Eagle Dance

All of the ceremonial dances of Cherokee tradition usually took place around the Sacred Fire. In the cold winter months, a dance might be held indoors. During those times a corn grinding stone could be used to represent the Fire. Corn was essential to life, and the grinding stone was considered a sacred item.

There are certain songs and prayers that are meant to be sung only in summer or only in winter, particularly the songs of the Eagle Dance. This dance is performed by one person only. The dancer holds an eagle feather fan made of two sourwood sticks bound together,where one is straight and the other is curved, for use as a handle.

The eagle feathers are tied by a medicine man to the straight stick. The curved stick is held in the hand of the dancer. As such, the dancer can use the fan without touching the feathers. Eagle feathers are so sacred to the Cherokees that most traditional people do not wish to touch one. When used in the Eagle Dance, the feathers are under the care of a medicine man, who hands the fan to the dancer. Afterward, the sacred feathers are returned to him. The Eagle Dance is only performed in winter, because of the power of the songs. If the songs were to be sung in the summer, the snakes might hear them and learn them, and become twice as powerful as they are now.

Murv Jacob

Origin of the Quail Dance

The Quail Dance originated as a fall ceremony. Ages ago the land suffered a great famine. There was no harvest of fruit and nuts, and the people and animals were nearing starvation. Some men from the village went out and fasted for four days and four nights. One had a dream that a big group of quail was gathered at a place not far from the village. The men then assembled the people and took them to the place where the birds were supposed to be. There they found the quail, just as the dream had predicted.

The people joined hands and made a big circle surrounding the quail, gradually moving the circle toward their village, herding the quail along with them. All parts of the quail were used. Their meat fed the hungry people. The oil was rendered and used as a hair dressing and skin ointment, and burned for light. The quail allowed the people to survive until the world was again green and fruitful.

Since then, the dance has been used to

remind every generation of how, when the Cherokees were without hope, the Creator gave them what they must have to survive.

Pat Moss

Cherokee Booger Dance

Traditional Cherokees often conducted dances indoors at someone's home. These took place at night in the winter months. The Booger Dance was an integral and much anticipated part of the night's entertainment. At a certain point in the evening, a predetermined number of the male guests would leave the party. Their departure started talk among the guests about the boogers, bringing on an air of excitement and agitation.

When the men returned, they came as ghosts of the old invaders of the

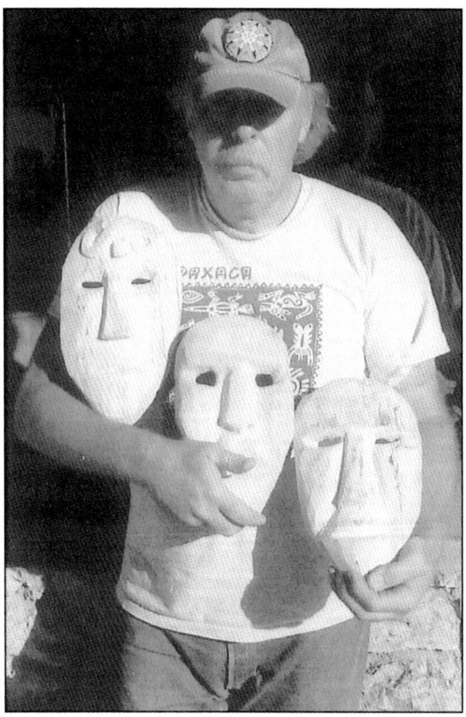

Carved Dance Masks, 2000. (Carvings by Murv Jacob. Photo by Edison Stinson.)

tribe, wrapped in blankets and wearing masks. The masks, made of buckeye wood and decorated with paints and assorted furs, might portray the faces of whites, blacks, asians, or enemy Indian tribes. Some masks were painted with smallpox sores or red measle spots to represent the diseases that "invaded" the Cherokees over the years.

The booger dancers spoke only in whispers to the host of the dance, who could then tell the onlookers what they said. They acted rude and argumentative, pretending to be drunk. They danced in a circle around the center of the room, and sometimes broke free to chase young women into corners, wielding dried gourds in a phallic manner. The girls pretended to be horrified at their antics. In the second stage of the dance, women joined the circle of booger dancers, stepping in between the men. Then the boogers left, and the other dances, such as the buffalo or the pigeon dance, resumed. The booger dance was a source of entertainment and pleasure, and was sometimes prescribed as a cure for illness.

Murv Jacob

The Friendship Dance

Cherokee Master Artist Cecil Dick once attended a Friendship Dance near Salina, Oklahoma in the 1920s. He described it as a formal event in which couples dance together, side by side in a circle. It is also called a "fondling" dance. The dance takes place in several stages. First, the couples go around side by side holding hands. Next, their forearms are crossed, so that both hands are clasped. Then the dancers have their arms around each other. The circle grows tighter, and the men may touch the women's breasts. As the dance continues, the touching grows more intimate.

The Friendship Dance is a very

old tradition that was not performed around outsiders. It was intended as a joyous celebration of good-natured and humorous eroticism. Cecil once painted a version of the Friendship Dance, which was purchased by Rennard Strickland. It was later donated to the Heard Museum in Phoenix, Arizona.

Murv Jacob

High Water Hospitality

It was spring and graduation time at the Male Seminary in Tahlequah. Little Sam and Florence Mayes planned to attend the ceremony and watch their relative, Lindsey Mayes, receive his diploma. They were traveling with all the children from their ranch near Pryor, a trip that would take an entire day in their wagon.

As is typical in northeast Oklahoma, a spring storm came up dumping several inches of rain in a short time. The wagon reached the bank of a creek swollen with flood water and could go no further. Soon another family arrived in their wagon and was stranded there as well.

The travelers were rescued by a full-blood Cherokee who invited them all to his home. Although the house was a simple lean-to consisting of only two rooms, the family made room for their guests to spend the night. All the women and girls stayed in one room, and the men and boys in the other.

The next morning the Cherokee woman cleaned several chickens and fried them up for her visitors. The creek had gone down overnight and the Mayes family went on to Tahlequah. They missed the graduation, but had an enjoyable visit anyway, thanks to the hospitality of their new found friends.

Sally Sanders Finch

Life at the Seminary

Devon Miheusah, in "Cultivating the Rosebuds," describes the daily activities of the young Cherokee girls who attended the Cherokee Female Seminary before statehood. About every two weeks, the teachers would take the girls to downtown Tahlequah for recreation and shopping. They might visit the opera house or one of several art galleries in town. Tahlequah had an ice cream "saloon" and a skating rink.

The girls spent their leisure time playing basketball and tennis, sitting beside the Big Spring that flowed through the campus, or just walking in the woods around the school. The Illinois River runs three miles east of the Seminary, and on Saturdays the girls often walked there and back. A student there, Eva Dameron, said that once the girls even tried to play football, but were so badly bruised that they gave it up.

At the Seminary, Friday was called "Sweet Friday" by the students because that was the day of the weekly spelling bee, and the girls loved nothing better. Once each semester, they invited their friends from town to attend an elaborate dinner at the school. The Seminary also put on an annual play at Tahlequah's Opera House. Graduation was a big event for the entire Cherokee Nation. The ceremonies lasted a full week and even included steamboat rides on the Illinois River.

Discipline was given in the form of demerits. As little as one demerit a week could cause a student to lose such privileges as visits home on weekends or shopping trips in town. Some of the punishable offenses were tardiness, passing notes, writing on walls, whispering during study hour, or keeping the lights on after 9:00 P.M. In 1907, several girls were suspended for meeting a group of boys in the seven acre pasture near the school.

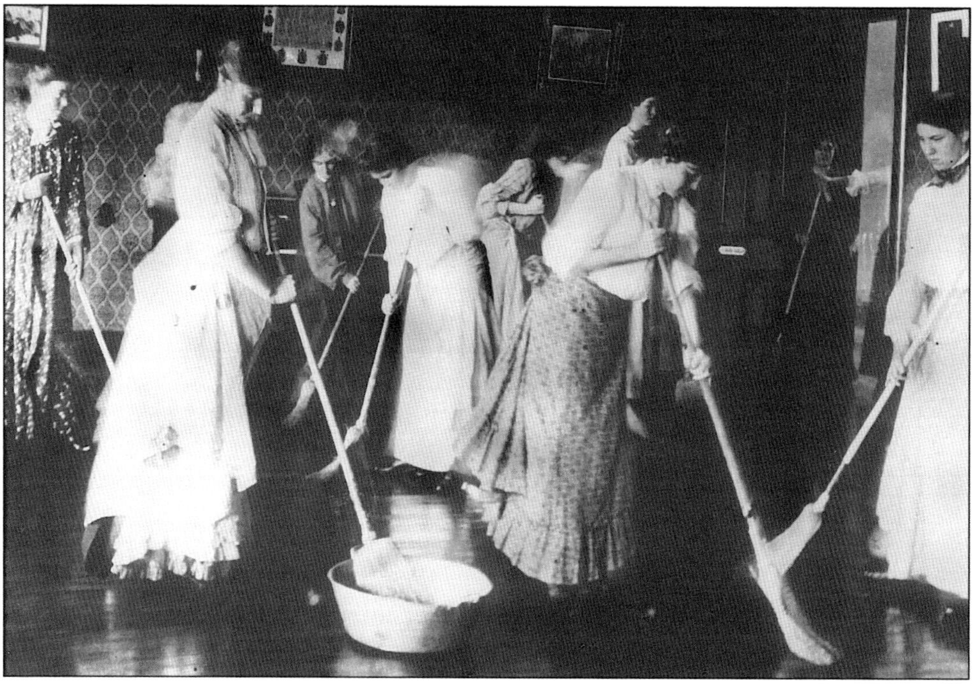

Seminary Students Cleaning, Late 1800s. (Courtesy Cherokee National Archives.)

Letters written to young men were strictly against the rules, and were almost always intercepted before they even left the building. At graduation time, the boys were allowed to send the girls flowers. The girls received so many long-stemmed roses, they had to keep them fresh in bathtubs.

The final commencement of the Cherokee Female Seminary was held on May 28, 1909. Receiving their diplomas were Sallie Bledsoe, Clara Melton, Anna Hanes, Minnie Fieland, Anna Truner, Narcissa Brown, and Electra Crittenden. The new state of Oklahoma had replaced the Seminary with the Northeastern Normal School. The undergraduate girls transferred their classes to the Cherokee Male Seminary until it burned in 1910.

Queen of the Cherokee Nation

In 1952, Columbia Pictures in Hollywood sponsored a contest to select the Queen of the Cherokee Nation. The winner received a huge trophy and a prize package that included a five-year contract to appear in western movies. Six semi-finalists were chosen from the 48 entrants to compete in the final Queen of the Cherokees pageant, televised on KOTV in Tulsa. Seventeen-year-old Charlotte Markham, a senior at Tulsa's Will Rogers High School, won the title.

Principal Chief W.W. Keeler sent Charlotte all around the Cherokee Nation making personal appearances. The construction on the Grand Lake of the Cherokees had just been completed, and a paddle boat, The Cherokee Queen, was launched on the lake. Charlotte spent two weeks aboard the boat greeting dignitaries from across Oklahoma. She appeared at numerous schools and football games, and danced for the grand opening of the Southern Hills Country Club in Tulsa.

At the beginning of each school year, Charlotte spent two weeks with the girls at Bacone College, teaching them how to sit, walk, dress, and behave like ladies. She represented the Cherokees at the very first Cherokee National Holiday, held in Tahlequah on September 6, 1953. That year she traveled to Hollywood to appear in her first motion picture, "Battle at Rogue River," the story of the Indian wars in Oregon Territory, starring George Montgomery.

Although she worked in a few more movies, Charlotte had little interest in the small parts she was offered, but was more intrigued by the production process. Between shooting, Charlotte studied pre-law at Tulsa University. She was an actress at both T.U. and the Spotlight Club, where she spent years portraying Mary, the little girl in the long-running play, "The Drunkard." While at T.U., Charlotte performed well-received comedy routines with graduate student Rue McClanahan.

Charlotte says that the I.C.O.T. Pow-Wow, held annually in Tulsa's Mohawk Park, attracted only a few participants in the 1950s. There may have been as many as 25 dancers from across Oklahoma, including a few older men and several children. Cherokee Queen Charlotte appeared with them and performed the War Dance, now called the Fancy Dance, wearing two bustles.

When not acting or traveling, Charlotte had a job modeling clothing at Vandiver's. August was "fur month," and the models wore heavy coats and snakeskin heels all afternoon in a department with no air conditioning.

The Queen of the Cherokee Nation competition was the first and last of its kind. Now a loved and respected Tahlequah resident, Charlotte still holds the title.

Charlotte Carstens

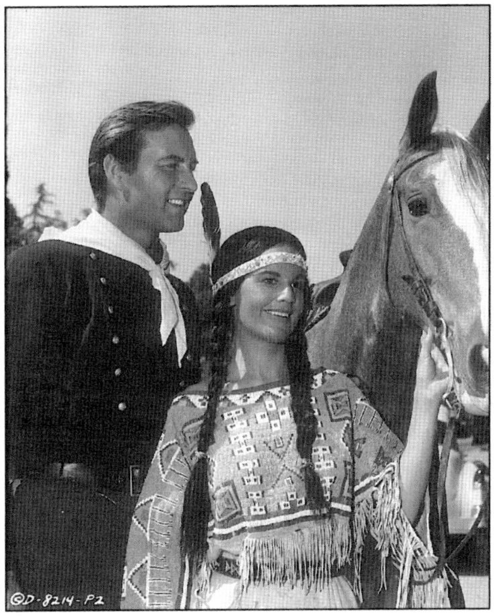

Charlotte Markham with Actor George Montgomery, 1953. (Courtesy Charlotte Carstens.)

The Cistern

Tahlequah's popular Cherokee Heritage Center was built on the site of the original Cherokee Female Seminary. For decades the few remaining brick columns stood silent as trees and brush overtook the graceful lawns of the school. At age 12, Roger Dunham discovered the ruins one morning while he and a friend were out riding horses.

The boys picked through the broken remains that could still be seen, finding nothing much of interest until they spied a big square rock on the ground. There was a hole in the middle big enough for a grown man to fit through, and beneath was a dark open space in the ground. It looked like the perfect place to find a hidden treasure.

Roger and his friend rode quickly back to town, then returned with lanterns and ropes. They lowered themselves into the blackness to find a tunnel lined with bricks. The only treasure to be had there was plenty of spiders and bugs.

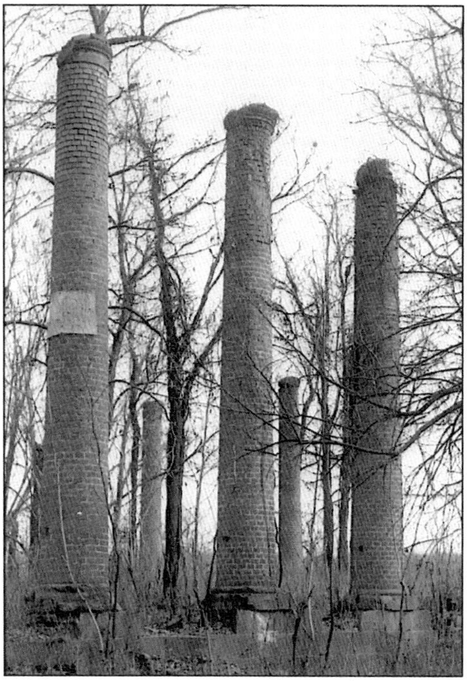

Ruins of Cherokee Female seminary, c. 1900. (Courtesy Cherokee National Archives.)

Some forty years later, Roger visited the Cherokee Heritage Center to watch the first Cherokee Medal of Honor awards ceremony. There on the lawn he saw that same big square rock, hole and all, standing upright with one corner buried in the ground. Hundreds of people must have seen it and wondered what it was. That old cistern cover stands as a tribute to the advanced culture of the Cherokees. But for Roger, it holds memories of childhood adventure.

Roger Dunham

Chips

Perry VanBuskirk grew up in the Rocky Ford community. Although his father Henry was a white man, he never interfered with the teachings his children received from his wife and her family. Perry's grandfather was John Rackliff, and his uncle was Sam Mellowbug, both noted Cherokee traditionalists. The children knew every inch of the surrounding countryside, and where to find the natural materials for making blowguns, bows and arrows. One of their favorite places to explore was a cave with its entrance halfway up the side of a large bluff.

As an adult, Perry still visits the cave. His good friend Tim Grayson, known for his ability to make bows and arrows, has often accompanied him there. He and Perry were walking together in the cave one afternoon and found themselves in a large open room. Perry stepped down on something that made a unique sound that both he and Tim heard. It was a perfect piece of chert, the rock used to make arrowheads.

Tim said, "That sounds like a good chipping rock." They carried it into the light and were impressed by the quality of the stone, and there was plenty more of it all around them. The two friends came back to the spot often to "chip blanks," by breaking off slivers of chert that they later made into arrowheads. They carried home bags of the blanks, making excellent points for bows and spears. On the cave floor they left behind thousands of tiny flakes and "worked" pieces of chert. Perry says that someday when the archaeologists find the place, they will think they hit the jackpot.

Perry VanBuskirk

Kathy's Family

Both sides of Kathy Dew VanBuskirk's family came across the Trail of Tears to Indian Territory. Her father's people came from Georgia and her mother's ancestors lived in Tennessee. Kathy's great-great grandfather was a Cherokee

Nation council member named Osceola Dew. He is buried at his old homesite on the Illinois River, along with his wife, Eliza Teehee. The name Teehee might sound like someone laughing, but the word in Cherokee means "killer."

Kathy's grandmother's name was Dirt Track. As far as Kathy knows, there are no other people with that name anywhere, and she wonders where the name came from since Dirt Track's mother's last name was Worm. It is said that when Sequoyah went looking for the lost Cherokees, his traveling companion's name was Worm. Kathy's great-great-grandmother came west in the Removal. When she was forced to leave her home in Tennessee, she wanted to take something with her to remember the place by. She chose a ceramic sugar cup. She carried the cup safely along the treacherous journey, hidden in her apron. Kathy's cousin still has it.

Kathy VanBuskirk

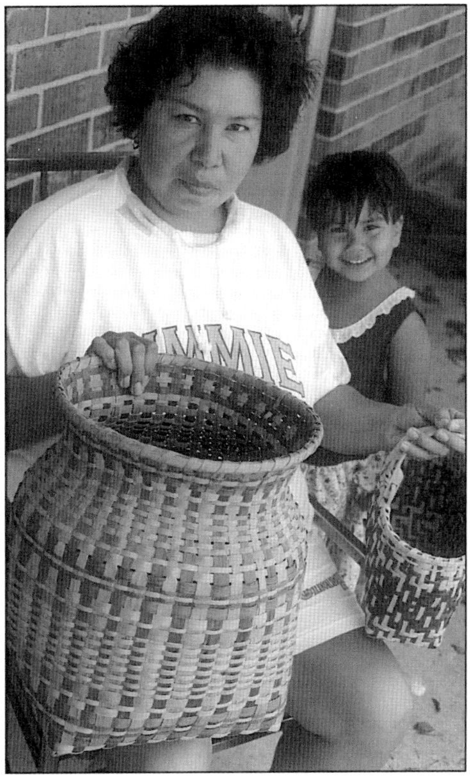

Kathy and Melissa VanBuskirk, 2000. (Photo by Murv Jacob.)

Miss Parthenia Gregory

Miss Parthenia Gregory, a spinster her entire life, was Virginia Vann's Oklahoma History teacher at Muskogee Central High School in the 1930s. As soon as Parthenia heard Virginia's name, she asked if she was related to "Chief" Joe Vann, or Rich Joe. Well, Virginia went home to ask her father Clem about it. Sure enough, Rich Joe was his great-grandfather. Rich Joe Vann had a son named William Vann, who had a son named Herman Johnson Vann, who was Clem's father.

Miss Gregory was hot on history, and especially liked the Native Americans of Oklahoma. She made a habit of asking the students in her history classes, "And who in this school is the direct descendant of Chief Joe Vann?" The students would chime out "Virginia Vann!" Like it or not, this became Virginia's claim to fame. Her younger sister Jean, not wanting that kind of attention, refused to take Oklahoma History.

Virginia Vann Perry

The Old Hen

After Virginia Vann had grown up and was working in Oklahoma City, her parents had a house in Muskogee, right next to Miss Parthenia Gregory's house, Virginia's old Oklahoma history teacher. Miss Gregory liked to bring people's attention to Virginia's father Clem, just as she had done to Virginia in her history classes. She described Clem as a "typical" Indian, who looked stern and would never smile. She once said that people might even find him frightening. Virginia couldn't imagine anyone being afraid of her Dad, and said as much to her friend Hazel. Hazel then told her that the first time she ever saw Clem he "scared her half to death."

One day, Clem had been injured as a load of pipe fell from a truck, crushing his foot. He was at home recuperating with his wife and his younger daughter, Jean. On that day his wife had brought home two live chicken hens that she planned to cook for Thanksgiving dinner. One of the hens wandered over to Miss Parthenia Gregory's yard, and was pecking around in her garden. Clem answered the phone when Miss Parthenia called to complain, and told his daughter, "Go over next door and get that old hen." Jean ran out and quickly came back, not with a chicken, but with Miss Gregory, the Old Hen!

Virginia Vann Perry

East Meets West

The Eastern Band of Cherokee Indians who now live on the Cherokee Reservation at Cherokee, North Carolina, are the descendants of those who escaped the tribe's removal to Indian Territory. Although separated by distance, many of their people have close ties with Cherokee friends and relatives in Oklahoma. Such a relationship exists between Oklahomans Perry and Kathy VanBuskirk and their friend Bill, from North Carolina.

Kathy and Perry have worked for several years at the Cherokee Heritage Center in Tahlequah, where they recruit and train employees of the Ancient Village. This museum, which is over 30 years old, is a recreation of a Cherokee village in pre-Columbian times.

In the first week of October, the Eastern Band celebrates its annual Festival. Western Cherokees attend this homecoming event every year. The VanBuskirks have often helped raise funds to allow the actors from Tahlequah's Ancient Village to attend. Kathy and Perry first met Bill in 1996 while he was in Oklahoma visiting the Cherokee Heritage Center. He made a generous donation toward the Villagers' trip that year, and invited the VanBuskirks to his home during the fall celebration.

Since then, the three have become great friends. All are well-versed in Cherokee culture, and are traditionalists. Kathy speaks fluent Cherokee and is a noted basket maker. Perry was taught to gather and use medicinal healing herbs by his grandfather and uncle. Bill trains and prepares the stickball team from Wolf-Town, or Soco, a community located near Cherokee, North Carolina. The Wolf-Town team has not been defeated in over 50 years.

Although the Eastern and Western Cherokees live miles apart, they share the same history, culture, and traditions. There is a powerful bond between them, a longing to be together, and a fond remembrance of their ancestral homeland.

Perry and Kathy VanBuskirk

Bloody Bear Tooth

A Cherokee descendant, John D. Loudermilk is one of the most prolific American songwriters who ever lived. Hundreds of his songs have been recorded by a variety of artists from Chet Atkins to Jewel. His many hit singles, like "Break My Mind," "Then You Can Tell Me Goodbye," and "Tobacco Road" are chart-toppers that will never be forgotten. John D. traveled to Tahlequah in the spring of 1999 to receive the Cherokee Medal of Honor from the Cherokee Honor Society. Guests at a party for the honorees were thrilled when he went to the stage and performed several of his hits, including "The Lament of the Cherokee Reservation Indian."

That song was entitled "Indian Reservation" when Paul Revere and the Raiders recorded it. At the height of its popularity, John D. received a phone call from famed radio disc jockey Casey Kasem at 3 A.M. He interviewed John D. about the Raider's hit.

John D. thought if Casey Kasem wanted a story, he would give him a good one. It went something like this: Loudermilk was driving through the snow in the mountains near the Cherokee Reservation in North Carolina. He had trouble with his car and pulled over to the side of the highway, stranded. Not knowing what else to do, he left the vehicle and set out on foot to look for help.

John D. came upon an Indian man who was standing by the road. He told John to follow him, and led him to the mouth of a cave. The cave was warm inside, and sitting around the fire were several more men. The leader of this group was a full-blood Cherokee named Bloody Bear Tooth. Although the men treated him graciously, he soon realized that he was their prisoner.

He slept on bear skins spread on the cave floor that night. From their conversation the next morning, Bloody Bear Tooth learned that Loudermilk was a professional songwriter. He told John D. that he would let him live if he promised to write a song about the Cherokee Trail of Tears.

John D. had made up every word of the story on the spot. Casey Kasem was so impressed with the story that he broadcast it across the whole country on his radio show, causing a sensation among music fans. Even today, wherever John D. travels people still ask him about that night he spent in the cave with Bloody Bear Tooth.

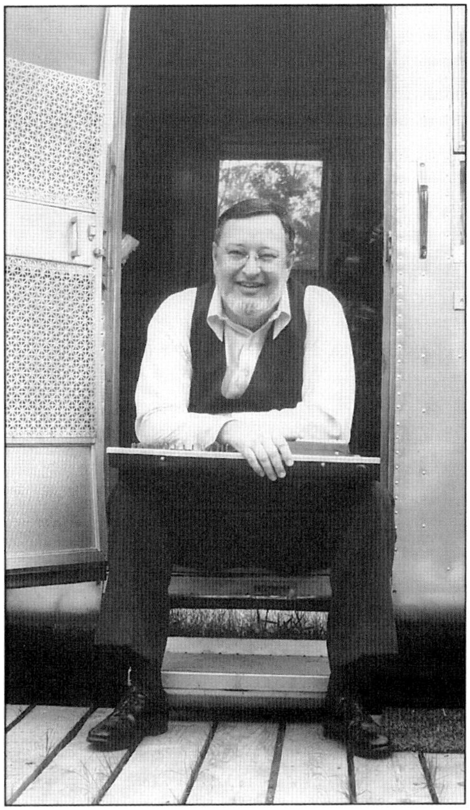

Songwriter John D. Loudermilk, c. 1980. (Coutesy Cherokee Honor Society.)

John D. Loudermilk

Garland's Gift

Former Deputy Chief and Cherokee speaker Garland Eagle has a beautiful singing voice, and works with a group of musicians who perform gospel songs in the Cherokee language. Garland tells this story of how he came to be a singer.

Like most men in their youth, Garland enjoyed a free-wheeling, partying lifestyle. When he was first married, he tried for a time to continue his wild ways, but the marriage suffered.

Then Garland turned to the Christian religion.

In those early days, Garland "couldn't sing a note." He began to pray, asking God to make him a singer, and promising to use his voice for praise and worship. His prayers were answered, and Garland became a singer, sharing the beautiful Cherokee hymns with his friends and neighbors.

Garland Eagle

Regrets and Hope

Twenty years ago, Robert Conley came to Tahlequah where he met his wife, Evelyn. He worked closely in those days with a young man named Chad Smith, elected in 1999 as Principal Chief of the Cherokee Nation.

When the Cherokees rebuilt after the Civil War, they attained a society that eliminated poverty while their people excelled in both education and commerce. Conley's grandmother was born in that Nation before statehood. His father missed being born there by thirteen years, and Conley by thirty-three. "Why did we miss it?" he asks. "Every day of my life I feel like I have been robbed. I didn't come here to live in Oklahoma. I am here because Tahlequah is the capital of the Cherokee Nation."

Conley believes that with Smith as Chief the Cherokees are inching their way toward a Nation reunited, as close as they have come since statehood. He says that above all, Chad is a Cherokee patriot - one who will do anything for the Nation, and who will go down in history as one of its greatest leaders.

Robert J. Conley

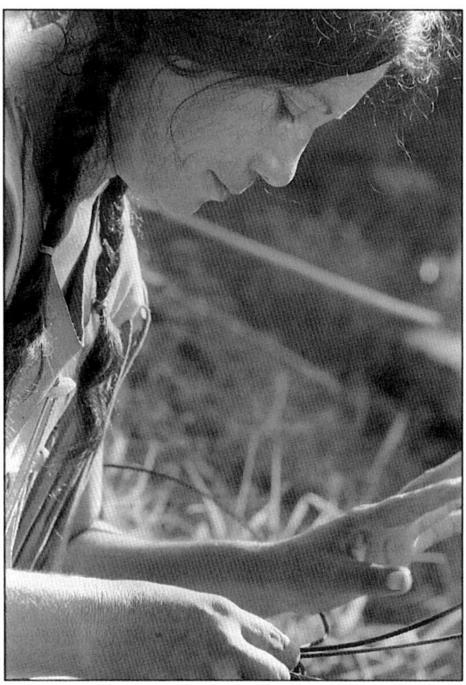

Artisan Betty Smith, c. 1970. (Courtesy Cherokee National Archives.)

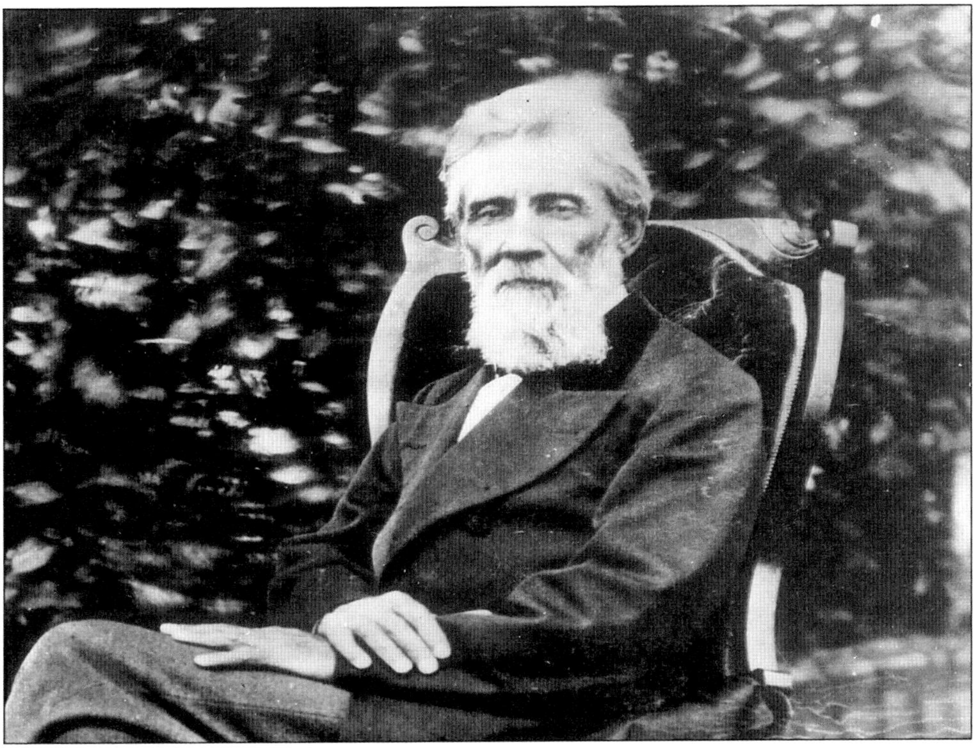

Principal Chief William Potter Ross, c. 1870. (Courtesy Cherokee National Archives.)

CHAPTER 2

HISTORICAL FIGURES

Through the centuries, Cherokee heroes, villains, leaders, and eccentrics have made their marks on the colorful history of the United States. Perhaps the most famous was Will Rogers, who was born in the Cooweescoowee District of the Cherokee Nation. He was named after Col. William Penn Adair, a beloved Civil War hero who later served as Assistant Chief.

The "Cherokee Cadmus," Sequoyah, was the only person in history to create an alphabet for a previously unwritten language.

Principal Chief Wilma P. Mankiller is one of the most highly respected and well-known women in the United States.

While Andrew Jackson was arranging the infamous Trail of Tears for the southeastern Cherokees, their contemporaries in Arkansas were living on sprawling plantations and ranches. In those days, it was said that Rich Joe Vann and his father before him were the wealthiest individuals in the entire western hemisphere. When the Civil War ended, the last Confederate officer to surrender was not some white Georgian, it was Brigadier General Stand Watie, a fearless Cherokee warrior.

The Lawgiver

Long before the Cherokees had written laws, or even a written language, they followed a concise code of oral laws. The man entrusted with the knowledge of the law was called "The Lawgiver," and once a year, he paid a formal visit to each Cherokee village. He stood upon the banked ashes of the Sacred Fire and recited all of the spoken laws to the people. On top of his head he wore the skin and feathers of a raven, the most wise of all birds.

Having heard the laws, a council and the village chief held a trial for people accused of crimes. They decided upon a proper sentence that could include punishment, banishment, or death.

Cherokee professor of law Rennard Strickland recorded a number of the oral laws in his book "Fire and the Spirits." An interesting example of the oral law is one regarding infanticide. A mother had the right to kill her own child without interference from any person. If the child were deformed or diseased, she could end its suffering. Yet any other person having killed that child would face punishment decided by a council from the mother's clan.

Murv Jacob

Old Tassel

Old Tassel was a prominent character of the old southeastern Cherokee Nation who signed three treaties; Wa-Ta-Gua, the Treaty of Sycamore Shoals, and the Treaty of Hopewell. According to his descendant, Brian Corntassel, the Treaty of Hopewell was the first and only "peace treaty" the Cherokees ever signed with the U.S. government because it was broken when the federal government brought death to the Cherokee who signed it. A U.S. soldier killed Old Tassel with his own tomahawk.

Brian Corntassel

Pretty Woman

Some believe that in ancient times the most important Cherokee leaders were women. The tribe adopted the practice of selecting male chiefs after white contact because Europeans disliked dealing with female leaders. Long ago, the highest ranking of the women was called the "Pretty Woman." As time passed, her title changed to "Beloved Woman" and then to

"Honored Woman."

There is an old story about a British officer who trespassed on Cherokee land and was captured and brought to the townhouse of the village. There he stood before the Pretty Woman, who had the power over his life or death. Her face was tattooed on both sides with the image of a rattlesnake with the rattles tattooed on her temples, and the bodies curved around her cheeks. The mouths of the rattlesnakes were tattooed over the corners of her mouth, so that when she spoke, they spoke. Imagine how the white man must have felt in the presence of one so exotic. It was written that she liked the looks of him and spared his life.

Artist and pipe maker Murv Jacob was taught this story by Cecil Dick. Murv says that the story comes to mind each time he has been in the presence of Principal Chief Wilma Mankiller. To him, she is the modern version of the Pretty Woman, who deserves his highest respect and regard.

Murv Jacob

The Vann Family Beginnings

John Joseph Vann, a descendant of Robert the Bruce, King of Scotland, came to Charles-Town (Charleston, SC) in 1750, where he served with the Royal Rangers as an interpreter to the Indians. His work took him deep into Cherokee lands, where he observed the annual Ripe Corn Festival. Part of the activities was the conclusion of a mating ritual in which young men and women made their intentions known through dance, and the women selected husbands from among their suitors. A woman of 30 years and a descendant of powerful Cherokee leaders, Wai-Li, cast her sights on the handsome white man John Vann. She danced around him until John was intoxicated with her charm. She then claimed him as her own and took him to her house.

John and Wai-Li were married in a traditional Cherokee ceremony. His brother Clement was brought into the extended family and other Scottish traders contributed to the gene pool, which included two more wives. Although given Cherokee names and clan affiliation by their mothers, the Scottish fathers gave the children Christian first names and surnames. John Vann, by way of his marriage, went on to become Chief of Tellico. He fathered James Vann (Chief Crazy James), who became wealthy by planting, trading, and making whiskey. His legacy was passed on to the legendary Rich Joe Vann, Golden Star of the Cherokees, whose son John Shepard Vann, born in 1826, was president of the first Constitutional Convention of the Cherokee Nation. Members of the Vann family can be found in most Cherokee communities. According to David Vann, a matriarch of his family lived to meet over 1,000 of her own descendants.

David L. Vann

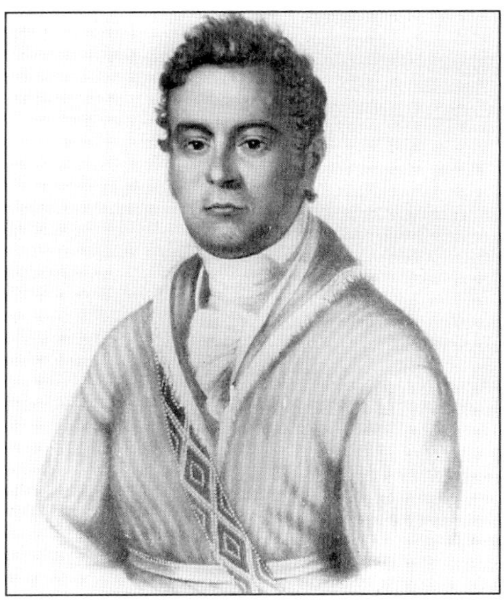

David Vann, c. 1800. (Courtesy Cherokee National Archives.)

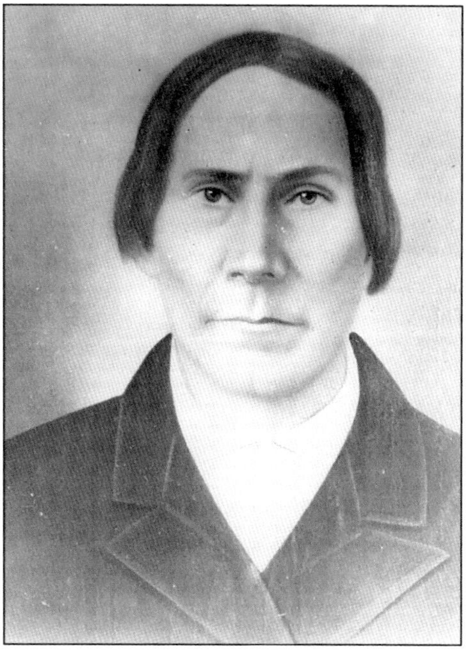

James Vann, Assistant Chief 1867–71. (Courtesy Cherokee National Archives.)

Prime Minister Priber

In the years before their removal to Indian Territory, the Cherokee people were visited by some interesting Europeans who profoundly influenced their way of life. One of the most unusual of these was Christian Priber, a visionary and humanitarian, who built a trading empire that lasted for 50 years between the southeast Indians, the English, and the French.

Priber traveled to the New World to find the perfect lifestyle. He was well-versed in languages and soon was speaking Cherokee. He befriended the Indians and taught them business ethics to use when trading with whites. Before long he married Chief Moytoy's daughter and gave his father-in-law the title of Emperor and called himself Prime Minister.

With his support, the Cherokees became great traders. He encouraged them live to peacefully and to refuse attempts of the whites to take their land holdings. In his perfect world, all would be equal in station, and none would own private property. He disdained both slavery and marriage. The English in the new colony of Georgia accused Priber of turning the Cherokees to the side of the French, and attempted to capture him. The Cherokees protected Priber and he remained their Prime Minister for another five years before his capture by an enemy Creek war party. Priber, who wanted to live in a perfect society, spent his final years in a Georgia prison.

Death of Doublehead

John Rogers, also known as "Trader John," was a Torie captain from Scotland who came to this country to fight in the Seminole wars. He married a Cherokee woman and came to live among the tribe in the southeastern Cherokee Nation. In 1807, Cherokee chief Doublehead sold tribal land to the white government, signed treaties with them, and accepted land from them. Trader John believed these activities were detrimental to the welfare of the people, and confronted Doublehead about this. Doublehead said to the white man, "You live by sufferance among us. I never see you in Council or on the warpath. You have no place among the chiefs. Hush and interfere with me no more."

Earlier that morning, Doublehead had sat upon his horse watching a game of stickball. A man rode up to him, pointed a pistol at his head, cocked the gun and pulled the trigger, but the gun misfired. Doublehead seized the man's gun, turned it around in his hand, and came down with the butt of the handle on top of the man's head, cracking his skull and killing him. His day was not going well, and the confrontation with Trader John had made things worse.

He made his way to a tavern, but was

trailed there by Trader John and two friends, Ridge and Hicks. A fight broke out, and one of them shot Doublehead in the mouth, cracking his jaw. The wounded man escaped to a nearby house and hid in the attic, but his attackers followed and found him. Doublehead was stabbed and hacked to death.

Sequoyah Rogers

Crazy James

Born 100 years before the Civil War, Chief Crazy James Vann was thought to be the wealthiest Cherokee of all. James accidentally shot his father to death, inheriting his trading network through which the economy of the Cherokee Nation was controlled. He brought in a whiskey still and began making and selling corn liquor. Profits soared from the sales, while the wealthy James drank regularly from the stock, gaining the reputation of a wild and crazy man and a nickname to match.

Due to his wealth, Crazy James became Chief of Tellico and a District Judge. He owned a tavern where trials were held, and those condemned to death found James both judge and executioner. James discovered gold in a stream on his land and began amassing a treasure. Though rich beyond belief, he constantly dreamed of being robbed and murdered for his gold. When he discovered that two of his house servants planned to kill him in his sleep, they were taken to his "court house" and made to confess. The co-conspirator was banished, but James tied the female ring-leader to a stake in front of the tavern and burned her alive.

In 1809, Chief Crazy James was bushwhacked at Buffington's Tavern by six men and shot to death. He was buried near his home, but not in the churchyard, as the missionaries considered him to be half devil. Legend said he was buried with a chest of gold, and years later, robbers dug up his grave to find only rocks.

David L. Vann

The Ridge

White men shortened the name of "The Lion Who Walks the Mountain Top," or Ka-nun-tla-cla-geh, to Ridge. General Andrew Jackson gave him the name Major after he led the Cherokees against the Creeks in the battle of Horseshoe Bend. Born near what is now Rome, Georgia, in 1771, Major Ridge was once voted the most influential man in that region. Thomas Jefferson, having heard Ridge give a speech in Cherokee, said of the orator, "I knew not what he said, but I cried for the eloquence of the man."

A member of the Treaty Party, Major Ridge was a signer of the Treaty of New Echota. This document determined the fate of the southeastern Cherokees,

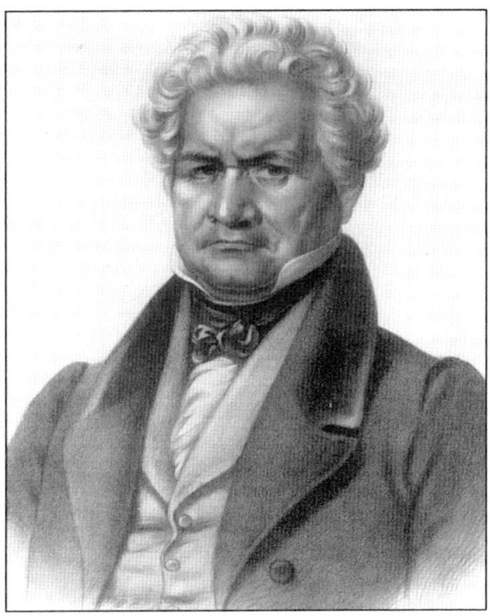

Major Ridge, c. 1830. (Courtesy Cherokee National Archives.)

allowing for their removal from their ancestral homeland to Indian Territory. Followers of Principal Chief John Ross resisted leaving until the forced removal of 1838–9. Ross's own brother, Andrew, signed the treaty and is said to have come up with the idea for it himself. Prophetically, as Major Ridge signed his name, he stated, "I have signed my death warrant."

On June 22, 1839, Major Ridge, his son John Ridge, and Elias Boudinot, brother of Stand Watie, were all ambushed and killed in the new territory. The killers were carrying out the provisions of the "blood law" that marked for death those who sold Cherokee land. Chief John Ross said of Major Ridge, "Once I saved Ridge at Red Clay, and would have done so again had I known of the plot."

One can only wonder what would have happened to the Cherokees had there been no agreement with the federal government to move west. Some historians are now saying that signers of the Treaty of New Echota may have saved the Cherokee people from total destruction.

Regarding the future of the tribe, Major Ridge wrote this statement in a letter dated February 27, 1826, to Albert Gallatin of Thomas Jefferson's staff. "Cherokee blood, if not destroyed, will win its courses in beings of fair complexions, who will read that their ancestors became civilized under the frowns of misfortune and the causes of their enemies."

Major Ridge, his son John Ridge, and General Stand Watie are buried in the Poulson Ridge-Watie Cemetery. Visitors to Southwest City, Missouri, turn west on Cherokee Street to Stand Watie Road, then right to the cemetery.

Paul Ridenour

Sequoyah and Cherokees in Mexico

There is much debate about the final resting place of Sequoyah, the famed Cherokee who created the tribe's syllabary. One story states that a group of Cherokees living in Texas in 1840 were driven from their homes there, and took refuge in Mexico in the state of Coahuila. They began a village there near Zaragoza. These were followers of Chief Boles, whose son was said to have married Sequoyah's daughter. Sequoyah went there himself in 1842, and died there in 1843. Some believe that Sequoyah is buried in Mexico, and have even spoken of finding and returning his bones to Oklahoma.

The village of Cherokees was attacked, robbed, and destroyed by Mexicans, leaving about 30 people homeless. Most of these went to live with Kickapoos, also in Mexico, in the community of Nacimiento. Today there are several Kickapoos there who say they are descended from Cherokees. The Kickapoos have stories that mention Sequoyah as a historical figure who may have spent time among their people.

In 1845, the head of the Indian Bureau in Washington DC put up $200 to fund an expedition to search for Sequoyah. Some believed that he had traveled to Mexico for the climate and was later buried in the Wichita Mountains. Others think he went to search for the lost Cherokees who left for the west in 1721 and were never heard from again.

Rich Joe's Arkansas Land

Andrew Jackson was an Indian hater and a racist. He would find two enemy tribes, supply both with guns, powder, and liquor, and let one tribe destroy the other. Then his army would ambush the victors on their way home. When Jackson began his campaign against the Creek Indians, ancestral enemies of the Cherokees, he was supported. During this war, Rich Joe Vann discovered that he could make large profits by supplying the army with cloth and finished clothing. He purchased a cotton gin and began production. When he delivered the goods, the army signed notes of indebtedness which Joe could later redeem for gold in Washington.

During Jackson's Indian Wars, Rich Joe collected over $1 million in federal IOUs. When the forced removal of the Cherokees to Indian Territory was underway, Joe took one of his steam boats to survey the new land and found it totally unsuitable, rocky, without water, and incapable of supporting crops and game. He traveled to Washington to plead for better land. The president refused to see him and sent a detachment of junior clerks to deal with him. After several weeks of negotiating, Rich Joe asked them how much they would take for the good land on the other side of the river. They laughed and jokingly told him $1 million. Rich Joe promptly opened his bag and counted out $1 million in federal IOUs signed by Andrew Jackson. He left Washington with title to two million acres in what is now Arkansas.

David L. Vann

Corntassel

According to some family members, Corntassel left the old Cherokee country with the Old Settlers in the 1820s, but he served as a wagon master during the Trail of Tears. He helped the Cherokees to make the treacherous journey at least four times, and some say it was seven. Corntassel was a blacksmith, and he carried pieces of his "luber," a machine used in his trade, from the homeland to Indian Territory with each trip until he had moved the entire thing.

Corntassel settled on Cherokee Nation land just west of Westville where the community came to be known as Green. It became "Old Green" when another community, also called Green, was established in Delaware County. From Highway 51 west of Westville, you can take Ross Swimmer Road toward Old Green. On the way, you will come upon a small cemetery with a sign that reads "Corntassel 1891." There you will find the grave of Corntassel and his family members. He was believed to be 117 years old at the time of his death.

Leon Corntassel

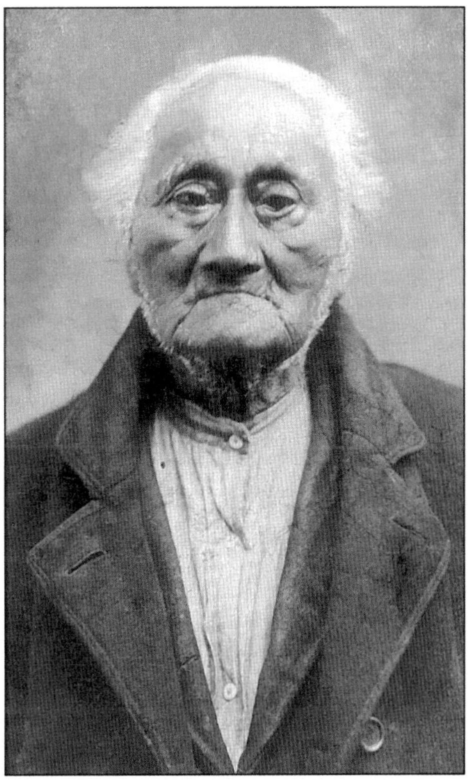

Corntassel, Late 1800s. (Courtesy the Corntassel Family.)

Susan Robbins Corntassel

It is said by family members that their ancestor, Corntassel, and his first wife were detained for a time in a stockade during the Trail of Tears. The wife became sick and died along the Trail. Corntassel had been close friends with a man known as "the Robin" who was killed, leaving his daughter, Susan Robbins, an orphan in the old Cherokee Nation. For the sake of his old friend, Corntassel arranged for Susan's passage to Indian Territory on a later trip across the Trail and married her.

There is some debate as to whether or not Susan was a Cherokee. Depending on who you talk to she is described in varying degrees from a white woman to a full-blood. Whatever her lineage, she and Corntassel started a family that now has many proud Cherokee descendants who keep their memory alive for future generations.

Brian and Leon Corntassel

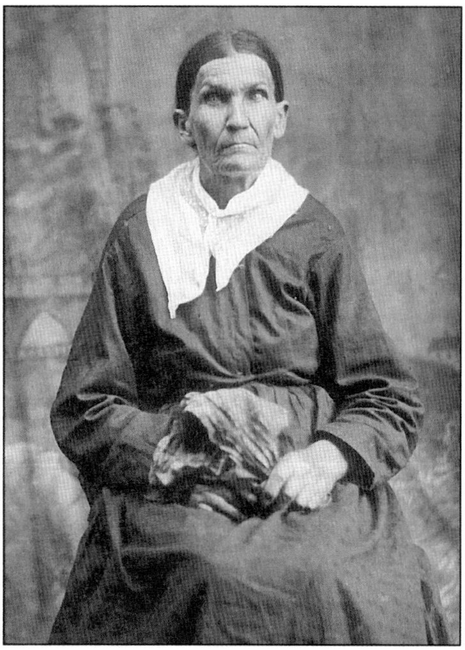

Susan Robbins Corntassel, Late 1800s. (Courtesy the Corntassel Family.)

Reverend Bushyhead

The Reverend Jesse Bushyhead was one of the most loved figures of Cherokee history. Born in Tennessee in 1804, young Jesse was a pupil of Evan Jones, the Baptist missionary who later revived the Nighthawk Keetoowahs during the Civil War. Jesse helped Reverend Jones to translate the Holy Bible into the Cherokee language, using the syllabary. He was known far and wide as one of the best translators in the Cherokee Nation.

In Indian Territory, Jesse remained neutral in the factional disputes between the followers of Principal Chief John Ross and the Treaty Party. His son Dennis Wolf Bushyhead was destined to become principal chief of the Cherokee Nation. His daughter Eliza was born on New Years Day, 1839, on the banks of the Mississippi River during the Trail of Tears. When Eliza passed away, after spending her life serving her fellow Cherokees, the headlines read, "Tahlequah's Most Distinguished Citizen is Dead."

John Vann, the Runaway

Rich Joe Vann and his wife Jennie Springston had four sons and four daughters. Their third son was John Sheppard (Se La U Le) Vann, born July 24, 1826, at Spring Place, Georgia. Following the Removal, Se La U Le met and married Elizabeth Pack Fields Coody in Indian Territory, 1846. Elizabeth was the daughter of Richard Pack Fields, and the widow of William Coody, better known as Buffalo Bill Cody. Elizabeth's son, John Vann, was born on July 8, 1854, near Fort Smith.

After Elizabeth passed away in 1862, Se La U Le married a white woman who made little John do "women's work" around the house and help out with his smaller siblings. Other Cherokee children made fun of him, so he decided to run away. He packed a sack of corn pone and bacon, went on a errand down the river, and never returned.

John headed for an old wagon trail going West. After a few days on the road, he came across a Dutch family named Van Horn. They were driving a covered wagon to Texas from Pennsylvania. Due to his features, the Van Horns thought he was a white child and treated him kindly. They had several children about his age, and invited him along on their journey. John told the biggest lie of his life and joined them on their trek to the Promised Land.

His hard-luck story went like this: When John was a baby, his folks were traveling West in a covered wagon and were "set-upon" by a band of hostile Indians. His parents, John and Elizabeth (Betty), were killed and his brothers and sisters were left to die. A kindly band of Cherokees came across the children and took them away to live on the reservation. So, when John was big enough, he ran away from the Indians.

John Vann later told his children, "We located on a small farm in Navarro County, near Corsicana, Texas. They were kind to me, and I worked the farm until I was 13. Now the [Civil] war was over, but times were real hard." Farmers had no buyers for their produce because nobody had any money. Banks were foreclosing on the overdue loans, and the carpet baggers were buying land for the balance of the loans and back taxes. You could work for food, and if you were very lucky, a roof over your head, usually in the barn, the stables, or the smokehouse. There was no work for freed slaves. They were left to fend for themselves in the woods along the rivers or in shanty-towns. Indians outside their territory were in constant peril of being murdered for the color of their skin. There was no work, no housing, nothing. John kept up the premise of being white so he could continue to survive in the post-war countryside.

In 1879, at the age of 25, John became the jailer in Kaufman, Texas. Now that he was a prosperous man, he could afford to build a house and take a wife. He married Sarah Matilda Hines, a full-blood Choctaw, and they had 10 children, five of whom survived infancy. John continued to help his farmer friends harvest their wheat, and in 1899, he was run over and killed by a farm wagon in the next county.

David L. Vann

The Watie Brothers

Another signer of the Treaty of New Echota to die in Indian Territory was Elias Boudinot, formerly Buck Watie, brother to Stand Watie. Boudinot was the editor of the first Indian newspaper, "The Cherokee Phoenix." The four-page weekly was written in both English and Cherokee, using the Cherokee syllabary. Working with missionary Samuel Worcester, Elias translated the New Testament and several religious hymns into the Cherokee language. It is said that "Amazing Grace" was sung so often along the Trail of Tears it practically became a Cherokee anthem.

On June 22, 1839, Boudinot was killed by a group of assassins near his home at Park Hill. He was struck in the head six or seven times with a tomahawk as his partner Sam Worcester shouted, "They have cut off my right hand!" Elias Boudinot was buried near where he died in the tiny Worcester Cemetery at Park Hill. A historical marker now stands at his gravesite.

A young Choctaw who witnessed the killing took Samuel Worcester's horse, Comet, to warn Elias's brother, Stand

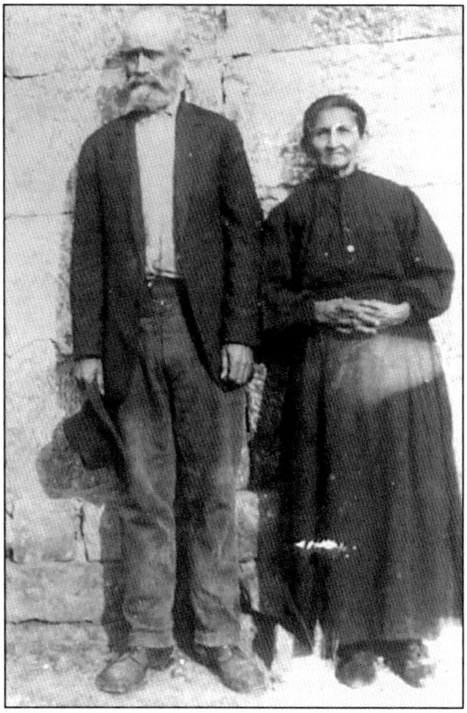

Elizabeth Miller Mann, Niece of Stand Watie, Late 1800s. (Courtesy Cherokee National Archives.)

Watie, who escaped a similar fate. Stand Watie is remembered as one of the most noted figures in Cherokee history. He was the first Indian ever to be found "not guilty" of killing a white man in self-defense in a white court. He was the only Indian to become a General in the Confederate Army, and the last General to surrender when the Civil War ended.

Paul Ridenour

Sam Houston

Sam Houston was a beloved hero of American History who was deeply devoted to the Cherokee people. He married Tiana Rogers, who was one-half Cherokee and the daughter of trader John Rogers. Houston was "adopted" by an act conferring citizenship as a Cherokee on October 31, 1831.

Sam and Tiana settled near the lower falls of the Verdigris River where they ran a small trading post. They called their home "Wigwam Neosho." Houston was deputized to travel to Texas and convince the Texas Cherokees there to return to the Cherokee Nation, and many of them did return. He joined in the Texas revolution and eventually became the president of Texas. He served Texas as both senator and governor. During Sam's entire stay in Texas, his Cherokee wife Tiana refused to join him.

Sequoyah Rogers

Rich Joe Vann's Demise

It was said that Cherokee Rich Joe Vann was once the wealthiest man in the western hemisphere. He purchased and raced horses and was a heavy gambler. He owned a fleet of steamboats which he frequently entered in races, piloting them himself.

Rich Joe used this fleet of boats to ferry thousands of Cherokee people to Indian Territory during the Trail of Tears. On October 26, 1844, he was engaged in a high stakes steamboat race on the Ohio River. His boat, the Lucy Walker, was losing ground, so he ordered the chief engineer, an ex-slave, to throw a side of pork meat into the boiler. The man refused, knowing that throwing fat in the fire would make too much pressure, causing the boiler to explode.

Rich Joe did not intend to lose that race so he produced a pistol and again demanded that the side of pork be added. The engineer had his men do as requested, then immediately jumped overboard. Moments later the boiler exploded, destroying the steamboat and killing all the fancy guests on board, including Joe's son-in-law,

Preston McKay. Rich Joe's body was never recovered, but two days after the accident, a dismembered arm clad in a purple silk sleeve and wearing a diamond signet ring was found in a tree, half a mile from the site. The ring and silk sleeve belonged to Rich Joe Vann.

David L. Vann

Major Ridge's Family

"The Ridge" is well remembered in his former hometown of Rome, Georgia. His home there has now become a popular attraction, the Chieftain's Museum. Ridge's wife, Susie Wickett, loved to smoke her pipe, and would refuse to attend white functions where her pipe smoking was unacceptable.

Their daughter, Sarah Ridge, was well acquainted with Sam Houston. She once got on a wild horse and continued riding it until its spirit was broken. After that, many of the young white men who knew Sarah wanted to marry her.

Paul Ridenour

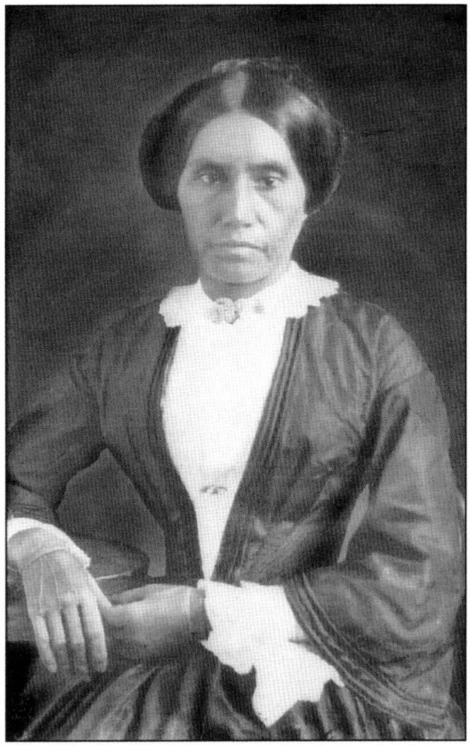

Sarah Ridge, Late 1800s. (Courtesy Paul Ridenour.)

DeWitt Clinton Duncan

At 10 years old, DeWitt Duncan accompanied his married sister Emily Beck across the Trail of Tears to Indian Territory. When DeWitt grew up, he became a writer who contributed a number of articles and original poetry to newspapers. His submissions were made using his Cherokee name "Too-qua-stee." Some of his best known titles are "Sitting Bull's Address to His Braves," "On the Eve of the Battle of the Little Big Horn," and "Ode to Sequoyah."

Dewitt also published a book entitled "Story of the Cherokee." The only known copy in existence today is preserved in the John Vaughan Library at Tahlequah's Northeastern State University. In his book, DeWitt wrote of a white man in Georgia who threw a Cherokee baby out of a burning house when the Cherokees were being driven from their homes.

DeWitt's older sister Emily had a baby daughter named Emily Beck at the time of the Removal. Emily Beck's grandson, Lawrence McAlister, once met with Tahlequah's famed historian Dr. Ballenger, who told Lawrence some interesting facts about his ancestors. He said that Emily Beck's parent had been out of their home when it was burned, and that a white man had thrown a baby out of that house. Emily's descendants now believe that DeWitt Duncan was writing about his family in "Story of the Cherokee." The baby saved from death by the white man was his own niece.

Larry McAlister, Jr.

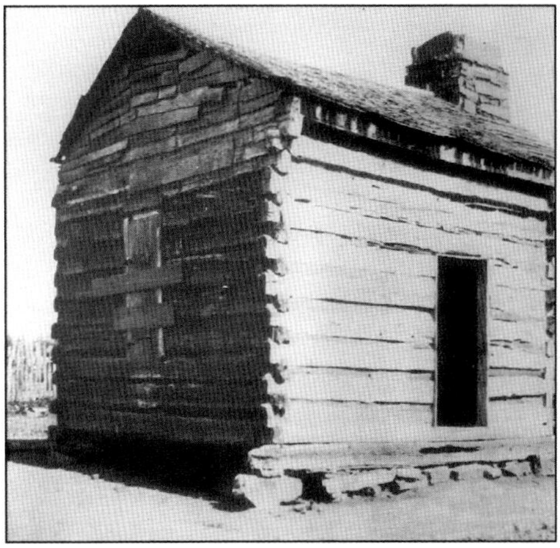

Sequoyah's Cabin. (Courtesy Cherokee National Archives.)

Sequoyah's Grave?

A Cherokee woman named Nakai was born in Stilwell, Oklahoma in the 1920s. As a child she was adopted by a Comanche family who lived in west Texas. She still resides there with her husband, cowboy and western artist Bud Breen. Nakai's story took place at Bracketville, Texas. Just to the south is Eagle Pass, home to a band of Kickapoos who live in Mexico. Among the Kickapoos are descendants of Cherokees who once lived there as well.

One day in her youth, Nakai was walking to school and came upon some workmen who were removing the surface of a road in her neighborhood. The men had uncovered the graves of five individuals. One appeared to be elderly, three were younger adults, there was one child and one baby. Nakai was intrigued by the clothing that remained on the bodies. The men wore turbans, sashes, and hunting coats. Their moccasins had a knot tied in the ends of the toes, and their leggings were held by red garters. The moccasins and the red garters proved the bodies to be dressed in traditional Cherokee style, as did the other garments. The body of the baby had been placed in a grapevine basket. This was the method of infant burial in the southeastern Cherokee tradition.

Nakai heard the men discussing what they should do about their find. Because this was an Indian gravesite, they decided to simply cover it back up and replace the road surface above it. Nakai discussed the bodies and the graves with the older women of her community, some who were a mixture of Kickapoo and Cherokee. An old woman told her that the elderly man in the grave was the "Cherokee who invented writing."

Pat Moss

Dr. Irwin Leoser

Just south of the Northeastern State University campus stands one of the oldest structures in the Cherokee Nation. It is a cabin that once belonged to Dr. Irwin Leoser, who came to Indian Territory with the Army, and was discharged at Fort Gibson. He helped to lay out the city of Tahlequah, and lived there until his death in 1877.

Leoser remained in the town through the Civil War. He was robbed and twice captured, but was always allowed to live because he was the only doctor in the area. Respected as he was, his cabin was also spared the ravages of the Civil War. He went on to serve as physician for the Male and Female Seminaries. Leoser Hall, a dormitory at Northeastern State University, is named for him as is Leoser Street, north of the campus. When traveling north on Muskogee Avenue in Tahlequah, turn right just before reaching the N.S.U. campus onto Goingsnake, then take the first street past the first house on your left. The Leoser cabin sits just ahead.

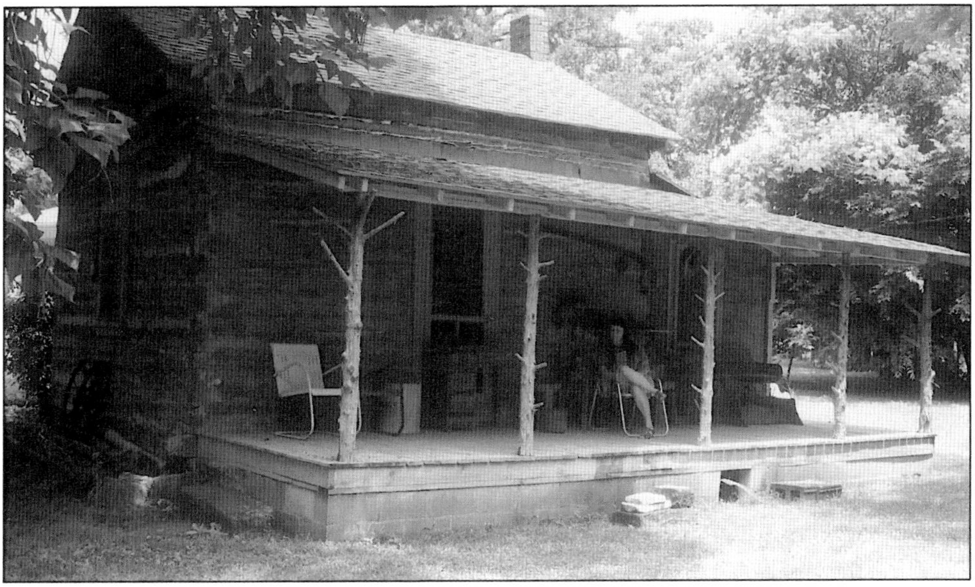

Leoser Cabin. (Photo by Murv Jacob.)

John Rollin Ridge, Novelist

After Major Ridge was murdered, his son John Rollin Ridge was eaten up with hatred. He left the Cherokee Nation for California, where he wrote for city newspapers. He sent letters back home to Stand Watie outlining elaborate plans to assassinate Principal Chief John Ross and take vengeance for his father's death.

In the 1850s John Rollin Ridge wrote the novel, "The Life and Times of Juaquin Murrietta." All movies and stories about the Mexican hero made since that time are based on Ridge's work.

The novel is the story of a brown-skinned man, persecuted by the whites, who emerges victorious in his adventures. Robert Conley calls it a marvelous work that must have done a world of good for Ridge, who was not able to do in the Cherokee Nation what the fictional character was able to do in the book.

Robert Conley

Stand Watie's Saddle Knife

Will Watie Wheeler was the son of John Finas Wheeler and Nancy Watie, a full-blood Cherokee of the Deer Clan. John was the first person to set the Cherokee syllabary into type, which he had cast in Cincinnati. He later became a typesetter on the Cherokee Phoenix, the tribal newspaper.

Will Watie served as his uncle Stand Watie's bodyguard. Stand made a promise that Will would one day inherit his much-admired saddle knife. When Stand Watie died, his wife remembered the promise and sent the knife to Will. Will passed the knife on to Will, Jr., who passed it on to Will Watie Wheeler III.

In 1979, when the younger Wheeler passed away, his wife Katherine presented the saddle knife to the Cherokee National Museum in Tahlequah. The knife, complete with a weathered leather sheaf, is inscribed "Col. Stand Watie from F.A. Rector." For years it has been a favorite of the museum's artifacts, and is often on display.

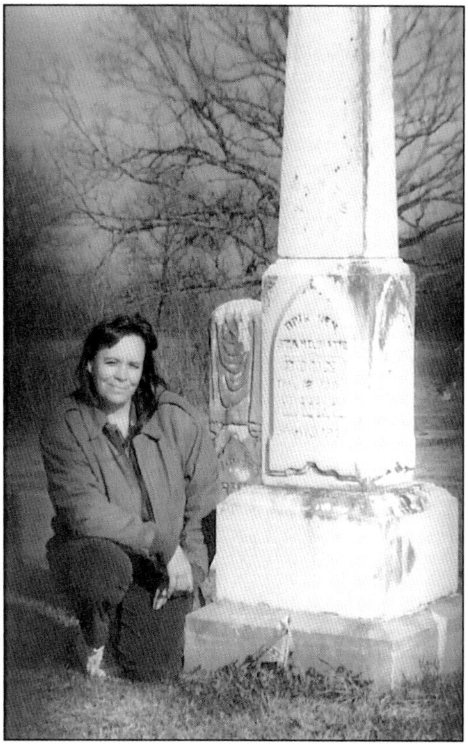

At Stand Watie's Grave, 1999. (Photo by Murv Jacob.)

W.C. Rogers, Principal Chief

The last elected chief of the Cherokee Nation before statehood was W.C. Rogers, a member of the Downing Party. Rogers was known among the Cherokees as the "merchant prince" because he owned trading posts in Talala, Skiatook, Vera, and Oologah. The original Skiatook was located on Bird Creek four or five miles north of where it stands today.

In July 1861, Rogers joined Company E of the First Regiment of Cherokee Volunteers under Confederate General Stand Watie. He was 15 years old and he drove an ammunition wagon for the troops. Rogers was interested in the old battle grounds and collected cannonballs and other memorabilia from Civil War sites in the Nation.

All the land documents issued during allotment contain the signature of Principal Chief W.C. Rogers. He once signed over 12,000 in one night. Rogers married Nan Haynie, known far and wide as Aunt Nan, the daughter of S.B. and Georgiana Haynie.

There is an unusual story about Chief Rogers, told by his grandson, Sequoyah Rogers. W.C. Rogers was charged for selling whiskey to the Cherokees and for assault. His bail for the assault charge was made by Clement Vann Rogers, father of Will Rogers. In July of 1893, Rogers went on trial for the murder of Lee Taylor, a U.S. deputy marshal. Taylor was a white man who was working around Skiatook to bring in whiskey runners. Rogers did not deny killing him, but claimed he did it in self defense.

It seems this deputy marshall had an eye for Rogers' wife, Nan, who was by all accounts a beautiful woman. Rogers said of Taylor, "He's like a dog you feed for awhile, then can't get rid of." On the day of the confrontation, Blackstone Tyner, a postmaster at the Skiatook trading post, took a customer by the arm and led him away, saying "You don't want to see this."

Rogers shot Taylor with a double barrel shotgun. He was tried in "hanging judge" Isaac Parker's court in Fort Smith, and found not guilty. Rogers contracted pneumonia during an epidemic in 1917 and died at Skiatook, Oklahoma.

Sequoyah Rogers

Jack Brown

The noted educator Jack Brown comes from a long line of respected Cherokee ancestors. His great-great-grandfather, John Brown, piloted boats on the Chattanooga River. It was said that he knew the river better than anyone else and could maneuver the crafts easily through it's treacherous rapids. His log cabin was used as a ferry stop on the river. Built in 1803, it still stands today as the oldest house in Hamilton County, Tennessee. John Brown also served as a Captain in the Indian Regiment under Andrew Jackson in the War of 1812. Little did he know then how his family would come to despise Jackson.

Jack Brown was born in 1887 at Marble City, Indian Territory. Jack's father, John Brown, was a Cherokee marshal who transported prisoners from the territory to Judge Isaac Parker's court in Fort Smith. He sometimes brought the prisoners to his home on the way there to spend the night. They slept on a pallet before the fireplace.

John Brown had his fair share of Cherokee wit and enjoyed using it. When his son Jack was born, John's sister Narcissa was in attendance. Narcissa had crossed the Trail of Tears and truly despised white men. Just to tease her, he named his new son Andrew Jackson Brown. The boy came to be known as Jack Brown. When he joined the Indian Service, he had the name Andrew Jackson legally changed to simply Jack.

Jack Brown's wife, Nola, was a wealthy descendant of the Choctaw, Greenwood LeFlore, a signer of the Treaty of Dancing Rabbit. This agreement allowed a group of Choctaws to remain on a small piece of land in the southeast following the Removal.

For over 30 years, Jack Brown served as the superintendent of the Cherokee Orphanage that became Sequoyah High School. The institution was first housed in the old Cherokee Insane Asylum building. After 1907, the State of Oklahoma provided care for its mental patients, and the Cherokees converted the asylum into an orphanage school, serving children up to grade six. Children who lived there were required to be one-half or more Cherokee and to have lost at least one parent. Brown strived to add one grade per year to the school until it became a high school.

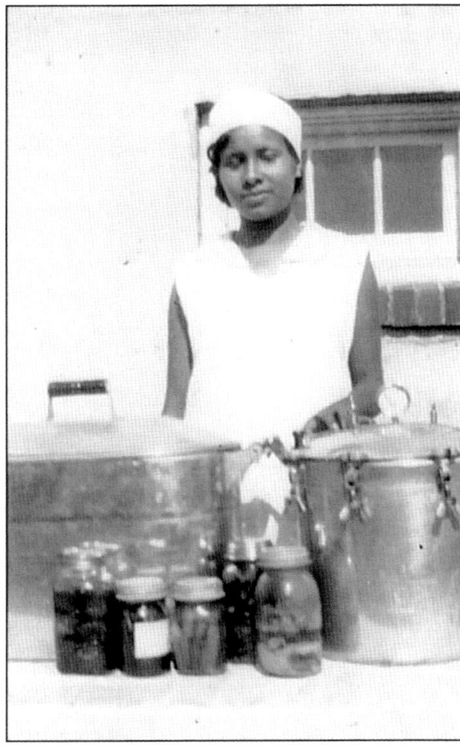

Annie Gritts, Sequoyah High School. (Courtesy Cherokee National Archives.)

Jack and Nola had a daughter, Marion, who grew up in their home on the grounds of the orphanage school. She remembers it as a wonderful place to live, where she had many friends to play with all through her childhood. Everyone there felt a sense of togetherness, and each older girl cared for a little girl, who she would bathe, dress, and groom. The older boys cared for the smaller boys in the same way. They all competed with each other to see whose little one was the best dressed. Today, Marion is a respected citizen of Tahlequah. Like her father before her, she works valiantly for the good of her beloved Cherokee Nation.

Marion Brown Hagerstrand

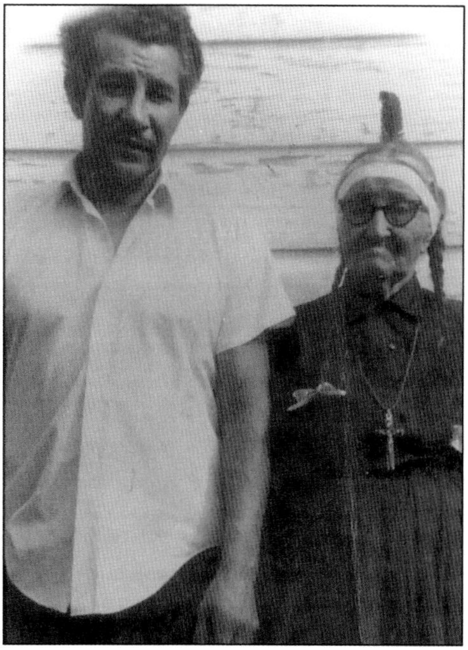

Sallie Toney Davis and Son. (Courtesy Talmadge Davis.)

Sallie Toney Davis

Sallie Toney and her twin sister Catherine were full-blood daughters of Susie Foster, who was the daughter of Sallie Guess, who was the daughter of Rebecca Bowles and George Guess, better known to the world as Sequoyah. The surname "Toney" came from the Cherokee "Too-noo-wee." Sallie married Robert Lee Davis, another full-blood Cherokee, and they settled along the southern edge of the Cherokee Nation at Porum Landing.

Sallie was sought after for her services as a midwife. She traveled with a country doctor for years, and delivered about 225 babies. "Aunt Sallie," considered a spiritual, traditional Cherokee woman, was a loved and respected member of the community. When people had problems or needed help finding lost animals, they went to Sallie for advice. Once she was visiting with her expectant daughter-in-law when she heard a screech owl outside. She told the young woman to cover her ears so that the owl would not mark her baby.

Sallie and her husband raised turkeys for some time on their allotment land in Porum. She loved animals, particularly dogs, and would take in any stray that looked hungry and needed a home. She used to joke with her grandchildren that she would make sure her dogs got fed even if the kids didn't. Sallie used snuff and refused to give it up until her death at the age of 96.

One of Sallie's grandchildren is the award-winning Cherokee artist, Talmadge Davis. He painted a beautiful portrait of Sallie, entitled "Quiet Dignity - My Grandma." Talmadge remembers when he was about seven years old and Sallie would wake him up early in the morning. She would send him to the woods with a .22 rifle to shoot some squirrels for breakfast. She would clean the squirrels and fry them up, and serve them with biscuits and gravy.

Sallie loved to tell stories to her grandchildren and Talmadge loved to listen. Using broken English, she often told a story of her ancestor Sequoyah and the White Butterfly. While visiting Dr. Abram's museum in Cherokee, North Carolina, Talmadge discovered among his collection a painting that featured Sequoyah, the White Butterfly and his grandmother Sallie.

Sallie always smoked a corncob pipe and wore a head-scarf on her head. The family has one photograph of her without it on. They fixed her up a headband with a feather sticking up in the back, and she posed for the photo with her son.

Although Sallie attended the Baptist Church, she was very traditional. Her funeral was attended by so many friends and acquaintances that dozens had to stand outside the church.

Talmadge Davis

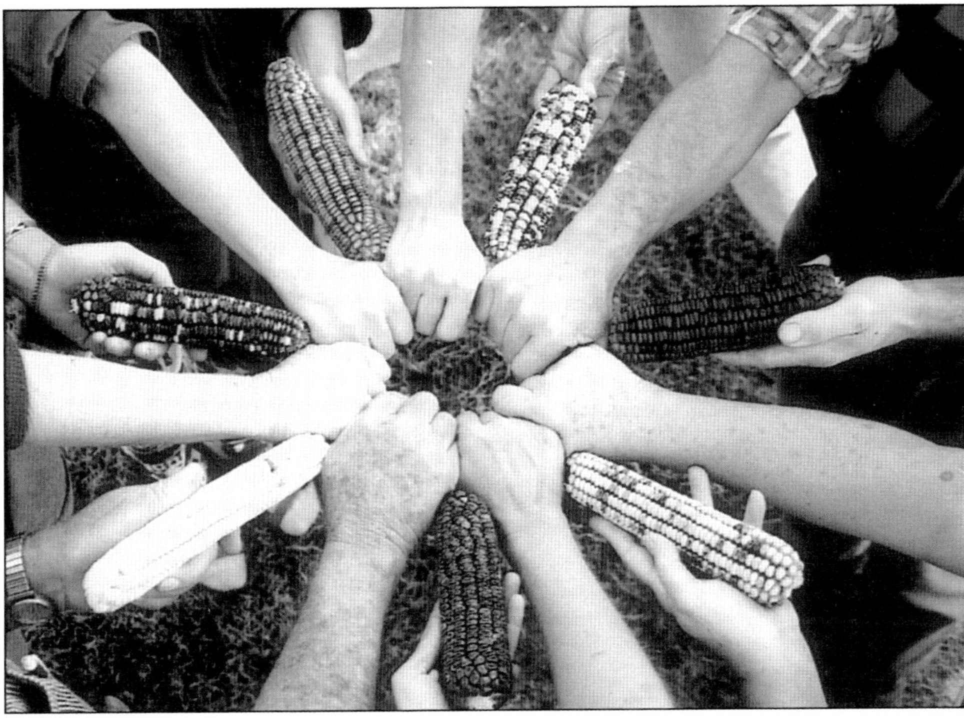

Sacred Seed Gathering, c. 1980. (Courtesy Carl Barnes.)

CHAPTER 3

THE NATURAL WORLD

The land of the Cherokees in Oklahoma is unequaled for its natural beauty. Its woodlands form one of the most diverse forests in the world, with countless species of trees, shrubs, grasses, and wildflowers. Here live all manner of wild creatures and game animals like deer, raccoons, squirrels, and rabbits. The forest is fed by clear, spring-fed creeks and scenic rivers.

The first blast of winter brings with it bald eagles from the north. Those who brave the crisp air for a canoe trip down the Illinois River see plenty of eagles. They may even see the work of traditional Cherokees who leave chopped fish in the shallows as gifts to the sacred birds.

Spring arrives in a spectacle of color as the air fairly buzzes with sounds of life. With it come terrific storms that both frighten and delight the locals. The heat of summer can be extreme. By the end of August, people are longing for the early days of October, perhaps the most magnificent time of year in Oklahoma.

People here have learned to appreciate both the beauty and the danger of their environment. All the fangs, fins, feathers, flowers, and funnel clouds of nature are synonymous with home.

A Strike of Luck

Robert Lee Sanders was a member of the Nighthawk Society of Keetoowahs. The organization held its meetings at night on the Illinois River in a special location. On occasion, the members would bring the women of their families to a spot near the meeting place where they built fires and prepared a feast to enjoy with the group.

Robert and his wife left home one evening on horseback after dark and headed for the Keetoowah meeting place on the river. It was a warm evening and an unexpected storm came up. Soon it was pitch dark and the pair got off the path. They reached a point where their horses would go no further despite their efforts to urge them on. A moment later, a huge bolt of lightning lit up the entire area. In the flash of light, the pair looked down the sheer face of a cliff on which they perched with their horses.

The couple found their way back to the path. Soon the storm was gone and they reached the meeting grounds without further incident. The ladies cooked a grand meal, the men went off a ways to have their meeting, and husband and wife made it home a little before daylight the next morning.

Sally Sanders Finch

The Peggs Tornado

If the busy town of Peggs had endured, it could well have exceeded its northern neighbor Locust Grove in population and growth. But on the afternoon of May 1, 1920, the city and surrounding countryside were laid waste by one of the fiercest tornadoes ever seen in Oklahoma. The same storm system killed several people in the town of Chelsea. Citizens in nearby Tahlequah and other communities remembered well the black cloud that lay, threatening and unmoving for hours, to the west.

When the storm finally let go, it descended with a fury upon Peggs, wiping out grocery and hardware stores, two cotton gins and dozens of homes. The town's bank, a beautiful cut stone structure, was swept totally away. Most horrifying was the loss of life. One-half of the population was killed or wounded. In all, 59 people died. Even underground shelters were of little use in the face of the tornado. In one storm cellar, a single person managed to resist the winds that ripped off the door, pulling another 12 people through the air to their deaths.

Famed Cherokee artist Cecil Dick was a young boy at that time, and lived in the Rose community, 12 miles north of Peggs. News of the storm's devastation traveled quickly, and the next day Cecil set out with his father, U.S. Marshall Andy Dick, to visit the scene. They followed the valley of Spring Creek to the road leading up the 100 yard ascent to the Peggs Prairie. As Cecil and Andy climbed higher, they encountered debris from shattered buildings and machines. Further on, trees were stripped of their leaves and impaled on their branches were the corpses of horses and cattle.

When Cecil and his father topped the hill nearing Peggs, they came upon a country church still standing where stunned survivors were bringing together the dead of the community. According to Cecil, the bodies were "stacked up like cordwood." There were no funerals, only prayers. Across the road from the church, neighbors worked together to dig graves as a new cemetery was opened for those lost to the storm. The smell of death in the summer heat and the horror of that day were etched in Cecil's memory. He recounted the tale to descendants and friends throughout his lifetime.

The Peggs community exists today with a few stores, houses, churches, and a school, but never recovered its former structure. Those exploring the surrounding woodlands will still find twisted metal grown into the trees or driven in the ground, and the foundations of homes, long since gone.

Murv Jacob

Selu

Dub West tells of the importance of corn in "Folklore and Legends of the Cherokees." Selu is the Cherokee word for corn, the tribe's most essential garden vegetable.

One of the most important of the yearly festivals was the Green Corn Dance. In Cherokee tradition, this was a time when prayers were sent up for happiness and peace, sins were forgiven, and criminals might receive amnesty. No new corn was tasted before the ceremony.

Seven ears of corn were always saved from the old crop to use as seed for the new crop. The corn was planted in little hills, with seven grains to each hill. After the last working of the ground, a priest entered a small structure placed in the center of the field. From this, he sang to the corn spirit, without looking in the field. Before long he heard the rustling of "the old woman" bringing the ears of corn into the field. This ritual was repeated for four nights. No one could enter the field then for seven more days. Then the priest would go in and find the young ears beginning to grow.

The trail between a person's home and the corn field was always kept cleaned and swept so that the corn would want to stay home and not wander off. When eating the cooked corn, the people never blew their breath on the ears to cool them, because to do so could cause a windstorm.

The Eagle Corn

Carl Barnes is a Cherokee traditionalist who works to preserve the ancient strains of corn that once sustained the native people of North America for centuries. Carl has studied Cherokee culture since he was five years old and his Grandfather Barnes first made him aware of his heritage.

Carl learned that several hundred years ago, the corn bore the symbols of the spirits. The shape of a buffalo, a dove, or an eagle would regularly show up near the top, colored portion of the seed, or kernel. After the white man interfered with the ways of the Indian, the symbols disappeared from the corn. But legend promised that one day the spirits would return, along with the symbols. This would be a time of reconnecting of the people with the land and the spirits.

Throughout his life Carl has tended the sacred Cherokee corn. Sometime in the late 1980s, the white eagle began to appear on selected kernels of the corn. The corn seed is a purple color, and the white figure of the eagle stands out unmistakably against the darker seedcoat. It looks as if a tiny, perfect outline of an eagle were cut from a white sticker, then pasted to the seed. As the years pass, the eagle becomes ever more clear and detailed.

Carl's carefully tended seed is the old corn from centuries past. He says the old seeds contain a powerful energy. He plants the seeds in a double-spiral pattern, like the double helix of the DNA molecule, with one side going clockwise and the other going counterclockwise.

Carl Barnes

Healing Springs

Known throughout the area for his memorable songs, musician Eddie Glenn is also a talented photographer and feature writer for the Tahlequah Daily Pictorial Press. While researching a story, Eddie ran across an article from 1881 in the Fort Worth Star Telegram about the seven healing springs of Tahlequah. The springs come together to form the creek that runs through town. In those days, people would camp on the banks of the creek in the warm months, and the Cherokee doctors would treat them with the healing water. The article went on to state that this was not a money making scheme, the practitioners did not brag or advertise, and the "patients" sincerely believed that they would be healed.

One spring emerges at the Methodist Home, northwest of town, and another wells up behind the houses on the south end of Seminary Avenue. These are joined by several more at Beta Pond on the Northeastern State University campus. One local Cherokee medicine man continues to use the water for healing, carrying home a fresh barrel every week.

At one time there was a bath house on the north side of Tahlequah where, for 25 cents, patrons could enjoy a hot or cold bath in the spring water. In Indian Territory, Tahlequah was called the City of Springs, and the Cherokee Nation was declared by some to be the garden spot of the world.

According to Dub West, there are older people who say that the oil spring that was discovered some miles north of Tahlequah had even better healing properties. It was said that if Ponce de Leon had found the oil spring, he would have truly found his Fountain of Youth.

In 1980, artist and traditionalist Cecil Dick performed a ripe corn ceremony on the town creek in Tahlequah. This is one of the seven sacred ceremonies of the year. Cecil roasted ripe corn to distribute at the Cherokee National Holiday. He felt that the bank of Bear Creek was the most appropriate place for the ceremony, even though his chosen spot was in the middle of the City Park.

Murv Jacob

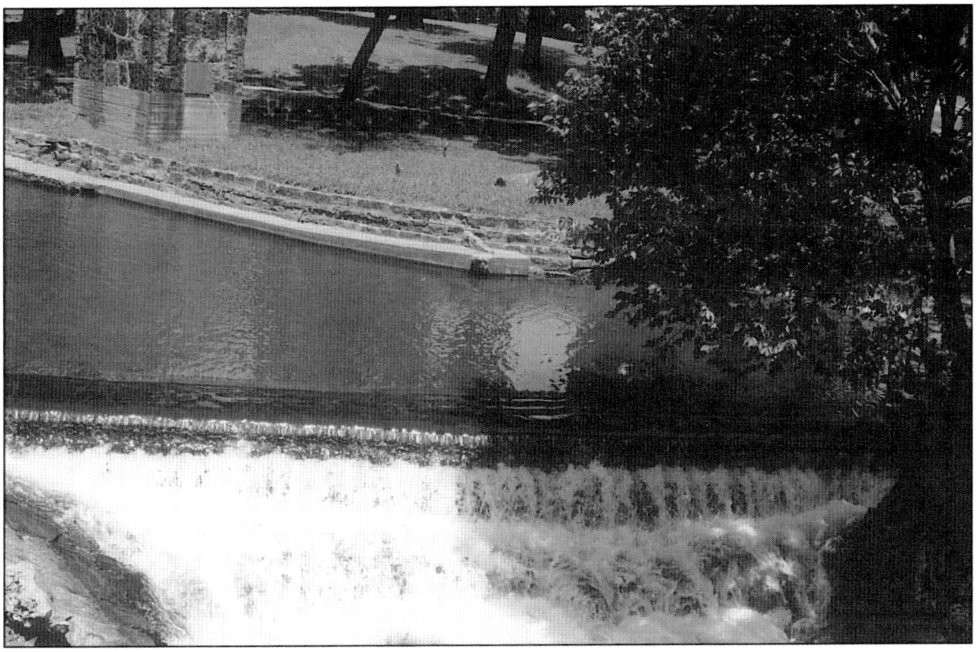

Town Branch Near Beta Field. (Photo by Murv Jacob.)

Tahlequah's Crystal

Quartz crystals are sacred to the Cherokee people. They are used by crystal gazers to divine needed information and for protection. Some crystals are extremely special and rare, and are hard to come by. One such crystal was said to exist with the remains of Stonecoat, a creature of legend. Another protrudes from the head of the Uktena, a powerful winged serpent. Before the Trail of Tears, a Seneca boy named Bullet set out to take the crystal from the Uktena. It is believed that he figured a way to do this, and succeeded.

There is an old story that the Cherokee people had such a crystal in their possession when they crossed the Trail of Tears to what is now Tahlequah. The people saw the beautiful springs that ran through the valley. They realized that this place would become the capital of the Cherokee Nation. The crystal they carried had a steak of red running through it. In its center was an artery, filled with blood. The crystal was buried, and still remains somewhere in the bed of Bear Creek, the stream that runs through Tahlequah.

Pat Moss

The Haunted Ravine

One evening at sundown, Charlotte Mayes was heading home on horseback to the family farm near Pryor, Oklahoma. A thunderstorm was brewing and the wind was picking up. Charlotte decided to take the only shortcut home, through a deep ravine in the woods which was said to be haunted. The wind was howling as she reached the entrance of the ravine, and it was beginning to rain. The horse had no intention of going in and Charlotte had to force him to go on. A few feet into the pass, Charlotte noticed how quiet everything had become. Inside the valley was an eerie dead calm, with not a leaf stirring, although there was a terrific storm all around. The horse was so skittish he jumped if he brushed against a leaf or stepped on a branch.

Horse and rider picked their way carefully through the stony silence of the ravine until they reached the steep incline leading out. There the horse broke into a gallop and the storm descended back upon them as soon as they left the ravine. Charlotte's horse did not stop running until they reached the farm. Charlotte was the niece of Principal Chief Samuel Houston Mayes and Principal Chief Joel Bryan Mayes. Her father, also named Samuel, was known as Little Sam.

Sally Sanders Finch

The Cloudburst

One July day in the 1920s, Leon Corntassel remembers a storm from out of the west that "set Mom and Dad to praying." The family lived in a house across the hollow from an old farm. It seemed that the storm came up out of the valley. Leon and his brother stood by the kitchen window and watched as the wind and rain pounded outside. A little plum tree at the edge of the yard took flight and hit the house right by that window. Whole groves of trees disappeared in the storm.

Off to the north, 15-inches of rain fell, and a 20-foot wall of water rushed down the valley near their home. A freight train had stopped in that valley between two bridges, but when the engineer saw the rising water, he put the train in reverse, and backed all the way up to safety. He waited 20 minutes and the water had gone, taking with it Willie Whitmire's corn patch and all his tools.

Leon Corntassel

Cat Tales

One day when I was a toddler, I was overcome by a heat stroke. My mother carried me inside our house and worked to bring down my body temperature, fearing that I was deathly ill. As she did so, she began to hear the frightful sound of cats, howling loudly at the front screen door, hanging by their claws all over the screen, crying to be let in. As I began to recover, the cats went away, but my mother was sure they were drawn to the house and were trying to get in because they knew I was near death.

Charlotte Sanders told her daughter about how people used to keep the bodies of dead family members on their porches before burial. A family that lived near Pryor had placed a deceased relative on their porch one evening. Soon afterward, they began to hear a panther screaming in the distance and coming closer and closer to the house. Instinctively, the family brought the body inside, barely getting the door shut as the panther landed on the porch.

It was customary in those days for neighbors and friends to go and sit up with a body all night. One night Charlotte was sitting with a body in the home of a friend. The only light was a kerosene lamp. Suddenly she heard a loud screech as a big cat jumped up on the screen door and just hung there by its claws.

Sally Sanders Finch

Chickens and Snakes

The Sanders family always had chickens, and those who raise chickens in Oklahoma can count on battling snakes. One night the whole family was awakened by loud cries of alarm from setting hens in the chicken coop. Robert Lee Sanders grabbed his gun, called for his wife Charlotte to bring a light, and set out after the culprit. The kids got out of bed and tore up the hill after them.

The chicken coop sat beneath a rock ledge where a big blacksnake was climbing up to make his escape. Although blacksnakes are not poisonous, they are a great danger to poultry, and will often kill a setting hen to get at her eggs. Charlotte Sanders did not intend to let this one get away. Dressed in a long nightgown and holding a kerosene lamp in one hand, she grabbed the snake by the tail and held it back while Robert Lee shot its head off.

On another occasion, the family heard Robert Lee's shotgun go off and ran to see what had happened. They came upon a huge rattlesnake whose head had been separated from its body. The head, with eyes glittering, was still opening and closing its mouth. The kids had a rat terrier who grabbed the rattler's body and began shaking it furiously, dislodging a whole frog from inside.

Sally Sanders Finch

All About Gigs

Gigging for fish is an art form that has been perfected for centuries by Native American people. It is the most popular fishing method of traditional Cherokees. The metal end of the gig is about 10-inches long with two 6-inch tines. Each tine has a sharp point with a barb, like that of a fishhook, two inches from the tip. Most gigs are handmade by a blacksmith like Cherokee Living Treasure Todum Hair, from the springs of old Model A or Model T Fords. The 10 to 12-foot handles are made of seasoned walnut wood.

Cherokees gig at night and the best

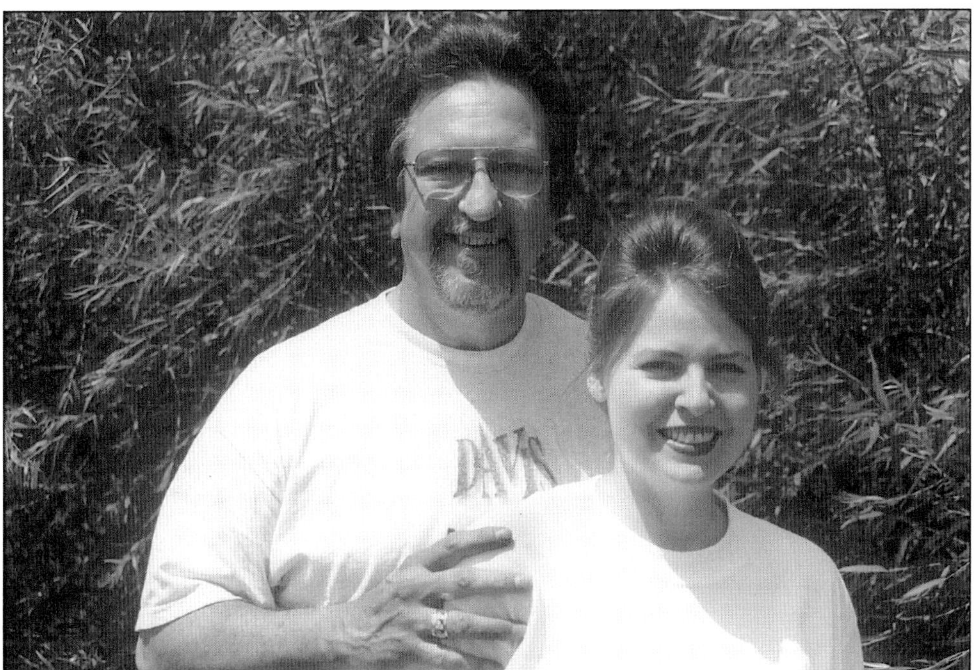

Wayne and Katherine Mitchell, 2000. (Photo by Murv Jacob.)

time is in the spring when certain fish are shoaling. Their flat bottom boats may be hand made of cypress sealed with tar. They keep the boats in water and never let them dry out, else they would leak. At the front end of the boat, a torch casts light on the water both to attract and illuminate the fish. Behind it, the gigger stands poised with the gig awaiting a target.

When a fish is spotted, the gig is aimed and thrown under the fish to correct for deflection of the water. Cherokees gig for drum, catfish, horny heads, carp, buffalo, and all sucker fish, but their prized favorite by far is the redhorse. Its meat has a delicious, sweet flavor.

To prepare a redhorse, they scale and gut the fish, then remove the head and cut score lines down through the rib bones crosswise, breaking the bones. The fish is dipped in corn meal and fried over high heat. The hot grease gets down into the score lines and disintegrates the bones, making them entirely edible. Sometimes Cherokees make little gigs out of kitchen forks for taking crawdads. They pull off the heads and bodies and throw them back to the bass. The tails are cooked shell-on in butter for a treat better than lobster.

Wayne Mitchell

Coon Hunting at Elk Creek

If there ever was a professional coon hunter it would be Ralph Dunham, lifelong resident of Cherokee County and lifelong hunter of coons. His all-time best and favorite coon dog was a blue-tick hound named Old Blue. Blue had a distinctive voice and loved nothing better than to use it on a treed coon. Many times Old Blue would stay treed deep in the woods all night, and Ralph would go back for him the next day. Ralph usually had partners who hunted with him. For years, a young full-blood Cherokee neighbor named Sheldon Smith accompanied him, and another hunting partner was Clifford Cantrell, a Southern Baptist preacher.

Coon hunting requires you to be fleet of foot and quick to think. Everywhere there are fallen logs and holes that can break ankles. It's dark and you have to hurry, never knowing what hazard the coon may lead you to.

One night Old Blue chased a coon and treed it inside an old deserted cabin at Chicken Creek, southeast of Tahlequah in the Cookson Hills. Ralph and two other hunters entered the dark cabin. Ralph was holding his gasoline lantern above his head, looking for the coon, but there were too many holes and places for it to hide. He climbed up on some boards to see better, then stepped down too hard and went on down through the floor. He found out then that there was a big hole beneath the cabin where a whiskey still had once been. Through it all, the lantern stayed lit, Ralph was unharmed, and the coon was caught.

Another night at Elk Creek, Ralph and the Reverend Clifford Cantrell and his dog were sitting down under a tree waiting for Old Blue. He had taken off through the night after a deer, and was in for some real trouble when he got back.

Pretty soon they heard Old Blue coming, but he stopped just before he reached them. Blue had treed six coons, and they were all in the same tree. Ralph had never taken so many coons at once, but Clifford had made a bet with some other hunters that he and Ralph could get back with the most coons, and insisted that Ralph take them all. With his left hand, Ralph held his light on top of his head in order to see his targets. With his right, he shot all six coons with his .22 automatic Sports King pistol.

The biggest coon Ralph ever caught was treed on the back steps of the then new Restaurant of the Cherokees. His daughter, Debbie, has the tanned hide.

Ralph Dunham

Coon Hunter's Daughter

One night Ralph Dunham decided it was time for his daughter Debbie, then age 12, to accompany him and their neighbor Sheldon, age 14, on a moonlit coon hunt through the woods. Even though it was cool weather, Debbie's mother made her rub kerosene around her ankles to keep the bugs out of her boots, and put on two shirts and a red jacket. The hunting dogs who went along were Old Blue and his blue-tick offspring Pete and Jack. Pete and Jack were in training that night, and so was Debbie.

To get to the good hunting woods, the trio had to first cross a pasture where there lived a big bull, or at least that's what Sheldon said. All Debbie could think of was that there was a bull in there and she was wearing a red jacket. By some miracle the bull never noticed the red and the group crossed the fence into the deep woods.

The first thing Pete and Jack did was chase a skunk into a patch of blackberry briars. They ran around the bushes barking like crazy while the skunk fumigated the whole area. The dogs finally lost interest in the skunk after much coaxing from Ralph and a new scent that assailed their nostrils. It was a big old possum. Sheldon took aim and shot the possum. Debbie was impressed by all this until it came time to move along. Being the one with the least seniority in the group, she had to carry the possum.

After a few minutes Old Blue let everyone know that he had picked up the scent of a coon. He streaked off into the woods with Ralph and Sheldon close behind. Debbie had a lantern in one hand and the tail of a heavy possum in the other and was struggling to keep up with the others. Suddenly something had hold of her right leg. The possum had come back to life and wrapped its four legs around her leg. Well this about scared Debbie to death, and she hollered for Ralph to help. By now the possum had fully recovered, loosed its hold on Debbie's leg, and was making every effort to get its tail free from her hand.

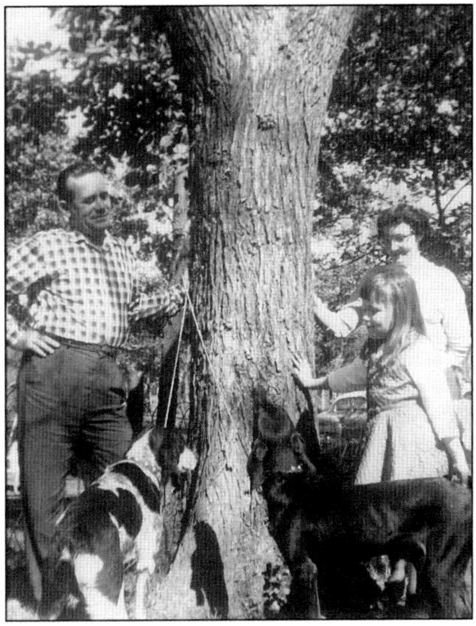

The Dunham Family and Old Blue, c. 1963. (Courtesy Loretta Dunham.)

"Don't let him go!" Ralph laughed. "Just hold him out straight beside you." With one shot, the possum was dead and Debbie, nerves frazzled, was ready to go home. Meanwhile, Old Blue was telling his master that the coon was treed and there was work to do. Debbie followed the hunters to the tree and gratefully laid down the possum and began to look up to catch a glimpse of the coon. Under that tree were three dogs and three people, and when Ralph shot the coon out of the tree, it landed directly on top of Debbie's head. Instantly, the three dogs were after it. When Debbie emerged from the mass of whirling dogs, it was with a new resolution. She never intended to go coon hunting again.

Debbie Dunham Duvall

Hunting Bears

Back in the southeastern Cherokee lands the mountains abound with bears, and the people still hunt them for both food and hides. Cooked properly, the red meat is a delicacy with a distinctive flavor that many traditional Cherokees enjoy. The hunters bring along big hound dogs, like black and tans or blue-ticks, to track the bears.

Perry VanBuskirk and Tim Grayson from Tahlequah went on their first bear hunt while visiting friends in North Carolina. When the hunting party arrived in the woods, Perry was handed two leashes with a pair of powerful hound dogs straining against them. Going up the first steep hill was easy because the dogs were pulling Perry behind them. When they started down the other side, they came upon a fallen log. The dogs leaped over it as Perry tripped over it. The leashes were looped around his wrists, and the dogs never stopped. Neither did Perry. The dogs dragged him on his stomach to the bottom of the hill. When he finally got them stopped, the seasoned bear hunters told him it was time to let the dogs go.

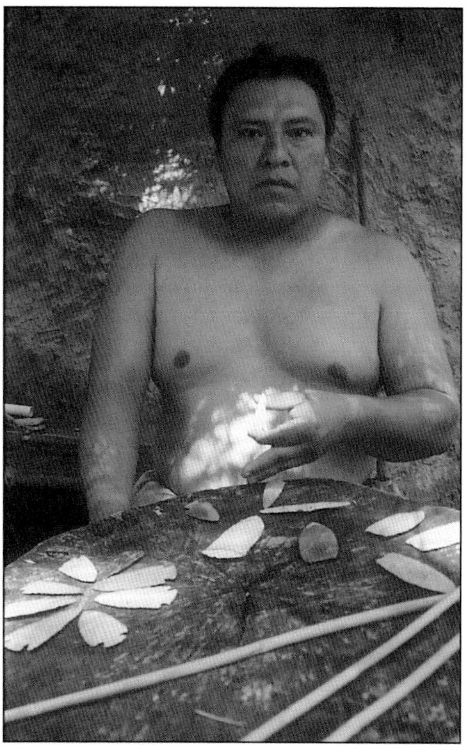

Tim Grayson, 2000. (Photo by Murv Jacob.)

In a little while they could hear that the two hounds had something treed. Perry and Tim headed toward the barking dogs. They worked their way to the tree, saw the dogs at the base and the bear in the branches, then realized that neither of them had brought along a gun. Meanwhile, their hunting partners had gotten a bear. Perry was offered the hide if he would skin it. Perry had always heard, and now found out it was true, that a skinned bear's body looks just like a human being.

An old story tells how a man entered the woods to find food for his hungry family. As he went further, his body grew hairy, and he dropped to all fours to travel through the woods. When he returned home, he resumed his human form. He told his whole family to follow him into the woods. They became the bear people, who would always be there to provide food for the Cherokees.

Perry VanBuskirk

Rattlesnake Steak

In the early 1970s, roommates Sam and Ernie lived in a small rented house in Tahlequah. Once while cave crawling the friends found a rattlesnake, captured it and began keeping it in an aquarium at their house.

Sam got pretty good at handling the snake, and would take it from the aquarium and carry it around with him. The last time he held the snake and put it back in the container, it bit his hand before he could pull back. Sam grabbed a razor blade from the bathroom, cut the wound and tried to suck out the poison, but it overpowered him and he passed out on the floor.

Ernie saw Sam fall and immediately called an ambulance. The ambulance attendants came to the door, but thinking the snake was loose in the house, were reluctant to go inside. Ernie dragged poor Sam out of the bathroom to the waiting attendants who rushed him to the hospital. Sam's heart stopped beating twice on the way, and he was told that had he gone another seven minutes without help, the venom would have killed him.

For some reason, while Sam was recuperating, Ernie kept the rattler in a tow sack. It stayed there for about two weeks, well after Sam had come back home. One evening they had the tow sack outside, and let the snake out onto the gravel driveway. They played with it until it began to strike at them, then they killed the snake, put it on a charcoal grill, cooked it and had rattlesnake steak for supper.

Neicey Dunham

Medicine Tales

According to legend, the animals of the earth turned against the people, who were always killing the animals for food and clothing. They had a great council and were able to make diseases that would cause the people to sicken and die. The plants of the earth cared for the people and for every disease the animals made, the plants made a cure. The Cherokees are blessed with people who know the plants and how to use them. These traditions have passed through generations and are still helping people today.

Some Cherokees believe that the old medicine people knew well before the Trail of Tears began that their people would someday be moved to what is now Oklahoma. They brought the healing herbs to this area long ago so the plants would be established and plentiful when their descendants arrived. Most of the medicinal plants found in Oklahoma are also found in the east. However, an herb used in Oklahoma to treat a fever might be used there to treat a stomach complaint.

Some plants, like Goldenseal, will treat a number of illnesses. It works as an antibiotic, but will also stop a hemorrhage. Placed directly on a cut, ground goldenseal will stop the bleeding. There is supposed to be one plant that, if you can find it, will cure anything. The trouble is, it will hide from you.

Perry and Kathy VanBuskirk

Whirlwinds

They say a tornado will never hit Tahlequah, but some might disagree with that. It was a stormy spring afternoon, and Nick Duvall and his friend Johnny were walking down Muskogee Avenue from the Junior High. They were about to cross Keetoowah Street when a little funnel cloud came down and ripped a big green awning off the front of the bike shop. The awning spun in the air a few times, then was thrown over the Cort Mall into the alley.

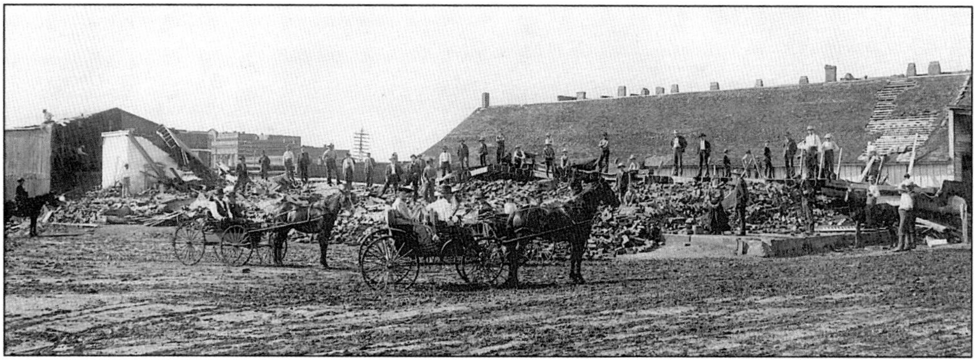

Aftermath, May 31, 1906 Tornado, Claremore. (Courtesy Rogers State College.)

Lela Krouse's house was hit once. Her furniture included a trunk that contained jewelry. The trunk sustained no damage at all, but a bracelet that was inside was twisted up and ruined.

On a hot, dusty summer afternoon Ralph Dunham and his wife Loretta both watched as a whirlwind came out of a clear blue sky. It pulled a good sized peach tree up out of the ground, twirled it in the air for a while, then tossed it down again.

Ralph depends upon the Oklahoma weather to do his tree maintenance for him. Just about every time one of the trees on his place needs topping, a good wind will come along and do the job. As he was leaving for a trip to Arkansas, Ralph commented that his big tulip tree really needed the top taken out. When he returned two days later, the treetop was lying in his driveway.

Ralph Dunham

A Fish Story

Neicey Dunham bought herself a brand new fishing rod and a Zebco 33 reel for her birthday. She was eager to try it out, and took her three daughters to Caney Ridge, on Lake Tenkiller, to fish off the boat dock. Rita, her youngest, was still a baby then. Neicey placed her in a folding play pen and got out the catfish bait.

Leroy Simons, a sports writer for the Tahlequah Daily Press, was out on a boat near the dock gigging for catfish. Neicie watched him as she sat waiting for a bite, until finally little Rita got bored and cranky. Neicey laid aside her pole to tend to her baby, and just then it was struck by something really big. Before she could catch it, her new fishing rod sailed off the dock and disappeared under water.

Neicey was downhearted and preparing to leave when Leroy, who was still gigging, shouted out that he had a big one. Neicie and the kids watched him pull up a 2-foot catfish that weighed about eight pounds into the boat. Then Leroy said, "Look, it's got a line in its mouth." Leroy pulled on the line and up popped Neicey's fishing pole, a little waterlogged but good as new. She still has it to this day.

Neicey Dunham

Nick's Cottonmouth

People who grow up in rural northeast Oklahoma learn at an early age to identify dangerous snakes, especially those in the water. The cottonmouth water moccasin, if provoked, can be aggressive and mean. If you see a fat, dark snake swimming with its backbone above the water, you can bet it's a bad one.

When Nick Duvall and his friend Carl Jones were kids in Tahlequah, they liked to hang around the south end of the Town Branch where the creek gets pretty deep and makes a good swimming hole. In those days, the area around the creek was thick with brush and a good place for winos to hide out and drink. Some even set up housekeeping there on the creek.

Nick and Carl were down there one time when a transient told the boys that a big snake was nesting by their swimming hole. They raced to Carl's house on their bikes and were back in a flash, armed with two BB guns and a two pocket knives. They searched all around but saw no sign of a snake. Pretty soon the boys got bored with that and jumped in the creek to swim a while.

Less than five minutes had passed when Nick saw the snake coming straight for them, with its entire back above the surface. He knew that was the way a cottonmouth swims. The boys hurried to shore and grabbed the BB guns. All that activity scared the snake and it slipped back into its hole in the opposite bank. The boys were fired up and took turns shooting at the hole, when finally the snake came charging out, ready for a fight. She was no match for them, and was soon killed. They waded across the creek to retrieve their prize, then wondered what they should do with it. Being inquisitive types, they thought they might as well dissect the snake and see what was inside it.

Out came the pocket knives and the autopsy was underway. About halfway down the snakes belly, a little sack popped out, spilling baby snakes all around the mother's body. They were perfect little cottonmouths, "all rolled up," but not yet ready to be born. Nick and Carl had no doubt then that this was a pit viper, and highly poisonous. They had learned that, in Oklahoma, only poisonous snakes give birth without laying eggs. Carl thought his mom might be impressed with their trophy, so he and Nick took the dead snake to his house. Carl opened up a wire coat hanger, pried open the snake's mouth, fangs and all, poked the wire through its bottom jaw and hung it up on his front porch. He did not know it then, but he was in for big trouble when his mom got home and found the snake. Meanwhile, Carl and Nick went back to the creek, ready for a swim.

Nick Duvall

Noodling

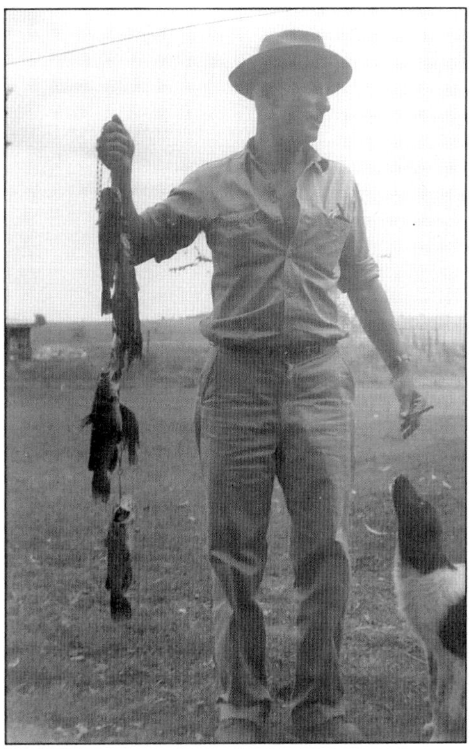

Hank Baker, 1958. (Courtesy Hank Baker.)

In the mud bank of the Illinois River, below the waterline, are hollowed out holes that go deep into the bank. On the first full moon of April, male catfish begin seeking out the holes for the upcoming spawning season. When the right hole is selected, the catfish spends several weeks clearing out the debris within it. He never leaves sight of the place until mating is over. His offspring will be born there.

Within this secluded space, the catfish is a prime target for noodlers. Noodling for catfish is an old Cherokee tradition that requires strength and know-how. The noodler feels along the bank with his hands until he locates a hole, holds his chest in front of the hole to keep the fish from coming out, and reaches in his arm sweeping the sides of the hole to feel for a catfish.

Until about the end of May, the catfish are docile and offer little resistance to the noodler's touch. He simply slips his hand through the catfish's mouth, getting hold of the gill plate. Then the fight begins. The fish rolls itself around the noodler's forearm, sometimes peeling off layers of skin. The fish could weigh 60 pounds or more and must be wrangled from its hole to dry land.

Once the mating catfish "go hard on a nest," when the eggs are present, they will fight off any intrusion with their very lives. The noodler's hand is mistaken for the black perch, a brave sunfish notorious for stealing the eggs of catfish.

People tell stories of noodlers pulling out cottonmouth water moccasins from the catfish holes. But they forget the cottonmouth breathes air and could not den up in the watery recesses.

Wayne Mitchell

Wildcat Whiskey, 1930s

Down in the woods around Shady Grove and Lost City, people knew the fine points of making wildcat whiskey. It was not legal to make and sell, but times were hard and whiskey was in high demand. The most common ingredients were shorts or bran like you feed to cows mixed up with water and any sweet substance that might be on hand, like apple juice or raisins. To this was added a little yeast to start the fermentation process. Ralph Dunham says the very best tasting "sour mash" contained watermelon juice.

When they were about 12 years old, Ralph and his friend Louis were out scouting around near Lost City and decided to drop in on Ralph's uncle. He was just running off a gallon jug of whiskey from his still, and as was done in those days, offered the boys as much as they liked.

Well, Louis did not know much about whiskey. He turned the jug up and took several huge gulps. When he put it down again, Louis could not get his breath. Ralph and his uncle carried him over to Spring Creek and threw him in the icy water, and the shock of it caused his body to breathe. For years after that, Louis refused to take a drink of alcohol.

Ralph Dunham

The Fireball

In the 1960s a four-lane highway was built in Tahlequah from the city limits east to Muskogee Avenue downtown. Before long the Sonic Drive-In was established, and it became the most popular spot in town immediately. Even today, the Tahlequah Sonic is the busiest and most successful of the chain in the country. A favorite pastime of Tahlequah teenagers was to "float the four-lane" and drive around the Sonic just to see who was there.

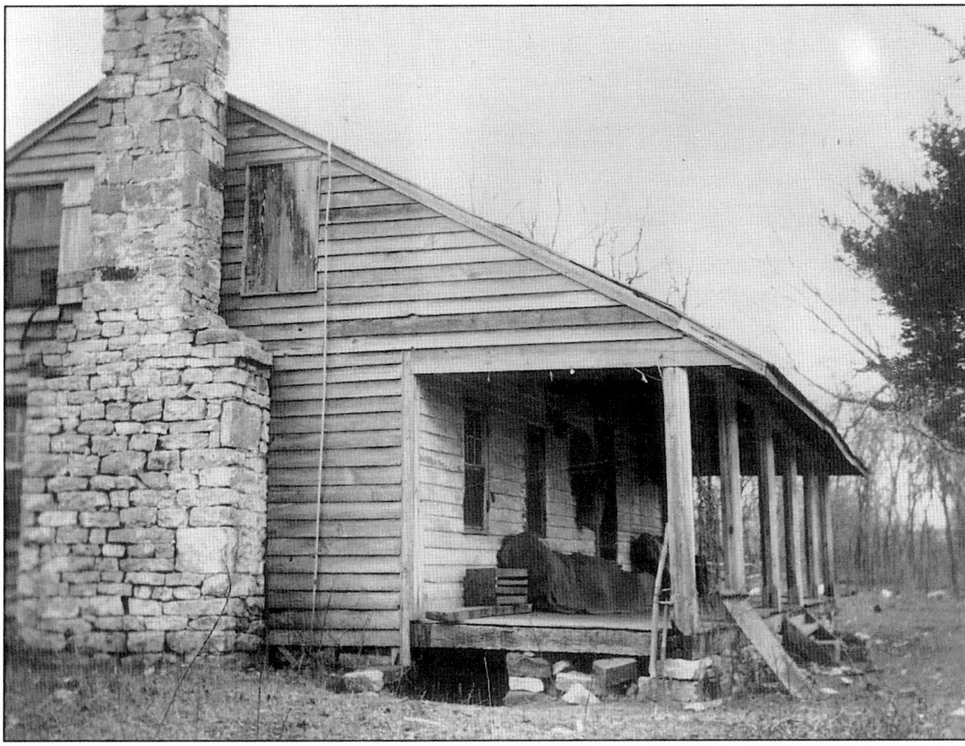

W.H. Hinton Home, Park Hill, 1930. (Courtesy Cherokee National Archives.)

One evening in 1969, Neicey Dunham and her friend Pam Russell were headed to the Sonic when they saw a huge ball of fire streak across the night sky. All traffic on the four-lane ceased, and people got out of their cars to watch its final descent off to the east. Neicey and Pam thought the thing had gone down close to the Illinois River, three miles east, and headed there to look for it. Later they heard the news broadcast about a large meteorite that had plunged into the ground in Arkansas.

Neicey was a flute player in both a rock and roll band and the Tahlequah Jr. High Band, and she was a good one. The next spring, the Tahlequah High School band was invited to march in the Cherry Blossom Festival parade in Washington DC. The streets on the parade route were eight lanes wide and the high school's band was not that big. So the junior high students who excelled were asked to go along, and Neicey was included.

When the parade was over, the band visited the Smithsonian Institute. There, in the center of an exhibit, stood the meteorite from Arkansas that Neicie and Pam had watched as it fell to earth. It had a hole in the middle, and standing on its edge, looked like a big gray doughnut.

Neicey Dunham

Outdoors with Joel

Joel Mayes Finch is named after his famous relative, Principal Chief Joel Bryan Mayes, and shares the family's sense of adventure and love of nature. Joel is a surveyor, and spends a good deal of his working days and leisure hours enjoying the great outdoors. Being outside in eastern Oklahoma for any length of time will assure a person

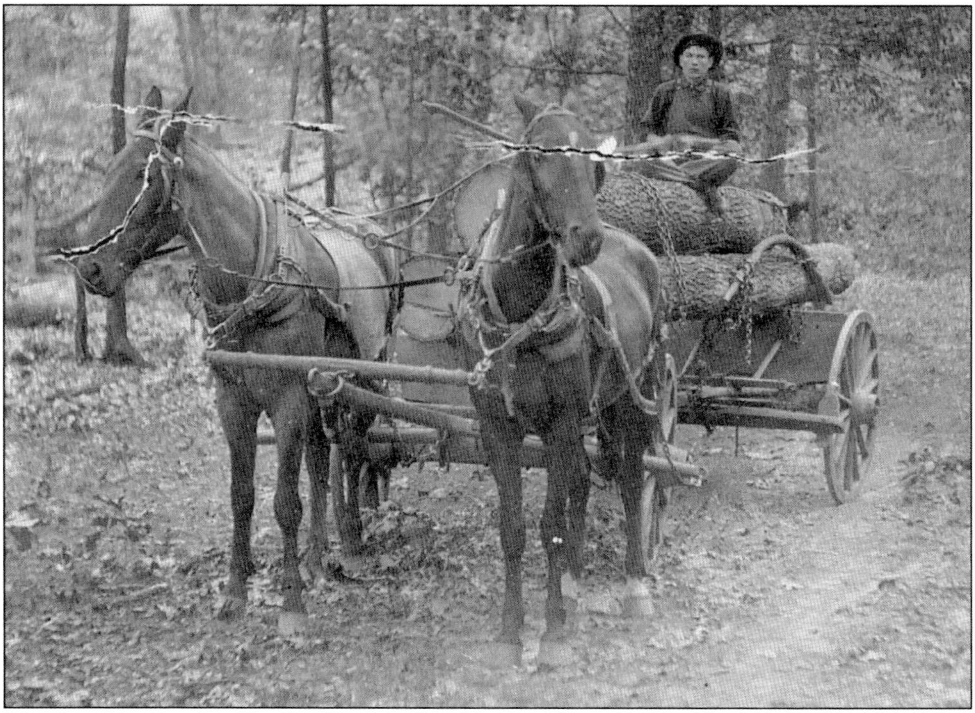

Hauling Timber, late 1800s. (Courtesy Cherokee National Archives.)

of direct contact with plenty of wildlife, and Joel has seen his share.

Joel was surveying in an area around Lake Wister, past the southern edge of the Cherokee Nation, where "there were so many snakes, you had to carry a gun." He and a co-worker had just trudged up out of a swamp onto a meadow of waist-high grass. Suddenly, he was face to face with a huge brown snake with most of its body standing straight up. The snake was hissing and waving back and forth, and it had a hood spread wide below its head. Both men, convinced it was a cobra, were so startled they threw down their gear and ran to get away. It then dawned on Joel that cobras do not live in Oklahoma, and he stopped running to look back at what he realized was a speading adder who was not alone. It was making a quick escape through the grass with its mate, having frightened off the intruders.

Joel was fishing in a pond near Stick Ross Mountain with an ultralight rod and reel when he hooked into a four-pound largemouth bass. It took two or three minutes of battling the big fish before it tired enough for Joel to reel him in. Just when he thought he had him, the bass jumped into the air, twisted from side to side, looked Joel right in the eye and spit the fishing lure out at his feet.

Joel and his wife were sitting on the tail-gate of their pickup after dark on a high bank above the Illinois River. They had pulled off Highway 10 near the old Echota House just to enjoy the evening air. The weather was chilly, and the river was quiet. They were looking out into the darkness when they heard something big hit the water on the opposite bank. Whatever it was, it was huge, and they could hear it making swimming strokes with what must have been arms. It quickly reached the bank below them, and they could hear it getting out of the water just as they scrambled into the truck, taking off as fast as it would go.

Joel Mayes Finch

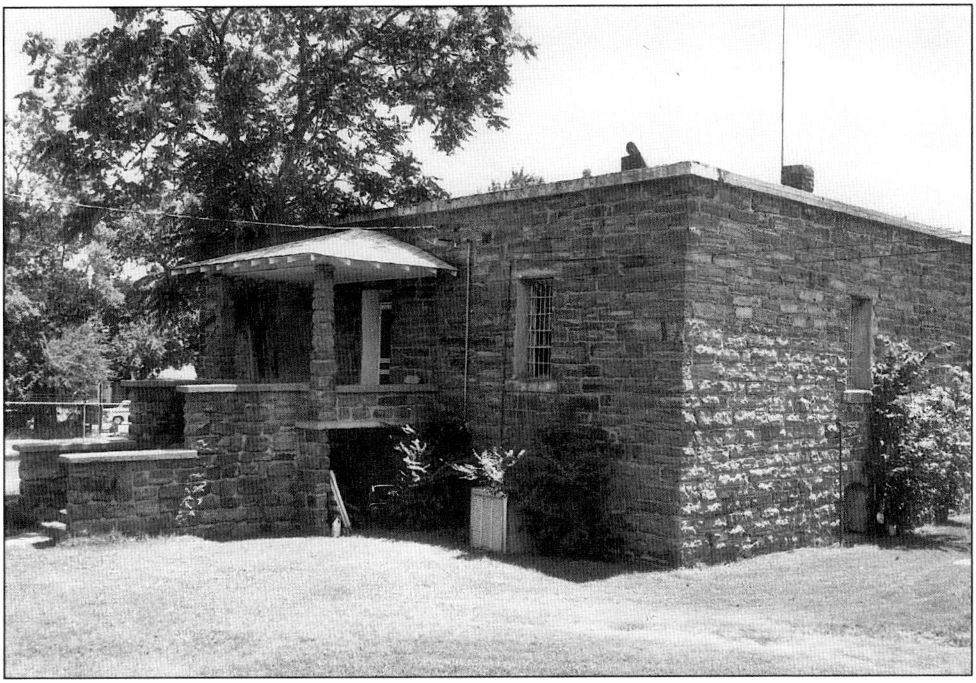
Cherokee National Prison. (Courtesy Cherokee National Archives.)

CHAPTER 4

OUTSIDE THE LAW

Before statehood, Indian Territory was a hotbed of activity for outlaws of every description. Wanted criminals from Arkansas, Kansas, Missouri and Texas often hid out in the Cherokee Nation where tribal peace officers had no jurisdiction over white lawbreakers. Instead, they were sought by deputy U.S. Marshals dispatched from the federal court in Fort Smith, Arkansas. It was not unusual for law-abiding residents of Indian Territory to find themselves face-to-face with notorious bank robbers and killers in those days. Just like in the western movies, many citizens in Tahlequah and other communities packed guns wherever they went. Cherokee figures Ned Christie and Zeke Proctor had the misfortune of being charged with the deaths of white men in Indian Territory. Both men fought back against Judge Isaac Parker's court, with surprisingly different outcomes

The Great Depression spawned a new generation of outlaws who came, not on horseback, but driving fancy cars and wielding machine guns. A gang could hide out in the wilderness of the Cookson Hills with little fear of being detected. They were tired of being poor, and so were many of the families who lived in Oklahoma. Some idolized the gangsters, especially Sallisaw's own Pretty Boy Floyd. When he was finally killed, people from all over the state flocked there to attend his funeral.

The Starr Family

Caleb Starr was a white man from Pennsylvania who moved to what is now eastern Tennessee where he met and married a Cherokee woman named Nancy Harlan in 1790. They had 12 children who grew up in agreement with their father's views supporting the removal of the southeastern Indians to the west. In 1834, Ezekiel Starr moved on west as his brother James remained in the Cherokee Nation where in 1835 he signed the Treaty of New Echota. Two years later, James joined Ezekiel in Indian Territory.

When members of the Ross faction assassinated Major Ridge, John Ridge, and Elias Boudinot for signing the removal treaty, their plan was to kill James Starr and Stand Watie on the same day. Yet both survived, and James went on to be elected a legislator from the Goingsnake District in 1841. The killings continued, however, and several attempts were made on James Starr's life. This enraged his son, Tom, who sought revenge. He was accused of murdering an entire family at Fort Gibson. The Ross faction put a price on Thomas Starr's head of $1,000.

As Tom remained a hunted outlaw, the Ross faction decided to make his father pay for his crimes. In 1845, James Starr was shot to death on his front porch, along with his son Buck who was crippled, as 32 men attacked his home. Tom Starr later said that he killed every one of the 32 except those who died before he could find them.

In 1846, the feuding factions of the Cherokees agreed that all offenses committed by Cherokee citizens up to that time would be pardoned. Many believed that this was a special pardon for the outlaw Tom Starr. He went on to fight for the South in the Civil War and became friendly with Quantrill and his men. After the war, Starr was visited at his ranch in the Canadian District by Coleman Younger. The ranch became known as "Younger's Bend," the birthplace of Tom's sons Henry and Sam, the future husband of Belle Shirley.

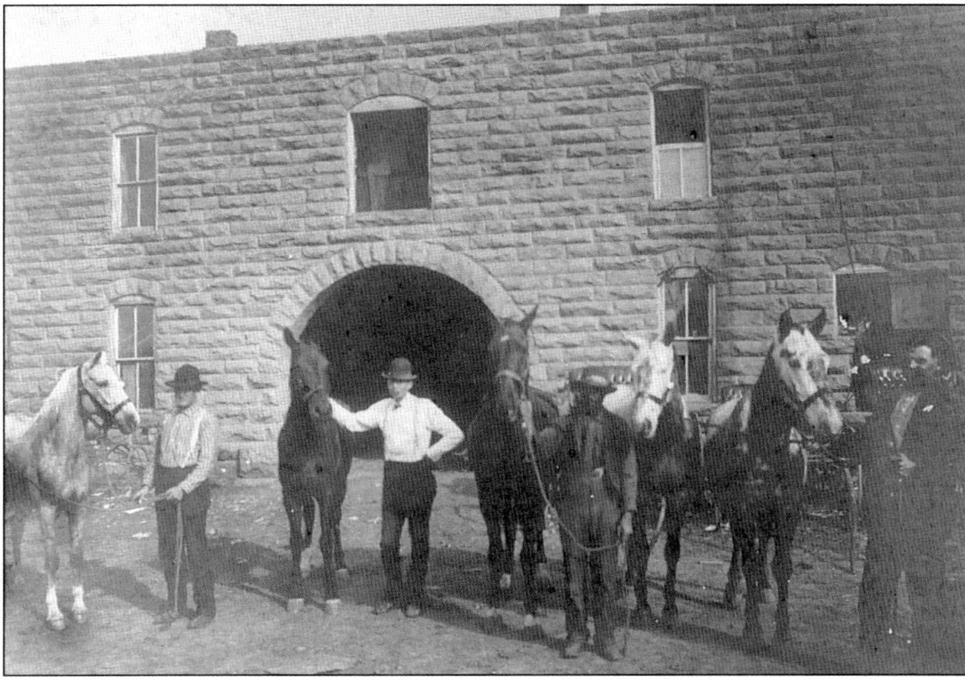

Clem Roger's Livery Stable, Cooweescoowee District. (Courtesy Rogers State College.)

Lesson from a Living Legend c. 1860.

The Cowskin Prairie is a large, naturally flat and clear tract of land which lies to the east of Grove, Oklahoma, and stretches near the Missouri border. In Civil War days, the area was a Confederate stronghold, and for a time Quantrill's Raiders conducted a training camp there for Indian Territory soldiers. A story passed through generations of the Winburn family tells of the day the outlaw Jesse James, himself a staunch southerner, visited the training camp. He tossed a silver coin to a young boy and told him to go find 12 pumpkins. These were placed atop fence posts in a row along both sides of the road.

Jesse mounted his horse and galloped down the path. In moments he returned, speeding toward the pumpkins with a gun in each hand. Bullets shattered all 12 as he streaked past. Jesse then told the soldiers, "If you boys are gonna whip those Yankees, you have to learn to ride and shoot like that."

Murv Jacob

Cherokee Bill

Part white, part black, part Mexican, and part Cherokee, Bill Crawford Goldsby was one of the most bloodthirsty killers and robbers of the old West. He terrorized the country until the reward for his capture reached $1,300. He was wanted dead or alive, but few lawmen were eager to risk their lives pursuing him.

Cherokee Bill was a member of the Cook Gang along with brothers Jim and William Cook, who were Cherokee citizens. In 1894, the Gang was hiding out on Fourteen Mile Creek near present day Hulbert at the establishment of Effie Crittenden. She was the estranged wife and a confirmed enemy of lawman Dick Crittenden, and the hired cook

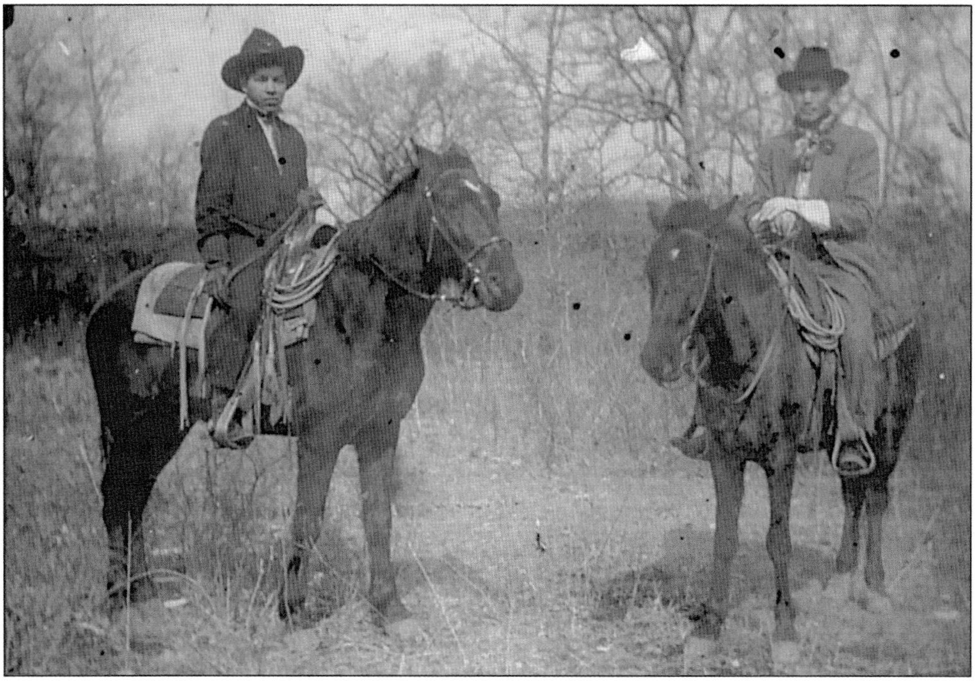

Horsemen in the Cherokee Nation, Early 1900s. (Courtesy Cherokee National Archives.)

at her "half-way house" was a brother-in-law to Jim and William Cook. The Cook brothers hoped to collect their share from the Cherokee Strip payment that was taking place in Tahlequah, but could not risk being captured there. Instead, they sent Effie Crittenden with a note from them authorizing her to collect their payment.

Somehow the sheriff in Tahlequah discovered the plan and sent a posse to Effie's place to capture the Cook Gang. In the gun battle that ensued, Effie's husband Dick was wounded and lawman Sequoyah Houston was killed, but Cherokee Bill and the Cook Gang escaped.

In 1895, Cherokee Bill was finally captured by Clint Scales and Ike Rogers, a deputy U.S. marshal. Tried for the 1894 murder of Ernest Melton, he received a death sentence and was placed in the jail at Fort Smith to await execution.

On July 10, 1895, Bill somehow obtained a gun and attempted to escape after shooting prison guard Lawrence Keating. The gunfire alerted famed deputy U.S. Marshal Heck Bruner and a large force of lawmen and citizens from Fort Smith. Over 100 shots were fired before another Cherokee inmate, Henry Starr, convinced Cherokee Bill to turn over the gun. On March 17, 1896, Bill Crawford Goldsby was hanged at the gallows in Fort Smith.

Ned Christie's Guns

Ned Christie was born on December 14, 1852, and raised in the Wauhillau Community, the son of Watt Christie and his principal wife. Watt had a total of eight wives and 11 children. Watt worked as a gunsmith and his services were sought by many, including his neighbors and outlaws traveling in the territory.

Watt Christie's blacksmith shop was a place where the men from the community met to discuss politics. Ned grew up listening to this talk, building and using guns with his father. By the time Ned was 10 years old, he was one of the best shots in the Cherokee Nation.

Watt Christie fought for the Union during the Civil War, and upon his return, presented his pair of cap and ball pistols to Ned. The teenage gunsmith converted the guns to five shot shell pistols.

Ned Christie grew up to be a statesman and worked diligently to protect the traditional Cherokee lifestyle of his neighbors and family. He openly opposed the idea of statehood and the coming of the railroad. When Deputy U.S. Marshall Dan Maples was killed in Indian Territory, Ned was blamed (many thought framed) for his murder and became a hunted outlaw, chased for years by lawmen from Judge Isaac Parker's court.

Christie built a fort near Wauhillau that was almost impenetrable. From its safety, he was able to hold off Judge Parker's many attempts at his capture. Finally, the use of dynamite and the resulting fire drove Christie from his stronghold, and he was shot as he tried to escape. Dan Maple's son was along with the posse. He filled Ned's body with unnecessary bullets as vengeance for his slain father overwhelmed him. It is said Ned Christie died with the pistols his father gave him in his hands.

Ned Christie is a legendary hero to many traditional Cherokees. Members of his family still live at Wauhillau. One relative dropped in to visit Tahlequah artist Murv Jacob after Murv had completed a colorful depiction of Ned Christie in the woods. After giving his approval to the likeness, the young man said, "You know, in all the stories about Ned he has grown to a tall 6-feet 2-inches. He really was about 5-feet 10."

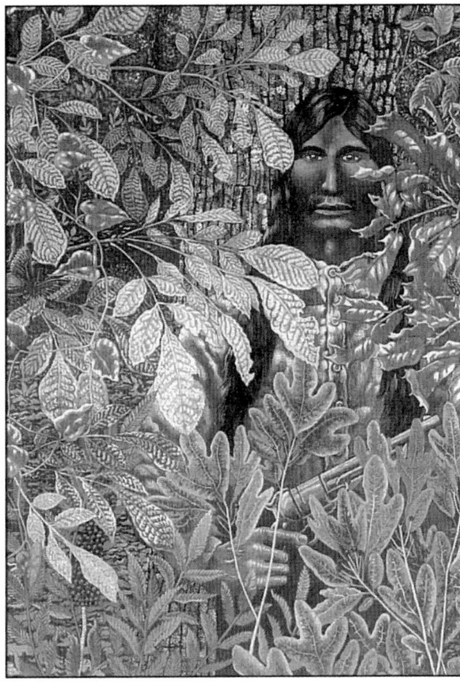

Ned Christie. (Artwork by Murv Jacob.)

Jesse Cochran, Outlaw Lawman

Jesse Cochran, Jr., was born in the Delaware District in 1847. His parents had journeyed across the Trail of Tears and settled there in 1839. His father, Jesse Cochran, Sr., was elected Sheriff of the district that first year.

The mother of Jesse, Jr., passed away shortly after his birth, and his father soon remarried. A son, George, was born to the couple, and raised as a close brother to Jesse. When Jesse was 26 years old he learned that his brother George had been shot by a white man. Jesse, in retaliation, found and killed a man named Rooks in Vinita. This shooting took place in 1873. Because Rooks was white, a charge of murder was filed against Jesse Cochran in the U.S. Court at Fort Smith, Arkansas. Jesse became a wanted man, who eluded capture until late in the year of 1875.

Cochran was held in jail until his trial in early 1877. The trial took place in the courtroom of Judge Isaac Parker,

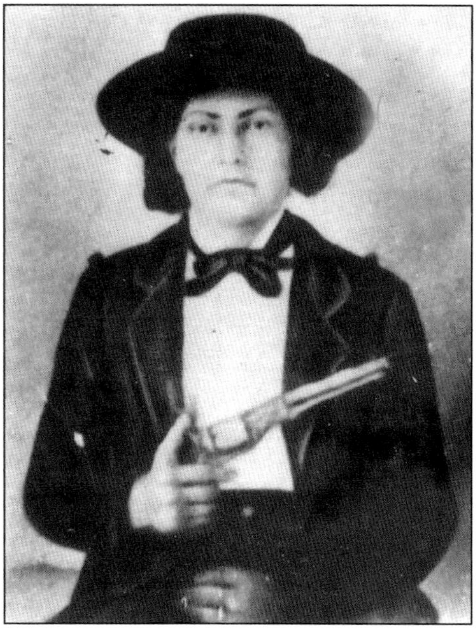

Jesse Cochran. (Courtesy Rogers State College.)

the "Hanging Judge." Surprisingly, the jury believed Jesse was justified in defending his brother and found the young Cherokee man innocent of the murder charge.

Jesse returned to Indian Territory and took up residence in the Cooweescoowee District, where he served as a deputy sheriff. He was elected Sheriff of the district in 1879. Jesse Cochran was a trusted lawman. In 1894, when the Cherokee Strip was sold, Jesse was chosen to oversee the guards of the $6 million as it was distributed to the citizens of the Cherokee Nation.

The Crittenden Brothers

Dick Crittenden and his brother Zeke had both served as Cherokee lawmen, surviving the 1894 shootout with the Cook Gang at Fourteen Mile Creek. But the brothers changed their ways and ran afoul of the law themselves. In October 1895, Dick and Zeke got drunk and began shooting up the town of Wagoner, wounding a local resident.

The story goes that Deputy U.S. Marshal Ed Reed was called on to stop the Crittendens' rampage in Wagoner. Reed came upon Zeke in the street and ordered him to surrender his weapon, but Zeke fired it instead. Reed returned fire and Zeke was killed. Across town, Dick Crittenden learned of his brothers death. He mounted his horse and rode quickly to the scene. Seeing the deputy there with his fallen brother, Dick shot at him. Reed fired back and Dick was badly wounded, dying the next morning.

Deputy Reed himself was killed a year later in Claremore. His father-in-law, Alec Cochran, had died from drinking bad liquor he bought from a merchant named Joe Gibbs. Reed intended to shut down the business of Gibbs and his partner J.N. Clark. As soon as Reed walked through the door of the store, he was taken down by two shotgun blasts.

On His Honor

Before statehood, the Cherokees tried and punished their own lawbreakers. If a crime should warrant it, an offender might be sentenced to hang by the Cherokee court. There was a courthouse located on Little Green Leaf Creek around the area that is now Camp Gruber. Behind the courthouse was a gallows.

A Cherokee woman who lived near the courthouse was sitting on her porch on a sizzling summer afternoon. She saw a young man walking down the dusty road toward her home. He asked if he might have a drink of water. The woman got his drink, then asked him why he was out walking at such a hot time of day. His reply was simple. "I'm going to the courthouse. I am scheduled to be hung today."

A person sentenced to death by the

Cherokees was sometimes released to his family for a set amount of time. He spent the final days getting his affairs in order and saying farewell to his family and friends. Then, having given his word to do so, he returned to face the executioner.

Wayne Mitchell

Blue Duck

Bluford "Blue" Duck was a Cherokee outlaw who grew up near Oologah in the Cooweescoowee District of the Cherokee Nation. In 1884, Blue Duck and his friend William Christie got drunk and went on a spree in the Flint District. A farmer named Samuel Wyrick was working in his field with a hired hand when Blue Duck rode up to Wyrick and fired several shots into his body, then turned to the hired man, shooting him as well. He and Christie rode on to the next house and tried but failed to shoot Wyrick's neighbor.

Blue Duck and Christie were arrested and tried in the Judge Isaac Parker's court in Fort Smith, Arkansas. Christie was released, but the judge sentenced Blue Duck to hang on July 23, 1886. His attorney, Thomas Marcum, appealed to the president of the United States to have his sentence reduced to life in prison. Marcum went so far as to have Blue Duck photographed with bandit queen Belle Starr in order to call attention to the case. Those tactics must have worked because Duck was taken off death row and sent to the Menard Penitentiary in Chester, Illinois.

The picture Blue Duck took with Belle Starr started so many rumors that the obscure outlaw enjoyed some public notoriety. Some said that Belle managed to get him released from prison and became his lover before the picture was made. Still others said that her husband Sam Starr killed Blue Duck in a jealous rage.

Although he had received a life sentence, Blue Duck was pardoned and released on March 24, 1895, less than nine years after his arrival at Menard. Author Glenn Shirley wrote that Blue Duck had been diagnosed with consumption and given only a month to live when he was pardoned by President Grover Cleveland.

The Goingsnake Massacre

The noted Cherokee Zeke Proctor endured the Trail of Tears and settled along the volatile border between Indian Territory and Arkansas. He was a vocal opponent of the federal government and wanted the Cherokee Nation to be a separate country. Proctor had two or more wives who lived with him near present-day Watts, Oklahoma.

Early in 1872, Zeke traveled to the Sequoyah District to visit his sister, Susan. When he arrived there, he found that Susan's husband, a white man named Jim Kesterson, had deserted her. Proctor took Susan back to his home. He soon heard that Kesterson had taken up with Polly Beck Hilderbrand, and was working at the Hilderbrand Mill on Flint Creek in the Goingsnake District. He was living with the other woman right under his wife's nose. At this, Zeke set out to defend his sister's honor.

Cherokee writer Robert Conley says that Zeke had been drinking at a place on the Arkansas border. The building sat right on the line, and there was an actual line painted on the floor dividing Indian Territory and Arkansas. It was legal to drink on the Arkansas side of the building. Having had plenty of whiskey, Proctor went looking for his brother-in-law, and found Kesterson and Polly together at the Hilderbrand Mill. Zeke took a shot at Jim. To protect

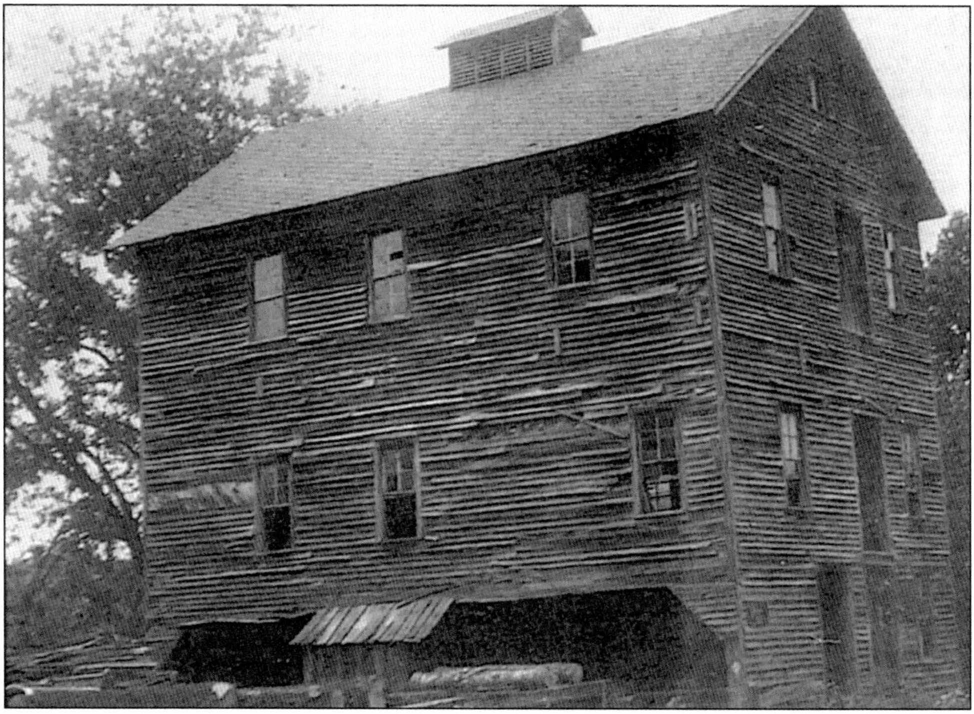

Beck-Hilderbrand Mill. (Courtesy Cherokee Studies Institute.)

him, Polly jumped in front of Kesterson at the last moment and took the bullet.

Realizing the trouble he was in, Zeke turned himself in to Cherokee authorities to avoid facing a white man's court. Since Kesterson was married to a Cherokee woman, the Cherokee court would have jurisdiction. The trial date was set for April 15, 1872.

The Beck family wanted Proctor punished and feared that he would be found innocent by Cherokees. On April 11, 1872, they pressed charges against him in the federal District Court. Deputy U.S. marshals were sent as a posse to attend Zeke's trial. They had been ordered to arrest him should he be found not guilty.

Word of the trial had spread, and onlookers crammed the small Whitmire School house where the trial was to take place. When the deputy marshals arrived, they were accompanied by members of the Beck family. Sut Beck broke through the door of the school and shot at Zeke, missing him, and then everyone began shooting. Nine people died at the scene and two of the wounded died later. Zeke Proctor survived with a gunshot to his knee.

The trial continued the next day, and Zeke was found innocent by his Cherokee peers. At the same moment he became a wanted man by the U.S. District Court. Arrest warrants were issued against every person on Proctor's side, including the dead ones. Neighbors and relatives took up the cause of protecting him from the white authorities. He remained an "outlaw" until finally Principal Chief Louis Downing and a delegation of Cherokees were able to convince Washington to grant him amnesty. Proctor went on to serve as a Cherokee senator and as sheriff of the Goingsnake District.

According to Conley, when the deputy marshals and the Beck family arrived at the trial, they began coming toward the schoolhouse in a group. At the same time Zeke Proctor's brother, Johnson Proctor, appeared in the doorway. He was shot down at once by one of the Becks, and the battle began. From then on, when Zeke would ride anywhere on his horse, he would lead his brother's horse along, saddled, beside him. Artist Murv Jacob has heard stories that Zeke would often be seen in animated conversation with the horse's invisible rider. Zeke Proctor died on March 16, 1907, of pneumonia.

Heck Bruner, Lawman

Deputy U.S. Marshal Eli Hickman Bruner was raised in Siloam Springs, on the border of Arkansas and the Cherokee Nation. A formidable lawman, Heck Bruner was involved in every major manhunt in Indian Territory between 1887 and his death in 1899. He was such a persistent hunter of outlaws that some would lay in wait for him to pass, hoping to kill him.

Bruner helped to bring down the Kelp Queen Gang, the Bob Rogers Gang, Ned Christie, and many, many more. There is a cemetery north of Vinita, Oklahoma with a little secluded corner called "Heck Bruner's Graveyard." It contains unmarked mounds within which lie some of Indian Territory's bloodiest bandits and desperados, all put there at the hands of Bruner.

In June of 1899, Heck Bruner and Vet Thompson were traveling east and needed to cross the Grand River at West's Ferry. The water was too high to cross on horseback and the ferryman was not at his post. Across the river a boat was tied, and Heck decided to go after it. He stripped off his clothing and started swimming across the river. Halfway across, he went under and never came back up. People in the territory could hardly believe that such a celebrated lawman died by drowning when so many had tried to take his life.

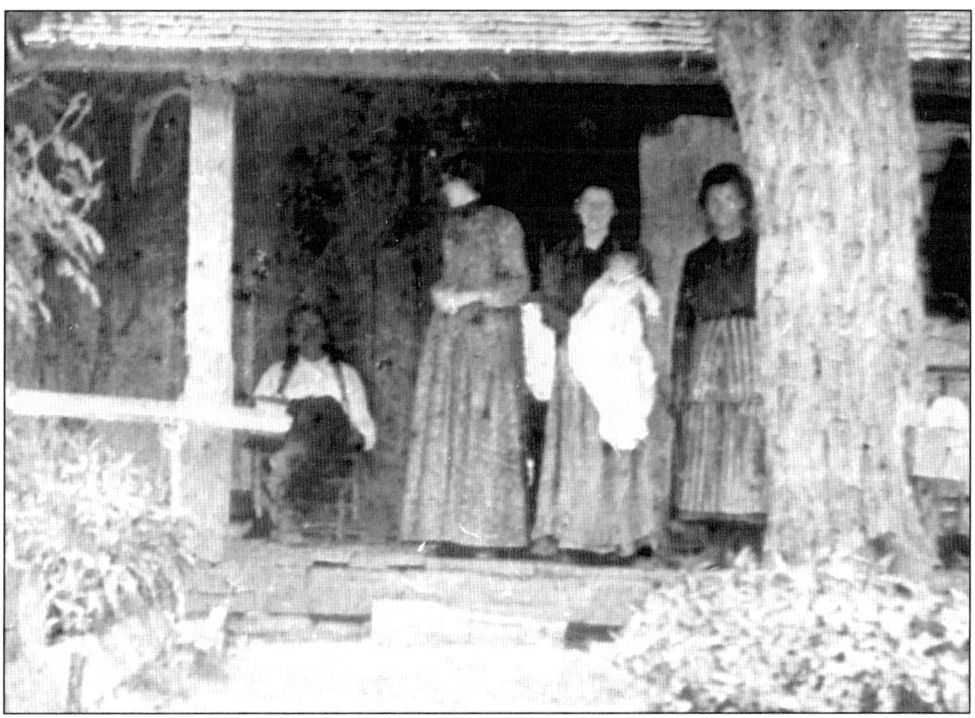

Zeke Proctor and Wives, 1903. (Courtesy Cherokee National Archives.)

The Shelly Brothers

John and Bill Shelly did not run with a gang of outlaws, they were simply thieves. In the winter of 1895, Heck Bruner was among a group of deputies who traced a number of lost horses to the Shelly ranch on Carr Creek east of Choteau. They waited until daylight, then approached the house. The Shelly brothers refused to go quietly and a shootout was soon underway.

After several minutes of steady gunfire, the deputies realized that they needed more than bullets as the men were well barricaded within. They loaded a wagon with hay and ran it up to a wall without windows. They set fire to the hay and soon the ranch house was ablaze. The Shelly brothers came out with their hands up. The deputies used the snow on the ground to put out the fire.

John Shelly had taken bullets in both legs, but Bill was completely unharmed. This seemed almost unbelievable to the deputies when they entered the smoldering house. It seemed every inch of the walls and floor contained a bullet hole. Over 800 rounds of ammunition had been fired into the place. The Shelly brothers were taken to Fort Smith and sentenced to eight years in prison.

Robbers Cave

To the south of the Cherokee Nation was a favorite hideout of local outlaws known as Robbers Cave. The cave, in what is now a state park, is located five miles north of Wilburton, Oklahoma in present-day Latimer County. French traders used the cave to store furs, and Civil War deserters from both camps used it as a hideout. Black Jack, a Cherokee, was the first known outlaw to stay there, and stories tell of visits by Ned Christie in later years.

The cave made a perfect hiding place. The entrance was narrow, but the main room was large and accommodating. There was a fresh stream of water running through it, and a hidden exit the outlaws used when escape was necessary. Those who knew the cave's secret passageways could hide out indefinitely.

One day, the famous Deputy U.S. Marshal Heck Bruner figured out where the secret exit was located and joined his contemporaries in setting a trap for the next unwitting gang of outlaws. Deputies stormed the front entrance while Heck and his friends waited at the exit. The entire gang was either captured or killed. Word of the ambush spread, and outlaws in the territory steered clear of their old hideout. Henry Starr was the last Cherokee outlaw known to take refuge in Robbers Cave.

The Price of Melon

When Charlotte Mayes was small, her parents had a big ranch of 1,500 acres. Her mother, Florence Nicodemus Mayes, raised a plentiful garden and cooked for the hired hands.

One day Florence was at the ranch house by herself, working in the yard, when a man came riding up on a horse carrying a big watermelon on the saddle in front of him. He had picked the watermelon out of Florence's garden and wanted to pay for it.

"No, you just go ahead and take it," Florence said. She kept refusing any payment, and the man finally got down off his horse and laid the watermelon in the grass. He went to her kitchen door, walked inside and laid fifty cents on the table. Then he picked up the watermelon and rode off.

Florence was reluctant to ask the man for anything, because she had seen his face before in the newspapers. He was one of the Dalton boys.

Sally Sanders Finch

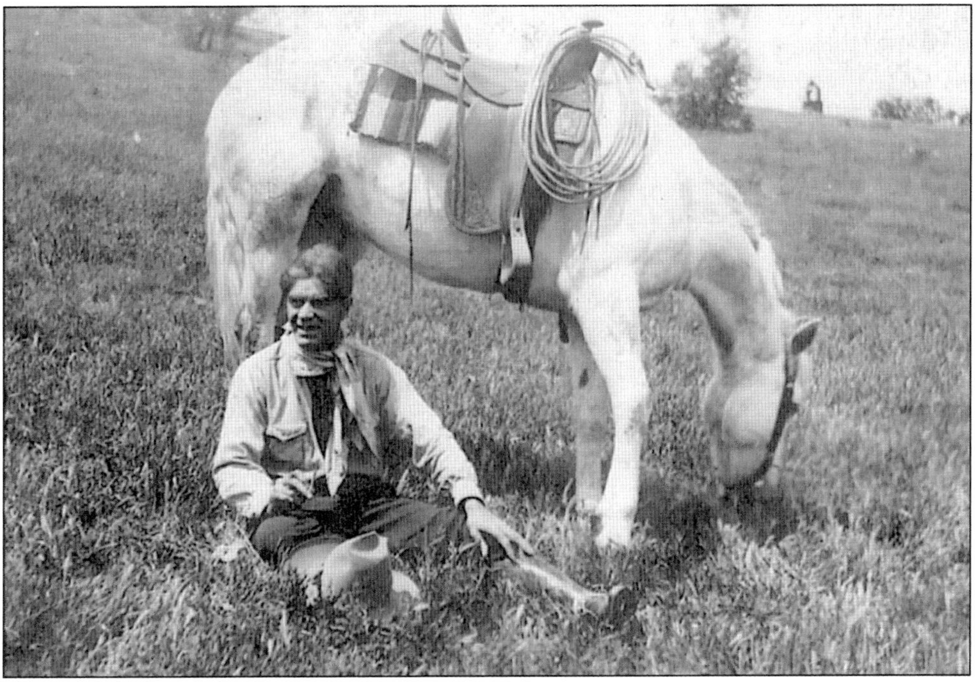

A Moment's Rest, Early 1900s. (Courtesy Cherokee National Archives.)

Gilstrap Meets His Destiny

Robert Conley tells how two stories about a deputy marshall come together with an odd twist. One story begins in 1905 with Conley's grandfather, Benjamin Franklin Conley, and his Cherokee sweetheart to whom he was engaged. "Benny" was a school teacher in the Gideon community, north of Tahlequah. One night he and the girl decided to go to a dance held in an individual family's home. People walked from all directions to attend these social events. Years earlier, they would have traveled on horseback, but there were not many horses left in the Cherokee Nation following the Civil War.

The couple stayed late at the dance, and decided to spend the night at a residence along the way. The owner of the home was a fullblood Cherokee woman who knew both young people and invited them in. They made pallets on the living room floor and settled down to rest.

The household was awakened suddenly by a "hell of a ruckus" out in the front yard. A deputy marshall named Gilstrap began pounding on the door. He was accompanied by a 17-man posse, several hound dogs, and a prisoner named Looney Bear. The whole assemblage barged into the home as Gilstrap announced to its owner that they would be spending the night. Soon the entire living room floor was carpeted with sleeping bodies.

Sometime around midnight, Benny and his fiance got into a spat and he asked for his ring back. She refused to turn it over, and the two began to wrestle around. The girl accidentally fell backward onto none other than Gilstrap, who came up in his long red underwear, with a gun in each hand, and proceeded to arrest everyone in the house.

At last all the travelers went back to sleep, and in the morning the deputy marshall said nobody would be arrested. But he got right in the face of

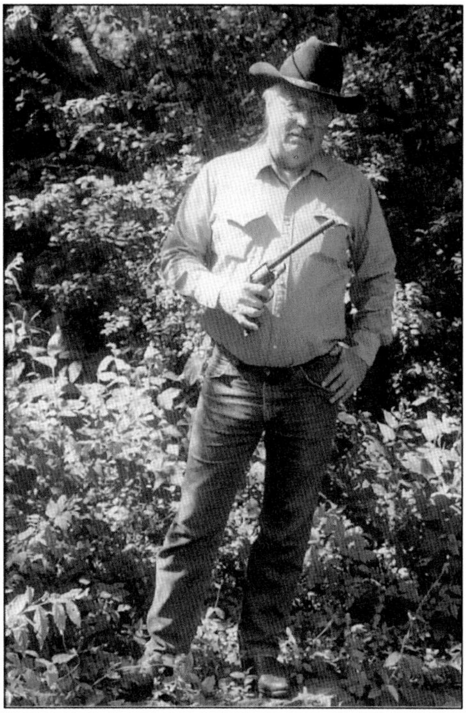

Robert J. Conley, Cherokee, 2000. (Photo by Murv Jacob.)

the Cherokee woman who owned the house and demanded to know, "Where's Charlie Wickliffe?" She said she did not know, but Gilstrap persisted with his questions and continued to harass her. Finally the woman said, "I don't know where he is, but I hope you find him, because when you do, he'll shoot you right between the eyes."

Benny took the girl home and a few days later read a newspaper article about the death of Deputy Marshall Gilstrap. He and his men had been ambushed, and Gilstrap's body was found with a bullet wound "right between his eyes." Not only that, his hound dogs were shot and laid across his body.

This story was all that Robert Conley knew about the outlaw Charlie Wickliffe until the late 1960s, when he ran across a True West Magazine story about the Wickliffe brothers, Charlie, John, and Tom. It stated that Charlie Wickliffe was wanted for killing deputy marshals. Conley was able to document all the elements of the Wickliffe story except the part about Deputy Marshall Gilstralp being at the woman's house, and her prophetic statement about the bullet.

One day in the late 1980s, Robert was visiting with Cherokee Master Artist Cecil Dick at his little studio in downtown Tahlequah. Cecil loved to share a bottle of peach brandy and talk about outlaws. Robert asked Cecil what he knew about Charlie Wickliffe.

Robert had not mentioned his grandfather's adventure with Deputy Marshal Gilstrap to Cecil, but at the mention of Wickliffe, the subject came up. It seems that Cecil's father, Andy Dick, was with the posse that had been ambushed when Gilstrap was shot. He remembered very well how Deputy Marshall Gilstrap came to be killed. The bullet that found him had ricocheted off a rock before striking him between the eyes. Had the Cherokee woman's words sealed his fate?

Robert J. Conley

Charlie's Casket

Tommy Belt told this story about Charlie Wickliffe and his brothers. While Charlie was still a wanted outlaw, his brothers went to the authorities and said Charlie had been killed. The three had been having a brotherly scuffle that got out of hand, and Charlie ended up dead.

The officials decided that representatives should go to look at Charlie's body to make sure he was really dead. When they arrived, the casket was nailed shut. The brothers told them that Charlie's face had been bashed in with a rock, and would not be recognizable anyway. The lawmen went back to town and said "Yeah, he's dead, all right," and let it go. The case was closed on Charlie Wickliffe.

Tommy said there was a big hog in that casket. Wickliffe kept quiet and went back in the woods around Kenwood to live out his life in peace.

Robert J. Conley

Hard Lessons from a Crap Game

There were not too many recreational activities open to the youth of rural Cherokee County in the 1930s that were not illegal. The following account was witnessed by a man who at that time was 15 years old.

A cattle rancher made a corner of his feed barn floor available to locals to "shoot craps," or gamble playing dice. On this particular day, a crap game was going between an older black man and a "mean man just out of the pen." Several teenage boys were watching as the ex-con began to win over and over. The old gentleman got to thinking the con was cheating him, and stood up to challenge him. The ex-con whipped out a knife and cut the older man's throat. He was "squirting out blood like a hog," and the kids carried him up the hill to the doctor's office, fearing that he would surely die.

The doctor managed to stop the bleeding and the boys helped him get to his home. The man survived his wounds and about two weeks later came walking into town. He was so pale he "looked like a dead white man." He continued to live, as did the ex-con who was never punished for his crime.

The Bank Robbers

In the 1930s, notorious criminals like Pretty Boy Floyd and Bonnie and Clyde frequented the Cookson Hills of Oklahoma. Two of their contemporaries, Ky Carlile and Troy Love, were wanted for bank robbery and had been seen in Cherokee County. Sheriff Grover Bishop and a group of deputy marshals set up an ambush for the pair on highway 82, a few miles southeast of the Keys community. In the gun battle that

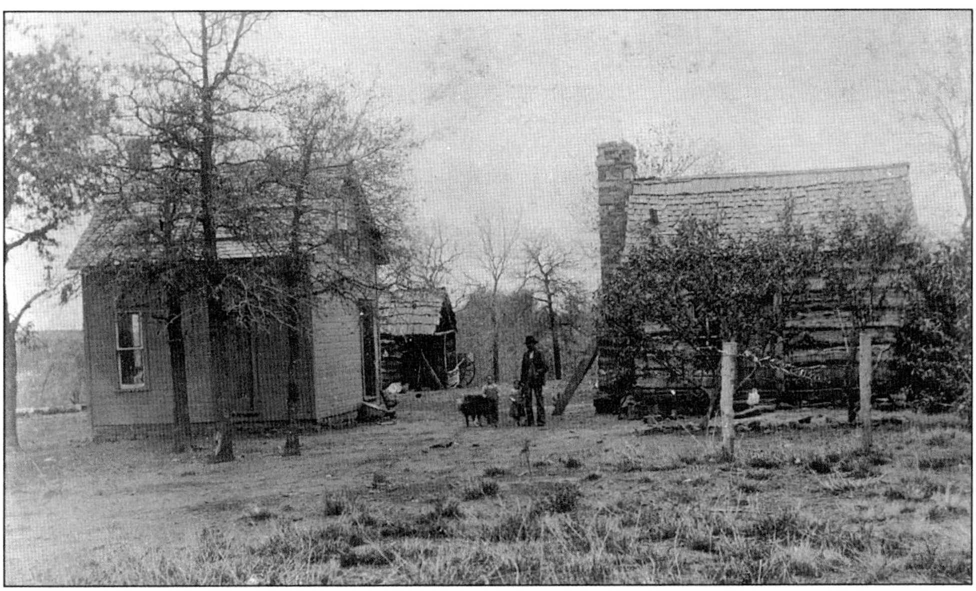

Homeplace in the Cookson Hills. (Courtesy Cherokee National Archives.)

ensued, two deputies were killed, but the crooks got away on foot.

The manhunt continued until the next day when authorities surrounded the men in a corn field about two miles from Keys. Knowing that the two were well-armed, the lawmen were reluctant to enter the field, but one deputy was eager to get them and kept pressing Sheriff Bishop to go in.

The sheriff was famous for bringing in criminals, and he always wore a big white hat. Bishop finally agreed to accompany the deputy, but first exchanged hats with him. Both Carlile and Love were killed, but not before shooting the deputy in the white hat. They must have died thinking they killed the famed Grover Bishop, but it was he who brought them down.

Bishop loaded the bodies into the rumble seat of his car and drove them to the Cherokee County courthouse in downtown Tahlequah. There he laid Carlile and Love out on the sidewalk to show his fellow citizens that "crime doesn't pay."

Wayne Mitchell

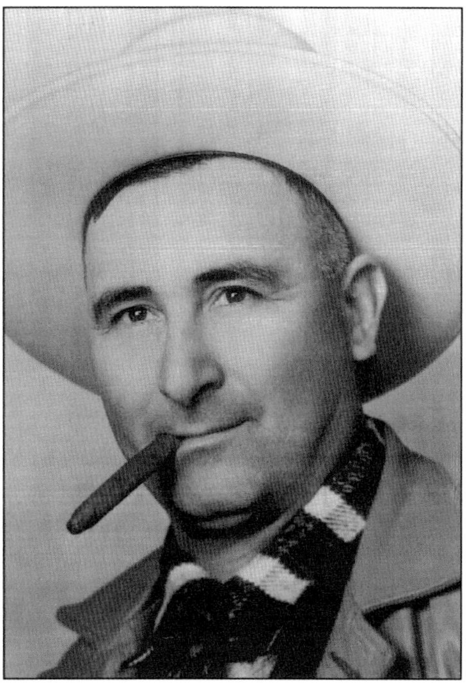

Sheriff Grover Bishop. (Courtesy Greg Blish.)

Ralph and Grover Bishop

Remembering the noted Cherokee County Sheriff Grover Bishop, Ralph Dunham says, "He was smart as an eagle. He was the best sheriff we ever knew." Bishop was an Arkansas native, once employed by the railroad. He worked as a waterboy for the surveyors of the Dawes Commission. Grover served as a deputy to sheriffs Sam Johnson and Jim Sanders before he took over the office. He was known for bringing in criminals, dead or alive, and knew many famous outlaws.

One afternoon the aunt of one of Ralph's teenage friends, Scotty Yeargain, sent Sheriff Bishop out looking for her nephew. When the sheriff arrived in Ralph's mother's front yard, asking for Scotty, Ralph pretended not to know where his friend had gone. Bishop detected the obvious lie and proceeded to "spin Ralph around and around like a top," then set him up on a waist-high porch and drove away. Ralph said he never knew that a man could handle a person like that.

Another time the teenage Ralph and his cousin Lester were in Tahlequah and wanted to go back home to Hulbert, but they had no car to drive. What they did have was a half gallon of home-made whiskey they planned to take with them. They walked about a mile west of town when a car pulled over to offer them a lift. Sitting in the car was Sheriff Grover Bishop. The boys jumped in, whiskey and all, and rode with Bishop to Hulbert, where he dropped them off without saying a word about the contraband.

Ralph Dunham

The Sheriff

In the 1930s, eastern Oklahoma was dangerous territory. Just a few decades had passed from the days of Isaac Parker, the "hanging judge" of the U.S. court in Fort Smith, Arkansas. Parker sent 120 outlaws to the gallows, of which only 86 were actually hung, but he lost over 100 deputies trying to bring them in. The same lawlessness Parker faced returned during the Depression with a rash of bank robbers and gangsters. A number of these were brought to justice by Cherokee County Sheriff Grover Bishop.

Ask any old-timer who was raised in Cherokee County about Grover Bishop, and you will hear that he was as good a fellow as you would ever want to meet. But he was deadly serious when it came to the law. He is reputed to have killed 17 people while in office, arguably more than Wyatt Earp or Billy the Kid. Bishop was a survivor and never gave a criminal the opportunity to kill him.

Even after Bishop retired from office, he never went outside his home without a gun. One day he was working by the corn crib on his ranch when a car pulled into the driveway. Out jumped a man and his son bent on revenge against him. The father, waving a club, told Bishop he had come to kill him. Bishop calmly pulled out his gun and shot the man in the chest, killing him. Investigators agreed that Grover had shot him in self defense, and the case never went to trial.

Sheriff Bishop was like a hero straight out of the old west. He was well-liked by those he served and won several bids for reelection. Even when she had reached a great age, Grover's second wife got a twinkle in her eye as she remembered her husband. She told of the night when she and Grover were walking along the streets of Tahlequah and a young tough accosted them. He flippantly remarked that if Grover were not wearing those guns he could handle him easily. Grover took off his gun belt, handed it to his wife, and gave the young man the thrashing of his life .

Wayne Mitchell

The Overpass

Visitors to modern day Tahlequah might notice that there are no overpasses on any of the highways in or around the town. These went the way of the railroad. In the 1930s, there was an overpass above the Frisco railroad line on Highway 62 south of Tahlequah. It was high enough that a car sitting on the opposite side could be concealed from view. This story is told by a woman whose brother owned a fast motorcycle and became involved in a dramatic incident at the overpass.

No one is sure why two individuals had decided to meet somewhere south of town that day, maybe to fight each other over a woman. One of the men was waiting down the highway in a car, and the other was in town. The young man in town approached the brother with the motorcycle and said, "Come with me and you'll see some fun!" Of course, the brother knew nothing of the planned fight and allowed the man to climb behind him on the motorcycle.

He was directed to head south of town, and was traveling at a fast pace when the motorcycle crossed the overpass. A car parked on the other side came into view. There was a man inside, and the next thing the cyclist knew, a shot was fired. He felt the bullet whiz past him, and began to drive faster. Then he felt his passenger's knees coming up on his sides and looked back to see blood flying from the rider's head as his grip loosened. By the time he stopped the motorcycle, his passenger was near death. He laid the man alongside the highway and raced back to town for help.

The young man died from the gunshot wound. There was never a clear answer as to why he was shot. As often happened, the shooter, a somewhat wealthy cattleman, went unpunished by the law, but fate did not treat him kindly. Once a big healthy man, he began to look pale and pitiful, losing weight and his good looks until he became a mere shadow of his former self.

Fastest Draw Alive

Wayne Mitchell is a Cherokee entrepreneur who lives on Lake Tenkiller. He worked hard to become successful in real estate and other pursuits, but when describing his childhood days he says, "We were dirt poor." The young Wayne admired the gunslinging heroes of history and the western movies and spent hour after hour learning the fast draw with his own toy gun.

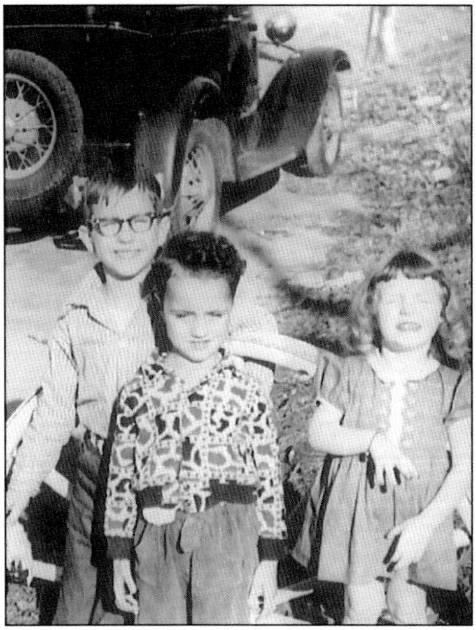

Wayne Mitchell (left) with Brother Larry and Cousin Alicia, 1960. (Courtesy Wayne Mitchell.)

In the television series "Gunsmoke," the show begins with James Arness drawing his six-gun in a shoot-out on Main Street. The person at the other end of the street in that scene was Joe Bodrie. Joe taught the stars how to handle, hold and draw guns for their movie gunfighting scenes. He was called indisputably the fastest human being alive with a gun.

Bodrie was a popular celebrity with fans across the country. Aside from training actors, he toured as a representative for General Motors. While promoting the GM cars, he thrilled audiences with demonstrations of his fast draw.

The day came when Bodrie made an appearance in Jonesboro, Arkansas. Seated in the front row and wearing his own replica of a six-gun, was 13-year-old Wayne Mitchell. Bodrie put on a fine demonstration of his ability to draw. When he finished, he asked if anyone in the audience wanted to challenge him.

Up from his seat came Wayne. He climbed onto the stage, got in position, and drew his gun, faster than Bodrie. The man said that was impossible and told Wayne to try again. Wayne beat him a second time, then returned to his seat. All Bodrie could do was shake his head and say, "There are only two things in the world faster than me...a Pontiac automobile and that kid in the front row."

When Wayne grew up he bought himself an 1873 Colt Peacemaker. It was a real gunfighter's gun with a hair trigger. Wayne was very good at handling it, and was once named the "quickest draw in Oklahoma."

Wayne Mitchell

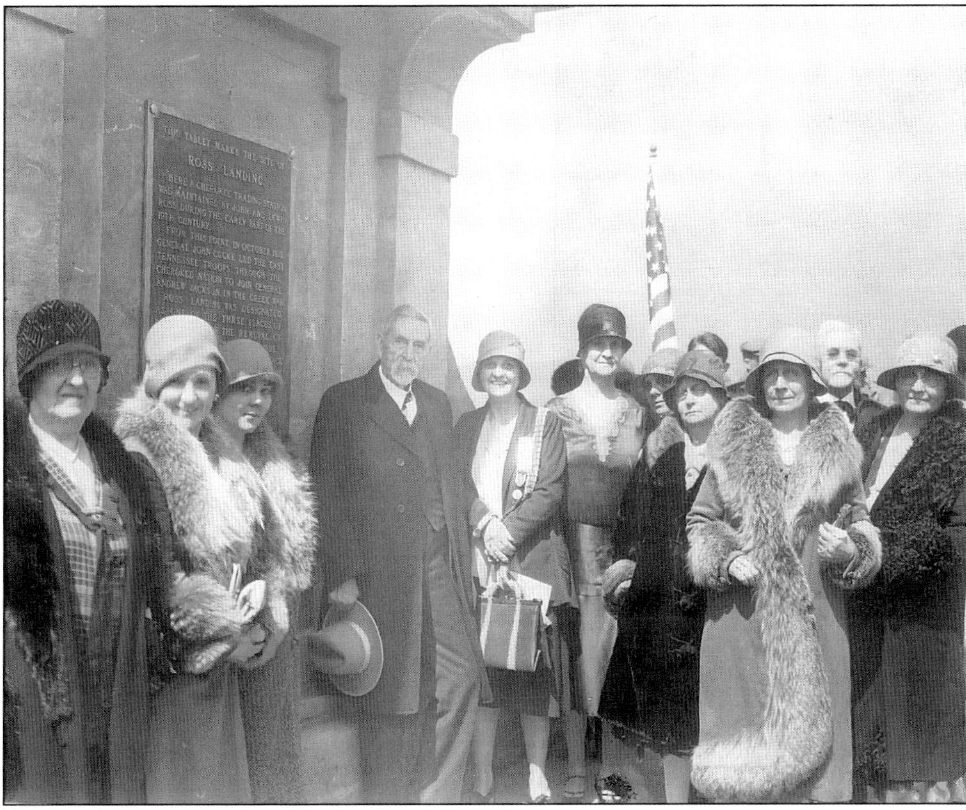

Robert Bruce Ross unveils the tablet commemorating Ross landing in Chattanooga, TN, March 2, 1930. (Courtesy Cherokee National Archives.)

CHAPTER 5

EVENTS

The history of the Cherokees is filled with tales of drama, adventure, tragedy, excitement, and humor. It is important to remember that their story did not begin with Chief John Ross and the Trail of Tears to Indian Territory. As traumatic as the Removal was, it was but a brief episode compared to the all the struggles and victories the Cherokees must have experienced during the centuries they have occupied this continent. Before the United States came into being, the Cherokees had conquered and dominated a land the size of France.

The division that began when the first Cherokees decided to move west in the early 1800s would have a profound influence on events yet to come. The Trail of Tears brought with it a tribe divided into factions as followers of John Ross stood opposed to supporters of the Treaty Party and the Old Settlers. The rift split open again during the Civil War. After the war, staunch southern sympathizers lobbied to separate the Cherokee Nation into two tribes. Fifty years later, the Daughters of the Confederacy unveiled a monument to "Our Confederate Dead" on the front lawn of the Cherokee Capitol that remains there to this day. Even now, a tiny confederate flag flies before the tombstone of southern war hero Stand Watie.

DeSoto and the Queen

In the mid-1500s, the Cherokees were governed by a queen or "Pretty Woman" whose name was Cofetichiki. The story of her capture by the explorer DeSoto was recorded by a Spanish priest.

DeSoto took the queen and all her handmaidens as captives because with Cofetichiki as his hostage, he could gain entry to any of the Cherokee villages. Cofetichiki owned a big cask filled with beautiful fresh water pearls which DeSoto plundered as well. One night the queen and her party managed to steal back the cask of pearls and escape to their home.

DeSoto and his men brought both death and disease to the Indians of the southeast. They were searching for spices and anything else of value. Desoto entered the Cherokee lands to search for the gold he heard was there.

DeSoto's men suffered greatly from attacks by various bands of Indians. Their arrows were made of river cane that would splinter in three or four directions inside the body. The first day the wounds were painful. On the second day, the muscles were paralyzed.

The white men's powder got so damp in the mountain air that their guns were useless against the Indians. So they melted down their guns to make lances and spear heads. When DeSoto was killed on the banks of the Mississippi by Choctaws, his men gladly departed the Indian lands.

After the invasion of DeSoto, the Cherokees charged the powerful Wolf Clan with the duty of guarding all entrances to the Cherokee lands. They protected their holdings completely from all intruders for the next 150 years.

Murv Jacob

Life Everlasting

In the late 1700s, the United States government attempted to destroy the entire population of the Cherokee people. Their soldiers were returning from the battlefield with smallpox. These men were quarantined, and those already exposed were ordered to deliver their infected blankets to the Cherokees. The deadly blankets were loaded onto wagons destined for the old Cherokee settlements.

Before anything happened, somebody in the Cherokee settlements had a dream. In the dream, the people were told that a certain plant would cure what was coming in the wagon. After the wagons had come and gone, and the Cherokees began to fall ill from the sickness, the medicine men went out to collect baskets full of the herb.

Everywhere in the villages, pots of water were filled with the herb and set to boiling. The solution was used to wash down the walls of the lodges, the clothing and eating utensils. Droplets were sprinkled everywhere on the ground. The people bathed in the water and drank it until they vomited. Many were cured and the Cherokees were saved from certain destruction. The modern name for the healing plant used to save the people is Life Everlasting.

Pat Moss

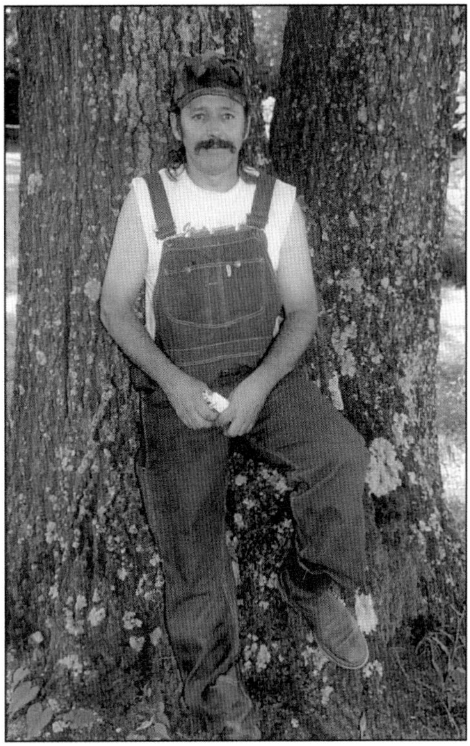

Pat Moss, 2000. (Photo by Murv Jacob.)

First of the Old Settlers

The first Old Settlers, who came to be called the Western Cherokee Nation, left their southeastern home to live in Missouri back in 1794. A group of Chickamaugas led by Chief Bowles had acquired quite a bit of money and were headed back to their homes when they stopped at Mussel Shoals to rest. A group of whites on a flatboat were docked there and they discovered that the Cherokees had this money. The whites gave them enough whiskey to get them good and drunk, then started selling them the goods from the flatboat.

When the Cherokees sobered up the next morning, their chief went to the white men to return the purchases and get back the money. The whites refused to give it back. Later, two more Indians went to negotiate with the whites. This time one of the boatmen lifted a pole and ran it through one of the Cherokees. In retaliation, the Indians killed every white man on the boat, but did not harm the women, children, or black slaves, who went on to New Orleans to tell the story.

Bowles had just finished signing a treaty with the whites and feared that the whole escapade would result in his group being shunned by both the whites and the Cherokees. So instead of going home, he led his group on to Missouri, where they remained until the great earthquake of 1811.

These Cherokees later settled in Arkansas and began dealing with the federal government as a separate tribe, the Western Cherokee Nation. It was to the benefit of the United States to work with them and establish a Cherokee presence in the west. This would help strengthen the white resolve of total removal of the southeastern Indians.

Robert J. Conley

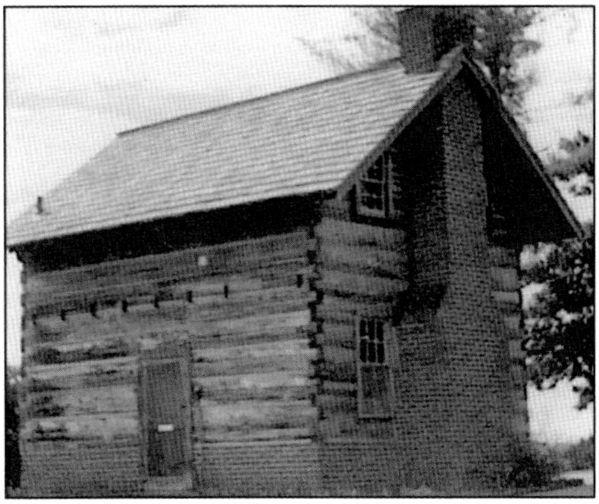

Spring Place Mission. (Courtesy David L. Vann.)

Missionaries at Spring Place

In about 1800, the Moravian missionaries came to Georgia to convert the heathen red pagans, without much luck. The missionaries finally approached Crazy James Vann and asked for permission to build a school and a mission. He agreed only after they promised to teach more reading, writing, and arithmetic than religion. He also required them to teach all children in the area, Cherokees, whites, half-bloods, and blacks, the same lessons in the same classrooms.

The site chosen for the mission was known as Spring Place. This was the beginning of education for the Cherokees. Although James swore he was not Christian and never would be, he allowed his slaves to help with the building. It is said that James Vann contributed more to the education of the leaders of the Cherokee Nation than any other citizen by bringing the Moravians to his people.

David L. Vann

Tecumseh Stamped His Foot

Around 1811, there came the most powerful earthquake the United States has ever known. It occurred, not on the west coast, but along the New Madrid fault line running through the central United States. The force of the quake rang the church bells in Washington DC. Chouteau had built a log fort in Indian Territory along the Grand River that was occupied by hunters, traders, and Osage warriors. Chouteau reported that the land surrounding his fort rose up in 20-foot waves, uprooting all trees and changing the course of rivers. The Quapaws say that the Mississippi River ran backwards for nine days.

The quake occurred at a time of great unrest among the Native American inhabitants of this continent. The whites in the southeast intended to have the Indian lands there. Facing constant pressure, some Cherokees began to move west in the early 1800s. Tecumseh, the great Shawnee leader, tried to organize the migrating Indians to join together and fight for their land. There were some Cherokees living along the Mississippi River in northeast Arkansas who had fled an epidemic of smallpox. Tecumseh's brother, "The Prophet," sent them word that unless they agreed to fight the whites, Tecumseh would "stamp his foot." This occurred just before the earthquake of 1811 struck that area with unimaginable force. The warrior Tecumseh was killed a year later fighting the Americans in the War of 1812. Traditionalist Pat Moss says that during that war the Cherokee people saw a giant eagle and an Uktena, the winged serpent, flying above their heads. Both creatures cast huge shadows on the ground. The Cherokees stood in the shadow of the eagle, because in their hearts they were told to do so. Because of this, they survived the War of 1812.

Murv Jacob

Mystique of the Western Cherokees

Historical novelist and Cherokee scholar Robert Conley says of all the cultures he has studied throughout his lifetime, the most fascinating are the Old Settlers of the Western Cherokee Nation. In the early 1820s, while John Ross and his contemporaries in the southeast were going about in tall hats and coat tails, a group of the Western Cherokees led by Captain Dutch raided an enemy Indian village in Texas.

They shaved their heads, stripped naked, painted themselves red, had a four day long war dance, then massacred the villagers. They then cut down a tree, stripped off its limbs and bark, painted the pole red, painted red the scalps of their victims, hung the scalps from the pole, then marched back to their homes singing victory songs.

These same people were living like southern gentry in plantation homes. When Sam Houston came west on a steamboat to Webbers Falls in Indian Territory, he was taken to the home of Western Cherokee John Jolly in a carriage driven by a black slave.

Sam Houston was a great favorite of the Cherokees, and John Jolly's relatives had adopted him into their family. Houston resigned his position as Governor of Tennessee and went to join the Western Cherokees. He was made a naturalized citizen of the band, and served as a delegate of the tribe to Washington DC. On a trip there, he appeared before Andrew Jackson dressed as a traditional Cherokee down to the last detail. Jackson was infuriated and questioned how Houston would dare to show up looking like a savage. Even the Western Cherokees, whose pet name for Houston was "The Big Drunk," made fun of his outfit.

There are few sources of information on these most interesting people. Conley says the only in-depth record is Grant Foreman's "Indians and Pioneers," published by Oklahoma University Press.

Robert J. Conley

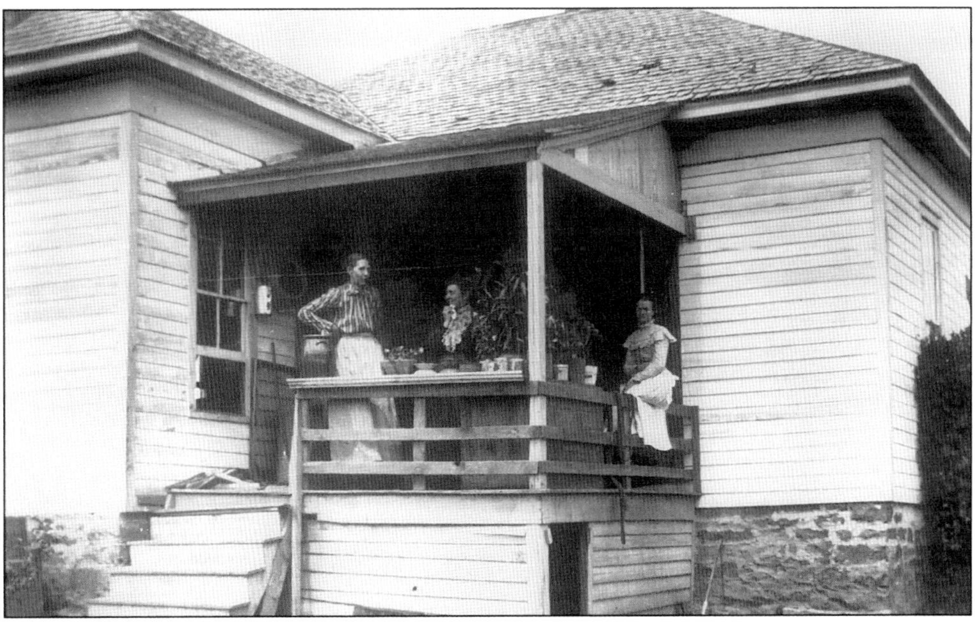

Neighbors, Early 1900s. (Courtesy Cherokee National Archives.)

Georgia Goes for the Gold

In the late 1820s, the state of Georgia began taking steps to insure that the rich lands belonging to the southeastern Cherokees would fall into their control. The discovery of gold in the Cherokee homeland spurred Georgia in this effort. To make matters worse for the Cherokees, the Georgians had a friend in the White House, President Andrew Jackson, who seemed duty-bound to remove the Indians to the west.

Although the Cherokee Nation had its own form of government securely in place, Georgia passed a law stating that the Cherokee government no longer existed. Knowing they had the president's approval, the Georgians passed another law making it illegal for an Indian to testify against a white man in court. Yet another law made it illegal for whites to live among the Cherokees. One such white man, Samuel Worcester, who would prove to be an important character in Cherokee history, was sentenced to four years in prison. When the Supreme Court ordered his release, Georgia simply refused to proceed, claiming that Cherokees had no right to use the United States courts. Georgia laid claim to the Cherokee lands and the gold therein.

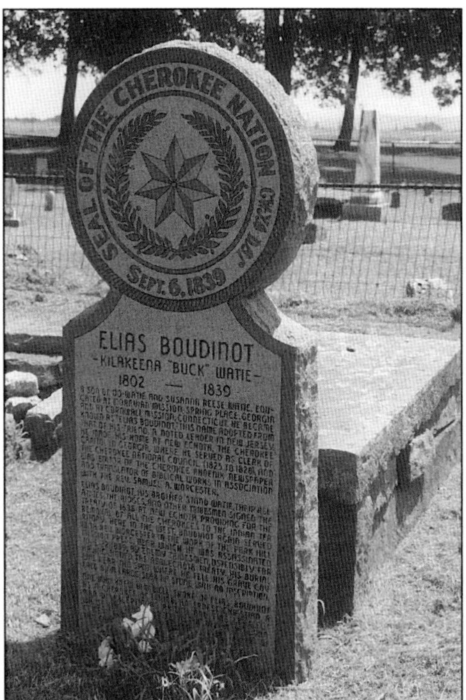

Elias Boudinot's Resting Place, Worcester Cemetery. (Photo by Murv Jacob.)

The Treaty

In 1818, Gahli Ginah Oowatie, whose name translated to Buck Deer Watie, graduated with honors from Spring Place, the Moravian mission in Georgia. A member of the Board of Commissioners of Foreign Missions named Elias Cornelius invited the brilliant young Cherokee to further his education in Cornwall, Connecticut. Buck and two other Cherokee youths made the trip on horseback. On the way, they were introduced to Presidents Jefferson, Madison and Monroe. While Buck was in Washington DC, the secretary of war promised to pay $100 per year for his tuition at Cornwall.

In Burlington, New Jersey, the travelers stopped at the home of the president of the American Bible Society. His name was Elias Boudinot. Elias and Buck struck up an instant friendship. Elias invited Buck to take his name, and from that time forward, Buck Deer Watie, brother of Stand Watie, was called Elias Boudinot. Years later, he would have a son named Elias Cornelius after the man responsible for Boudinot's good fortune.

Boudinot completed his studies and returned to Georgia. In 1826 he married Harriet Gold, a white woman he had courted in the east. The next year he became acquainted with the missionary, Samuel A. Worcester, who accompanied the couple as they moved to New Echota, the capital of the Cherokee Nation. There the men began work on

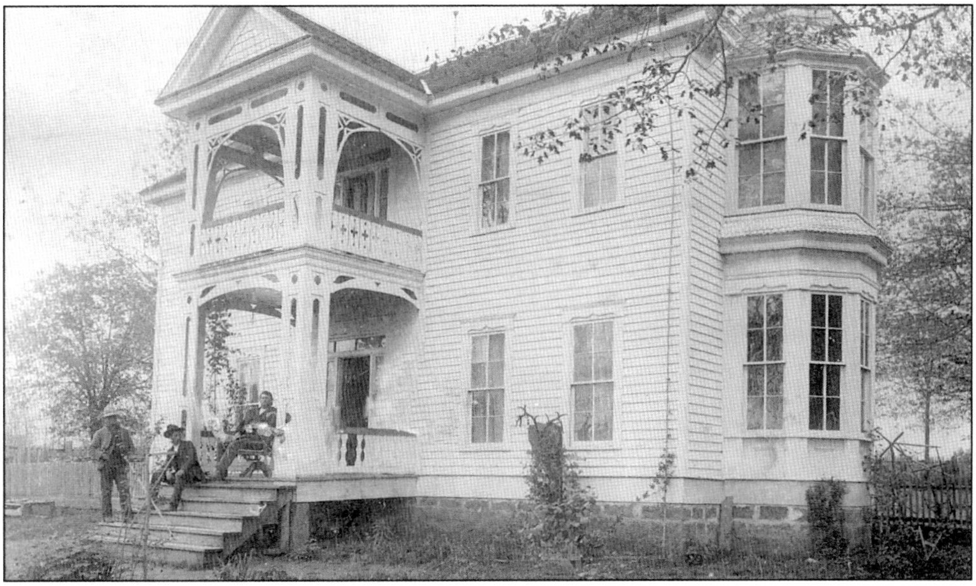

Elias Cornelius Boudinot Home, 1889. (Courtesy Cherokee National Archives.)

the Cherokee Phoenix, the first Native American newspaper ever published.

Elias became involved in the struggle with the United States over the proposed removal of the southeastern Indians, and at first stood defiantly against it. But he came to realize that there was little choice left for the Cherokees and thought it best to agree to a treaty with the federal government. The Treaty of New Echota, that allowed for the removal of the Cherokee people to Indian Territory, was signed in the parlor of Elias Boudinot's home on December 9, 1835. The signers included Boudinot, his uncle Major Ridge, his cousin John Ridge, and Andrew Ross, the brother of Principal Chief John Ross.

The Treaty Party—A Viewpoint

Robert Conley offered this example to describe his feelings about the signers of the Treaty of New Echota as a group of three sat talking on his patio. Suppose some Russians came in this yard and said, "Will you three sign a treaty that says we can take over the United States of America?" And supposed we signed the treaty, and from then on, everyone in the world said that treaty was valid. That is what the Treaty of New Echota was like. Those who signed had no right to sign it. They were not representatives of the Cherokee government, but they signed it, and it was accepted.

Robert J. Conley

At Old Fort Gibson

A soldier who died on active duty at Fort Gibson served in the U.S. Army for over 20 years. Not until the soldier's body was being embalmed did officials discover it was a woman.

In the National Cemetery at Fort Gibson there is a special group of graves called the "Officer's Circle." One of the grave stones bears the name of Tiana Rogers, wife of Sam Houston. She was said to be a relative of Sequoyah.

The renowned American writer Washington Irving spent time at the old fort. He traveled there down the Texas Trail from Kansas City. Soldiers from the fort escorted him through the territory where he recorded the lifestyles and living conditions of the different Indian Nations. In Irving's work, "Tour of the Prairies," he mentions visiting with Cherokees of the Rogers family.

Sequoyah Rogers

Incident on the Trail

A teenage southeastern Cherokee girl named Narcissa and her mother were washing their family's clothing at a creek near their home one day. Laundry day was long, and Narcissa's mother had brought along cooking pots in order to prepare a noon meal. The two were hard at their work when the soldiers came upon them. The women would never see their home again.

The soldiers marched the terrified women to a stockade filled with other Cherokee people who had been driven from their homes. Mother and daughter soon realized that they were more fortunate than many because they were allowed to carry their wet wash and cooking utensils with them. Others within the stockade had come with only the clothes on their backs.

Soon Narcissa and her mother left the stockade to begin the treacherous journey across the wild country to the west. One day a soldier who was guarding the Cherokee captives spied a beautiful young girl among the group. Narcissa watched him torment the girl, making unwanted advances and enraging her family.

That evening, while the people rested and ate around the campfire, Narcissa heard the whooshing sound of a knife. It came out of the woods and plunged into the offending soldier's back, killing him. The other soldiers blamed the killing on a certain young man who they confined until morning, then took him into the woods and shot him to death. The soldiers refused to allow the young man's family to bury him, forcing them to walk on as they left his body there on the ground.

The horror of that experience left Narcissa with a deep hatred for the white people who invaded her life and destroyed her home. She especially despised white men, and never forgot those soldiers on the Trail of Tears. As an older woman, she was finally able to associate with some of her white women neighbors.

Marion Hagerstrand

The Agreement

Following the Trail of Tears, a large pole barn was constructed on what would become the Capitol Square in downtown Tahlequah. It was here that Principal Chief John Ross held the great council meeting of 1839. A message was sent to the Western Cherokee Nation inviting them to attend, but instead they held their own council meeting at Manard Bayou near Fort Gibson.

Chief Ross sent messengers there, to request again that a delegation travel to the meeting in Tahlequah. A small group of the Western Cherokees went, and Sequoyah was among them. While there, those few individuals signed the articles of agreement that united the two groups into one nation. The remainder of the Western Cherokees never got a chance to agree or disagree with this decision. Ironically, this was the same tactic used by the federal government when the Treaty Party signed the Treaty of New Echota, initiating the Trail of Tears.

Robert J. Conley

White Gold

Judge Thomas Lewis Rogers came to Indian Territory as an Old Settler and set up the first salt industry west of the Mississippi River. The salt mine was located where Spavinaw Creek ran into Six Bulls, later called the Grand River. The work was hard and the men had few tools. The salty water was brought up from wells, then poured into shallow "salt kettles" that were eight to 10 feet across. The kettles sat atop huge furnaces and the water was boiled off, leaving the salt crystals. In those days, salt was among the most valuable commodities.

A second salt mine, located at Salina, was owned by John Rogers, who later sold it to his brother-in-law and future Texas President Sam Houston. After the Trail of Tears brought the bulk of the Cherokees to Indian Territory, Principal Chief John Ross claimed the mine as national property and put Robert Ross in charge of it. John Rogers fled to Mexico to avoid being killed by the Ross Party.

Sequoyah Rogers

Gold Fever

The citizens of the Cherokee Nation were not immune to the lust for wealth that swept the country, sending Forty-Niners packing to California in search of gold. Neighbors from the Arkansas border towns convinced the Cherokees to build a road through their land so that the Arkansas gold seekers would have a direct route west. The road became known as the Cherokee Trail.

Future Principal Chief Dennis W. Bushyhead was among those who went to seek their fortunes. He left with a party of 13 people for the hazardous journey west. The group was assailed by cholera, and 10 of the travelers, including Return Jonathan Meigs, died on the same day. Bushyhead also survived an epidemic of smallpox. He remained in California until 1868, entirely missing the Civil War, before returning to the Nation. There he was elected principal chief in 1879.

Another future chief who tried his luck in California was Joel Bryan Mayes. George Washington Adair, father of Col. William Penn Adair, also went west for a time. One of the few who returned to the Cherokee Nation with any wealth was Charles R. Hicks. He had sold his claim to prospectors from the East Coast for $75,000.

Mayes Takes the Capitol

In 1887, following a heated campaign, it was no simple matter for Principal Chief-elect Joel Bryan Mayes (of the Downing Party) to assume his duties or even to enter his office room at the Capitol. The National Council consisted of two houses, the Council and the Senate. By law, they were to meet and arrange for the inauguration of the new Principal Chief. The majority of the senators were of the National Party, whose candidate and current Principal Chief Dennis W. Bushyhead had lost the election. The Senate, in order to keep Bushyhead in office, refused to meet with the Council. Both parties were at a standoff, and the date for the inauguration passed as tensions increased.

Armed National Party members had been guarding the courthouse for days. One afternoon in January, 1888, a heavily-armed group of Downing Party members waited until most of the guards had gone home. They forced their way into the Capitol, broke down the door to the executive office, and physically carried Chief Bushyhead

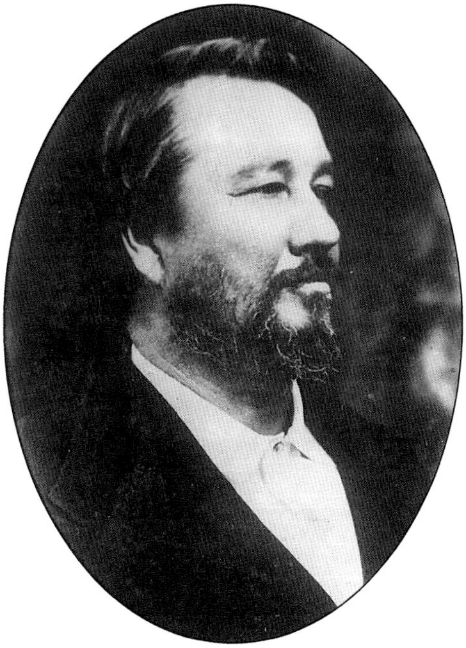

Principal Chief Joel Bryan Mayes, c. 1890. (Courtesy Cherokee National Archives.)

out. The president of the senate, a Downing Party member, swore Mayes in as Principal Chief.

For days the town talked of little else. One morning a strange item appeared in a downtown storefront window. It was a plaster cast of a foot with the big toe missing. The shop owner told the gathering crowd it was the foot of Hoolie Bell, with the toe broken off from kicking the Chief's door down.

Joel Mayes Finch

Chief Bushyhead was a big man, weighing at least 350 pounds. When the Mayes supporters decided to storm the capitol, Hoolie Bell led them across the yard and into the building. They kicked down the door of Bushyhead's office to find him seated in his chair. The group pushed both him and the chair over backward. He remained in the sitting position as two men took the back of the chair at his shoulders, and several others took the chair by its legs. They carried him in this awkward manner down the stairs and out the door onto the Capitol lawn. They sat him up in his chair under a tree where he remained until it started to get dark. Then he walked the few blocks to his home.

Historian and writer Robert Conley recounts the loss of Chief Bushyhead's residence from the city of Tahlequah. His home was the last one standing that had belonged to a principal chief elected before statehood. The historic building was ordered taken down by a local banker to make room for an expanded drive-through service at his bank. The banker was a Cherokee Nation council member and an official of the historical society. Although many Cherokees would like to have seen the Chief's home restored, the building was cut in half. It was sold in two pieces to a full-blood Cherokee from the Briggs community, who supposedly put it back together.

Robert Conley

More About Bushyhead

The late Cherokee historian Leon Gilmore elaborated even more on the removal of Bushyhead from office. After the election, it was up to the Principal Chief to call for a Council meeting to ratify the election, but Bushyhead refused to call the meeting.

Highway Robbery

When the Cherokee Strip payment came to Tahlequah, between June 4 and June 16, 1894, Principal Chief Col. Johnson Harris urged his fellow Cherokees to be careful and try to save their money. He warned them against "indulgence in any kind of intoxicating drinks. The too free use of these has been the prime cause of bloodshed in our country." Each person in the Nation received $365.70. With all that money circulating around, every kind of "entrepreneur" came out of the woodwork. Record numbers of horses were sold, a circus came to town, and the dance halls stayed open all night to accommodate the gamblers. The money attracted the most outlaws ever seen in the Nation at one time, including the Dalton Gang, the Cook Gang, Cherokee Bill, and Jim French.

A young man named Levi Sanders had been drinking heavily and caught a ride with the stage coach headed from Tahlequah to Fort Gibson. He sat up front with the driver until they cleared the outskirts of town, then pulled out a pistol, ordering the driver to stop. Next he lined up the passengers and proceeded to rob them, although he got very little in goods. When a young gentleman passenger made a suspicious move, the drunken Sanders shot him, then ran off down the road. He pulled the gun again on the first person he saw and stole a horse.

As bad luck would have it, a much respected townswoman, Nancy Duncan, and her son Felix were approaching the rider in a wagon just outside Tahlequah. Sanders must have intended to shoot at everyone he met. He aimed at Felix, but shot the mother instead, killing her. Felix Duncan then proceeded to empty his rifle into the gunman, ending the young man's misguided attempt at robbery.

The Dawes Commission is Born

Having visited Indian Territory and the Cherokee Nation in the 1880s, Senator Henry M. Dawes of Massachusetts made the following remarks. "The head chief told us that there was not a family in the whole Nation that had not a home of its own. There is not a pauper in that Nation, and the Nation does not owe a dollar. It built its own capital, and its schools and hospitals. Yet the defect of the system was apparent. They have got as far as they can go, because they hold their land in common. There is no

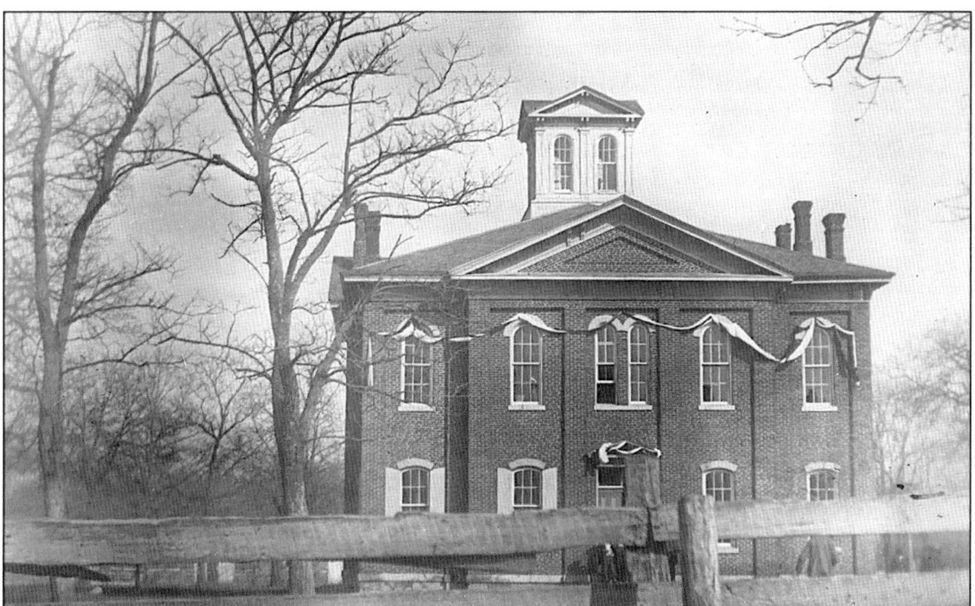

The Cherokee Capitol, 1898. (Courtesy Cherokee National Archives.)

selfishness, which is at the bottom of civilization. Until these people will consent to give up their lands, and divide them among their citizens so that each can own the land he cultivates, they will not make much progress." On February 8, 1887, President Grover Cleveland signed the Dawes Act, and land allotment for the Cherokees became a reality.

Senator Dawes gave much credit for the initiation of land allotment in Indian Territory to the Women's National Indian Association. Formed in 1879, this group was not made up of Indian women, but white women from across the United States. This ambitious organization was a close relative of the Women's Christian Temperance Union. In their minds, nothing could have been better than nice little plots of land for all Indian families.

Dick Halfbreed

In the late 1800s, there lived a Tahlequah merchant named Richard Fields, who was known by the locals as Dick Halfbreed. On a number of occasions, Dick had spoken favorably of the idea of allotment of the Cherokee Nation's lands to individual owners. The fullbloods were dead set against allotment, and one hot summer night three of them decided to kill Dick Halfbreed.

A church service was being held in the old Masonic Lodge building, and Dick was seated near the front of the building. The three fullbloods met in a vacant lot on the south side of the building. One of them took a gun to the open window, looked in on the churchgoers, and aimed the pistol at the back of Dick Halfbreed's head. Just as the shot was fired, Dick turned his head. The bullet went through his nose and knocked his right eye completely out.

Dick said later that when the bullet struck him, his soul left his body and hovered around the ceiling for a while, then returned to the wounded body. Only then did he feel the pain of his injury. Dick Halfbreed recovered from his wounds and moved out of Tahlequah. Although everyone in town knew who they were, no charges were

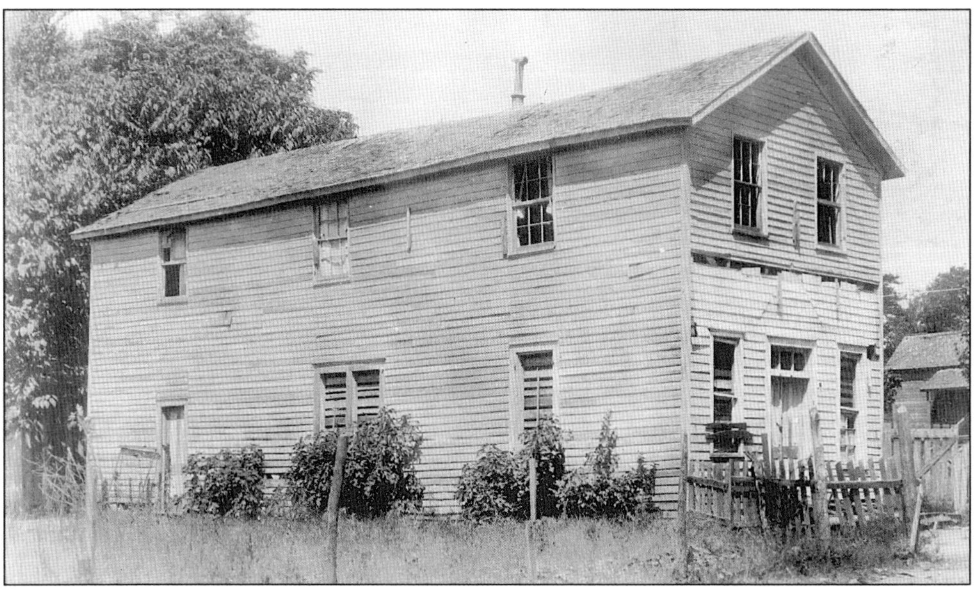

First Masonic Lodge, Built 1853. (Courtesy Cherokee Studies Institute.)

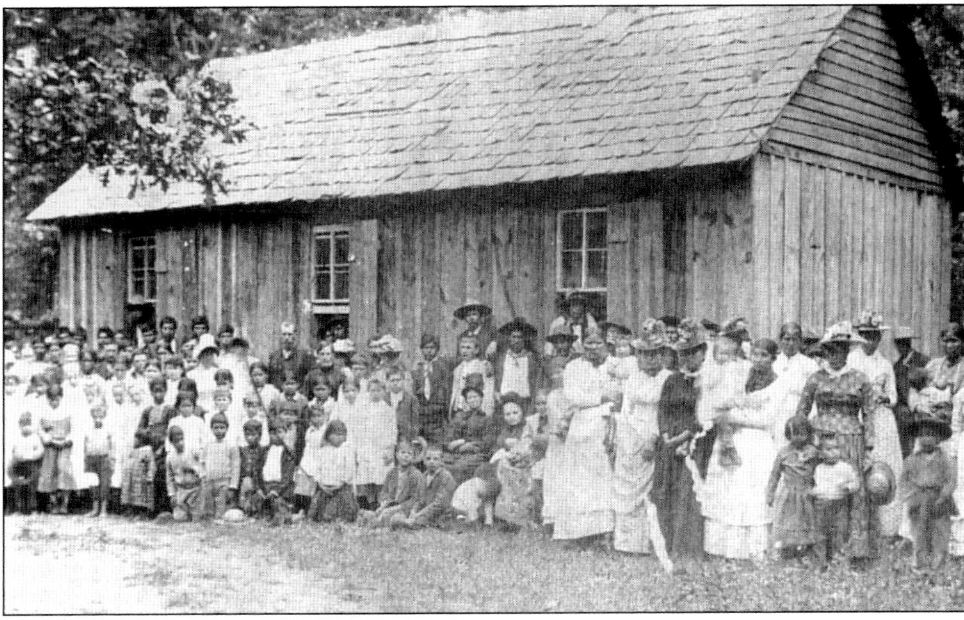

Elm Springs School, Park Hill, 1889. (Courtesy Cherokee National Archives.)

ever filed against his assailants.

Around Tahlequah

There is supposed to be a big cavern underground in Tahlequah, part of which goes under Central Elementary School. In the 1800s, some children got lost in the cave, and its entrance was sealed off from the public.

Incorporated in 1852, Tahlequah is the oldest town in the Cherokee Nation. Fort Gibson once claimed that spot, but it was incorporated as "Keetoowah" five years later.

During the late 1800s, croquet was the most popular sport in Tahlequah. In the warm months the men would play croquet for hours. Tahlequah had more musicians, mostly fiddle players, than any other place around. The same holds true today, but today's musicians are mostly guitarists.

In 1888, Tahlequah was described by a Mr. Vogel as a one-street town of about 750 inhabitants. He said that the first time he went there, the people "eyed him with suspicion," and practically everyone there was wearing a gun.

In 1895, a fire broke out downtown. It started in Wilson's Stable and spread to all buildings between Shawnee and Delaware Streets on both sides of Muskogee Avenue. The city council passed an ordinance stating that no more wooden buildings could be constructed in the business district of downtown.

Officials of the Dawes Commission arrested several prominent Cherokee citizens for refusing to sign the rolls. Included were Redbird Smith, Charles Sexton, John Beamer, and Jeff Lowie. All these men had served the Cherokee Nation in some official capacity. The men said they did not mind so much being arrested, but were infuriated when jailers cut off their long hair.

On August 2, 1902, a solid gold railroad spike was driven in at the Tahlequah train depot to officially complete the track into town. Three days later, the first passenger train arrived there.

On May 24, 1922, the Ku Klux Klan had a parade through downtown Tahlequah. Two thousand people from the area showed up to watch as over

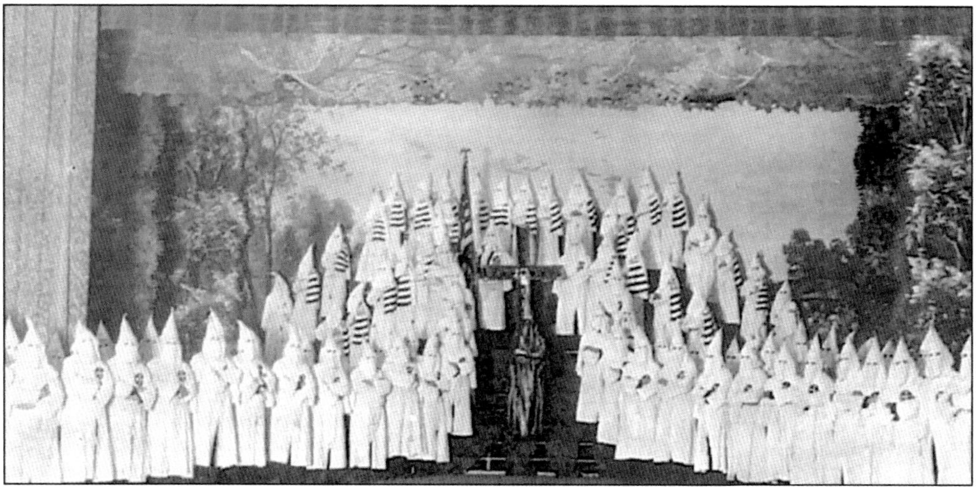

KKK Meeting, Tahlequah, 1925. (Courtesy Cherokee Studies Institute.)

150 klansmen drove past in their cars. Representatives of the Klan visited a local church in full costume, dropping a sizeable donation in the collection plate.

The Porum Range War

Four Davis brothers came to Indian Territory in the early 1900s. Jack Davis and a man named Pony Starr were running cattle together near Porum. Another rancher in the area by the name of Hester accused Davis and Starr of stealing some of his cattle, and began making threats on their lives. Hazel McClure's uncle, Charlie, was one of two deputies who were sent to the Hester home with an arrest warrant.

A group of men from the Hester ranch disarmed the lawmen and locked them up in the smokehouse. Then the band of men headed for Pony Starr's ranch with intentions of killing both Starr and Davis. A shootout followed between the two sides. Starr's men were unharmed, but two of Hester's were killed, one of them his own son. Afterward, Davis and Starr turned themselves in to authorities in Eufaula. A train was sent from Muskogee to pick up the dead and the wounded. Davis and Starr were released, but Hester's men were charged with intent to kill. It was interesting to note that the range war made headlines in the Muskogee newspapers, but the sinking of the Titanic, which occurred at the same time, did not.

Time passed, but Hester was still thirsty for revenge over the death of his son. Hazel McClure's uncle, the deputy who sided with Starr and Davis, was assassinated. Hazel went to sit with the body, which was being kept iced down in a casket. Molten ice water dripped from the coffin. After that, Hazel could not stand the sound of dripping water.

Virginia Vann Perry

Depression Times

For a time during the Depression, Sequoyah Rogers stayed with his mother in the weighing house of a cotton gin. The gin was located at Catoosa, Cherokee for "high hill." There was an old barn at the cotton gin where the bales were stored, and its top story was inhabited by pigeons. At night, Sequoyah would climb into the loft and catch enough pigeons for his mother to cook for the next day's meals.

When Sequoyah was about seven years old, he and his mother moved into the basement of Hillside Mission, about nine miles north of Skiatook. From there, they would pull a little red wagon to the town of Vera where they picked up commodities like dried beans, rice and grapefruit juice.

Upstairs in the mission lived a very old man who made a great impression on Sequoyah. His name was Solomon Abbot and he was a writer. People around there thought it almost unbelievable that such a man lived among them in those hard times. Abbot kept a tiny office stacked with books. When Sequoyah would go up and visit with him the old man would show him the books he had written. Sequoyah has never forgotten that.

Sequoyah remembers going to dances way down in the bottoms east of Sperry. The dance ground was called Spybuck. The most famous of the dancers there came from a family named Supernaw. They were claimed by the Osage, but were actually Delawares. The dancers circled around a big fire, and Sequoyah remembers several occasions when one or more fell into the fire, having had too much liquor. Although some of the men drank, many of the elders sat within a big tepee, eating and smoking peyote. The locals called them "peyote heads."

At the age of 15, Sequoyah enlisted in the Marine Corps. At his insistence, his mother signed the papers saying he was old enough to join. He was in boot camp when the Japanese bombed Pearl Harbor.

Sequoyah Rogers

Virginia's War Effort

Virginia Vann graduated from high school in 1936. Times were hard then in northeast Oklahoma, and jobs were scarce. She went on to continue her education at Warner where Lorene Davis, a family friend, looked out for her.

During the World War, Virginia was compelled to do her share in the war effort. She boarded a train to the west,

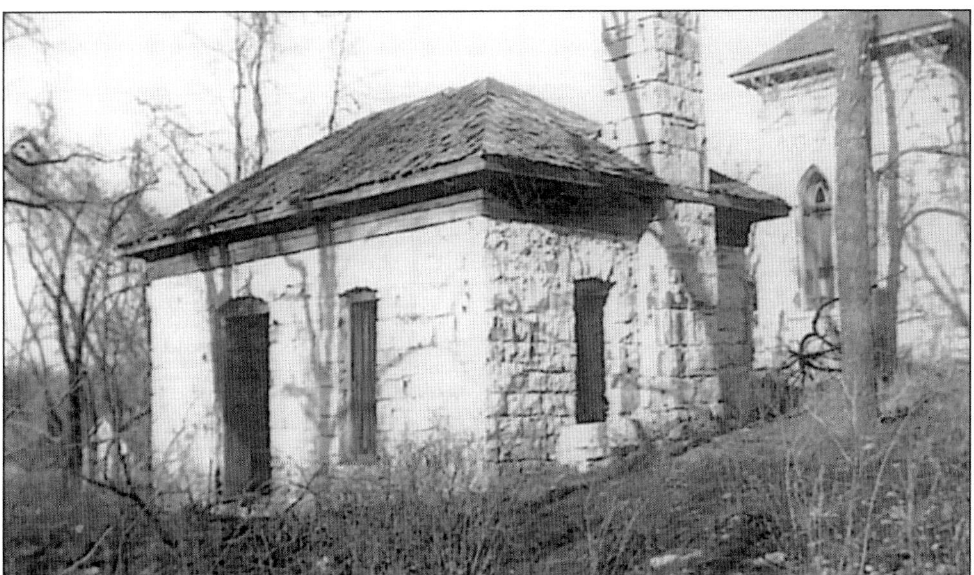

Old Mission Outside Grove. (Courtesy Cherokee National Archives.)

arriving at Richland, Washington. She was employed, along with young and old from all across the nation, at the Hanford Engineer Works. Before long Virginia realized that she was working on a secret project, and all operations were "hush-hush." She spent her days at a section of the construction site called "Excess Material." Everyday, she was tested for radiation contamination, but none was ever found. Virginia was helping with the beginning experimentation and construction of the atomic bomb.

The workers stayed in a sort of camp where there were dormitories and recreation halls for the women that were separated from those of the men. The barracks building where Virginia roomed was surrounded by a tall fence and a gate. The fence was electrified, and all husbands and boyfriends who visited the residents had to check in at the gate.

In order to gain access to the women's recreation hall, the men had to have a date with one of the residents. Young Virginia was single, and became popular indeed. Big name bands would perform there for dances and the workers looked forward to the time spent socializing.

The men's recreation hall sold beer to the workers, who would sometimes get pretty rowdy. One evening a brawl broke out at the men's hall which continued until officials turned high powered water hoses on the men to cool them off. The argument got started over whose home state was the best in the nation.

After a year's service, Virginia felt she had done her patriotic duty and headed home by train. She bought a ticket to Kansas City where she stopped for a short visit with a friend. There were so many soldiers traveling through there that Virginia could not schedule the trip to Oklahoma. She went to the station and tried anyway, offering a $10 bribe to a redcap if he could sneak her aboard. The redcap advised her instead to find a soldier and pretend to be his wife.

Virginia thought the redcap's idea might work, so she went looking for a meek and mild looking soldier. Sure enough she found one who halfheartedly agreed to the venture. Neither of them thought to ask where the other was going, and when they got up to the conductor, Virginia had to think fast. She told the conductor that her "husband" was going for active duty (which he actually was) and she was heading home to Oklahoma. The soldier and Virginia were sent to two different trains.

Two sailors from Oklmulgee, Oklahoma had heard the conductor telling Virginia she would need to go on alone. They believed she was being separated from her husband, and valiantly stayed by her side the whole trip, even getting up to fetch her dinner.

Virginia Vann Perry

A Distant Volcano

Kathy and Perry VanBuskirk had retired for the evening and were lying in bed when Perry said, "Did you see that!" He had been looking out the window when he saw what looked like a big ball of fire in the sky. The next morning they found out that it was the explosion from Mount St. Helens eruption's.

The family lived in a concrete block home that must have been near one of the many fault lines that run through Oklahoma. Soon after the eruption, a shock-wave came through their land and shook the walls of their home. They said it sounded like a truck had hit the house. The whole family ran outside. The shock-waves weakened, but continued for two or three weeks after the eruption.

Perry and Kathy VanBuskirk

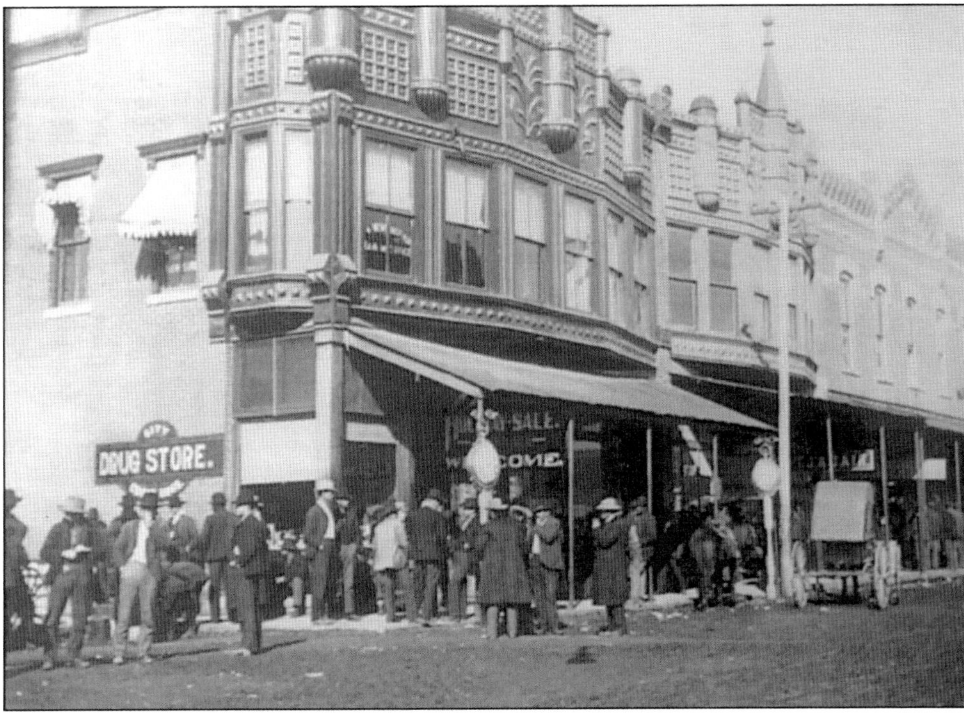

Downtown Tahlequah, late 1800s. (Courtesy Cherokee Studies Institute.)

CHAPTER 6

LIFE IN THE CHEROKEE NATION

Perhaps the most wonderful stories about the Cherokee Nation come from the recollections of ordinary people who live there. Sharing their memories, they bring the true essence of their experiences to light, to be understood and appreciated by others. They take us back to a time when life was simpler yet more difficult, and people had less but enjoyed what they had more.

The Cherokee Nation has attracted residents from all backgrounds and walks of life to its bustling towns and quiet communities. Some of its counties rank among the most poverty-stricken in the United States. Even so, the people come because this is a wonderful place to live, especially for retirees. They join Cherokee neighbors whose families have been here for generations.

Cherokees from around the world return annually to the Nation and celebrate their heritage at the Cherokee National holiday. The holiday marks the anniversary of the Cherokee Constitution, adopted on September 6, 1839, and falls each year on Labor Day weekend. This is a time of homecoming, when Cherokees get together to share memories of the past and dreams of the future.

The Clan System

In the 1500s, after European explorers first visited the Cherokee settlements, the lands were closed off for 150 years to any and all intrusion. The Wolf Clan sat guard at every passageway into their territory. Meanwhile, the smaller Indian tribes whose homes lay on the east coast were being ravished by marauding groups of white men. They were the Dutch, the French, the English, the Spanish, the Portuguese, and the Swedish, who plundered and burned Native villages, taking slaves and stealing anything of value.

At the same time, the whites were fighting among themselves as well. If an Indian tribe were to make a treaty of peace with one group, they were automatically at war with another. Many coastal tribes could not survive the onslaught, and exist today only as place names on a map.

The remnants of those displaced people became homeless wanderers. Those who trespassed upon the Cherokee lands were captured and taken to the tribal leaders who decided their fate. They might be killed, sent away, or adopted into the Cherokee tribe. If the adoptee was a man, he became a member of the Wolf Clan. Women were taken into the Bird Clan. These two clans remain the largest in the Cherokee Nation to this day.

The clan affiliation of a man became irrelevant once he was married. The man left his own extended family to stay with the woman's clan in her village. He lived among her people and depended upon their support. As such, spousal abuse by a man against a woman was eliminated. If a man should mistreat his mate with her entire clan there to defend her, he would likely be put to death.

In the warm months, children ran about carefree and naked. They dressed only after reaching puberty. They lived without fear because the entire clan was their extended family, and each member was committed to the children's welfare. Children grew up with a strong sense of family, community, and identity.

Just as the Wolf Clan secured the tribal borders, every clan had its particular duty to the tribe. The work was divided evenly and each group could be counted on to do its share. Thanks to the clan system, the operations of the tribe ran as smoothly and as flawlessly as a beehive.

Murv Jacob

Spare the Rod

When white men first came to know the southeastern Cherokees, some were appalled by the tribe's lack of discipline of the children. The whites thought them most unruly. The little Cherokees were always throwing rocks, shooting arrows, riding horses, behaving wildly, and having way too much fun. When the men complained to the parents, they replied very simply that their children were just being children.

Sequoyah Rogers

Tahlequah Cemetery

According to Dr. Ballenger, the land for the current Tahlequah City Cemetery was purchased for $50 and was first used in 1888. The first person to be buried there was a young man named Bert Jones who was killed while showing off with his pistol. Bert had been present when some people were looking over the new cemetery land, and was heard saying that he found it gruesome and would hate to be the first person buried there.

In 1905, families who had relatives in the old cemetery were told to move their graves to the new location. The old cemetery was located at the present site of Sequoyah School. It is said that some graves were left there by families that failed to remove them. Ghost stories still are told by those who believe they have encountered spirits at the school.

In the mid 1960s, the junior high school was located at what is now Central Elementary. On the north side of the school was a semi-circular drive where the kids got on and off the buses. At just the spot where hundreds of children's feet had jumped from bus to earth, something began to surface from

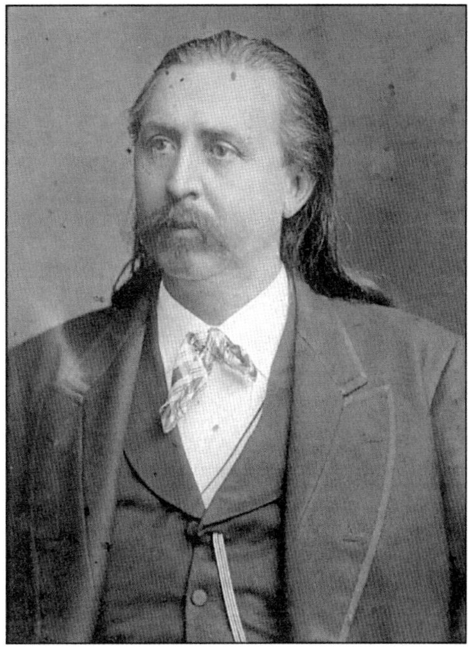

Col. William Penn Adair, 1830–1880. (Courtesy Cherokee National Archives.)

beneath the dust. Three very old grave markers had appeared, causing excited chatter among the kids. This occurred just before the end of the school year, and was soon forgotten as the summer break began. The dusty area today lies beneath several inches of asphalt. Maybe the graves are still under there.

Take a walk through the Tahlequah Cemetery today and you can find the final resting places of some of the greats of Cherokee history. Three of our chiefs lie there; Dennis Bushyhead, Joel Mayes, and Col. Johnson Harris. Deputy Chiefs George Lowery, Richard Taylor, and Col. William Penn Adair are there as well, along with the Reverend Evan Jones who traveled with the Cherokees across the Trail of Tears.

Hard Times at Old Green

Leon Corntassel was born in 1917. At the age of 15, his father passed away and he went off to the Chilocco

Indian School where he graduated in 1935. He was on his own from then on, and got his first job at Woolaroc Lodge in Bartlesville, Oklahoma. The Lodge is now known as the Woolaroc Museum. He remembers how his family managed through the hard times of the 1920s in northeastern Oklahoma.

The Corntassels of Old Green had two cows and a horse. Cream was in high demand in those days. When the cows were milked, the cream was allowed to rise to the top of the container, which was skimmed off and sold. The cream was transported by train to Neosho, Missouri, then on to Springfield.

The money made from the sale of cream was the only income the family had for a time, but they had a large garden that helped sustain them the whole year. In the spring and summer, wild berries like huckleberries and blackberries grew in abundance. In the fall, the family would shell bushels of walnuts and hickory nuts. The mother made "kanuchi" from ground hickory nuts and hominy grown in her garden. Leon says there were hazel nuts in the area for a long time, but now the trees have all died out.

Leon Corntassel

Message of Death

Mention the screech owl to anyone from an old family in the Cherokee Nation, and you are sure to hear stories of misfortune and death. The tiny owls are said to be the bearers of bad news, and their cries will instantly bring fear to believers. Some traditionalists have been known to kill owls, while others say the owl is harmless.

Sally Finch remembers this event that took place on an August night in 1938. It was so hot inside the house that Sally's family, except for her father, were sleeping on the screened porch.

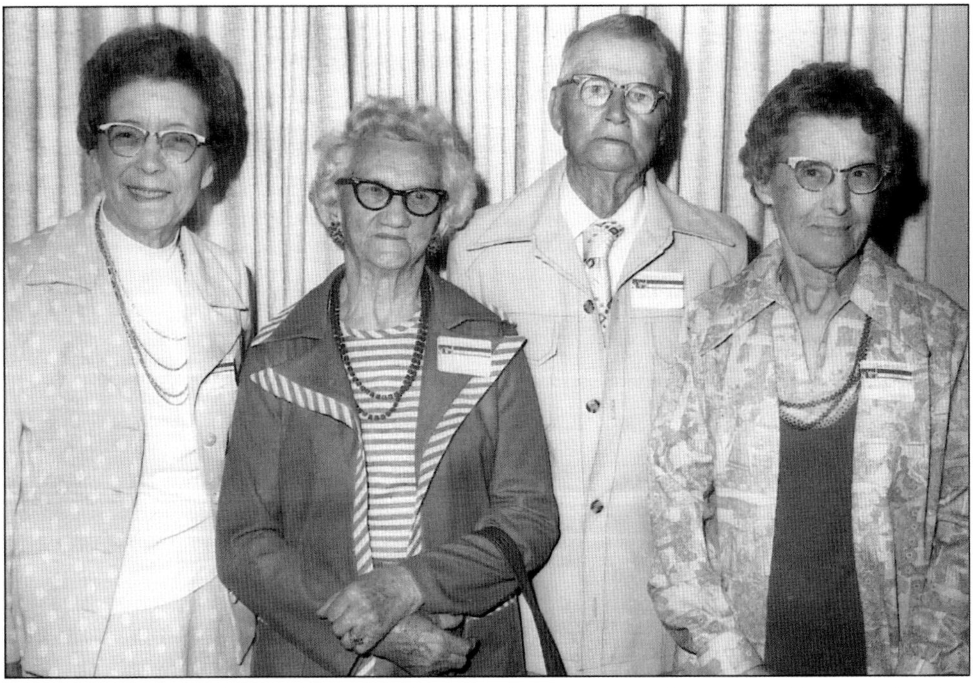

Seminary Association Officers Pearl Mayes Langston, Susie Martin Alberty, Charles Ross, Charlotte Mayes Sanders—Sally's Mom, 1977. (Courtesy Sally Finch.)

Her father had gone to be with his mother, Sallie Clay Sanders, who lived at Old Wauhillau, who had suffered a stroke. The children were all nervous and miserable in the heat.

At about 10 P.M., a screech owl began to scream from a big oak tree that stood near one corner of the sleeping porch. The family tried to scare the bird away. Sally's brother even tried screeching back at the owl, but it would neither leave nor cease its call.

Finally, Sally's mother said, "Well, your Grandma's dead. This is a death message." Pretty soon they saw the lights of a truck coming down the road toward their home. It was the owners of the filling station five miles away. Theirs was the nearest telephone. Sally's father had called and asked them to send a message to the family that his mother had passed on at about 10 p.m. that night. After the truck left, the owl left, too.

Sally Sanders Finch

Grandma Mattie and the Owl

Mattie Evans went to live with her daughter Martha Dickenson in her old age. She shared a bedroom with her granddaughter Loretta, who loved her deeply. Loretta remembers Mattie as a tiny, delicate lady, who always wore dresses down to the floor. When Mattie got her pension check, she and Loretta walked to town to go shopping. In the summertime, they would often buy a big watermelon and carry it back home. When they got near the house, Mattie would break it open and she and Loretta would eat the center heart, saving the seedy part for the other kids.

As Mattie aged, she kept a chamber pot in the room near the bed she shared with Loretta. Very late one night, Loretta woke up suddenly. Mattie was on her chamber pot, and a screech owl sat in a lilac bush outside. The two spoke to each other, and every time the owl would cry out, Mattie would say, "I'm coming, I'm coming." A few days later, Mattie passed away peacefully in her sleep.

Loretta Dunham

Father and Teacher

Sally Sanders' first school was a one room building lit only by its windows in the daytime. There were eight rows of desks in the room, one for each grade. This was an Indian day school, and Sally's father, Robert Lee Sanders, was the teacher.

Robert kept his teacher's desk in one corner of the room. He would have the kids gather round him as he opened a book, and using an unsharpened pencil, point at words and read them aloud. He would have the children repeat each word to him. This is how he taught reading and English. Children in all eight grades were allowed to participate in the lessons.

At Christmas time, Robert and the bigger boys would go out and chop down the biggest cedar tree they could find for the school. All the decorations were hand made by the children, like chains of red and green construction paper that were draped around the tree.

Before the Bureau of Indian Affairs came into being, commodities were brought to the school each month by the U.S. Indian Service. These were used to provide lunch for the students. In addition to the regular staples, special items for the whole family were included with the Christmas delivery. There were gloves for the women, socks for the men, and both socks and gloves for all the children. They brought crates of oranges, apples, and big, juicy pears, along with pounds of old-fashioned Christmas candy.

Sally and her sister Betty helped their mother prepare the gifts to hand out at the annual Christmas program at the school. There were no bags for the candy, so they stuffed the unwrapped pieces in pairs of new socks for each child. Fibers from the socks might stick to the Christmas candy, but the kids "ate the fuzzy candy anyway."

Every student in the school was required to learn a Christmas poem and recite it at the program. Robert taught the kids to sing all the best-loved carols. When the big night arrived, the wall lamps were lit and the whole community was welcomed into the crowded little school house. Sally said, "You have never seen such happy faces. When Daddy sang 'Joy to the World,' he looked 10-feet tall to me." Then the poems were recited. Sena Johnson always recited "Twas the Night Before Christmas" because she was able to memorize the whole thing. Every person in the room received gifts, fruit, and candy.

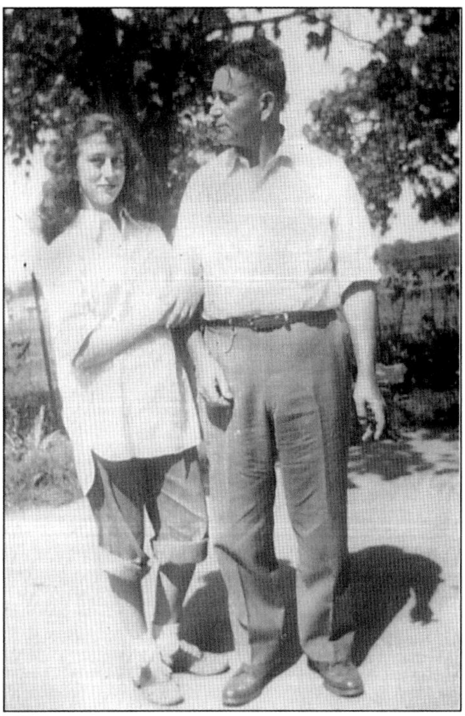

Sally and Robert Lee Sanders, 1946. (Courtesy Sally Sanders Finch.)

Robert Lee Sanders taught at Indian day schools in Kalihoma and Mulberry Hollow (near Stilwell). Later in his career, he moved to Sapulpa, Oklahoma, where he served as boys advisor at the Euchee Boys Boarding School. When the boarding school was closed, he began teaching in public schools.

Sally Sanders Finch

The Hero

Frank Dickenson was left with a son and a daughter to care for when his first wife passed away. As many did in those days, he married his wife's younger sister. Martha gave birth to five more daughters and two sons. Each of the family treasured their hero Frank. It seemed he could do anything, but when he was away, everything went to pot.

The family lived in a big house in the woods, lit only by kerosene and Alladin lamps. When Frank wasn't there, it didn't take much to get everyone in the house really scared, and Martha was just as bad as the kids. One night they thought they heard something in the house. As if on cue, they all decided to run outside. Martha grabbed a kerosene lamp and jumped over the seven steps from the front door to the ground. The lamp gave a little comfort until Frank came home.

The family never knew what a doctor was. Frank was a seventh son, and his family had great faith in his healing ability. He always kept a bottle of apricot brandy on hand. When the kids caught cold, they were sent to bed with a hot drink of lemonade and brandy. If Frank ever cut himself, he took a box of salt and poured it into the cut. The children's cuts he doctored with kerosene.

Donna was the baby of the family and

slept with her parents. When she was just a toddler, Donna contracted whooping cough and became terribly sick. Late in the night she began shaking with fever and choking, unable to breathe. Frank worked and worked over her, but nothing he did could help. The whole family watched and prayed as Frank finally gave up and laid Donna down to die. Her big brother Jud had been out on a date and walked in at that moment. He picked the baby up by her heels and shook her. A large clump of something dislodged from her throat, and she was able to breathe. Jud became quite a hero, too.

Loretta Dunham

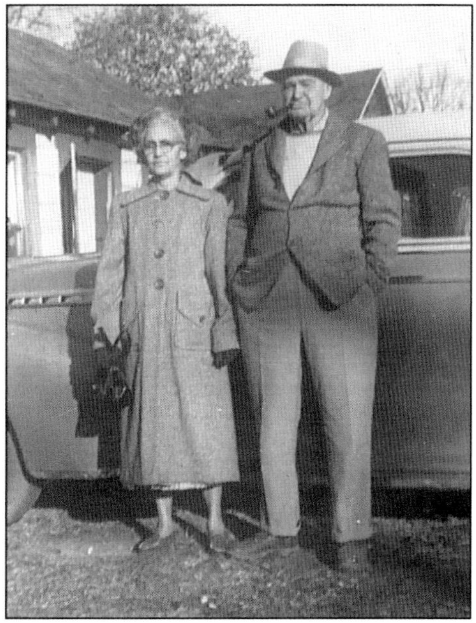

Martha and Frank Dickenson, 1958. (Courtesy Loretta Dunham.)

Virginia's Folks

Virginia Vann Perry is a respected member of the Trail of Tears Association, and a welcome volunteer at Native American museums and organizations in northeastern Oklahoma. She is often accompanied by her sister, Imogene, known by friends as "Jean." Virginia is an avid historical researcher and genealogist. A direct descendant of the famed Cherokee, Rich Joe Vann, she shares interesting stories about her family.

Hazel McClure and her sister married two of the Vann brothers. Hazel's husband was Clement Vann, a name that has popped up several times in Cherokee history. Clement, or Clem, was 38 years old and Hazel just 17 when they took their vows. They bought a home in Nowata, Oklahoma.

Clem worked and Hazel kept the home. There was a young man in the neighborhood who liked to talk with Hazel, and each day he would ride up on his spotted pony for a chat. She told Clem about these daily visits, and he promptly purchased the pony from the young man.

While living in Nowata, a thief entered their unlocked home. Clem's wallet was taken out of his pants pocket, along with 18 to 20 of his "everyday" gray silk shirts. When he really wanted to dress up, he wore striped silk.

The couple moved to Porum, Oklahoma, by wagon. The journey took them two days and nights. Clem got into the cattle business there, and ran his herd on the Braxton Ranch. On November 30, 1919, a daughter, Virginia, was born, followed by another, Imogene, on March 9, 1921. Within a few years, the price of cattle began to drop. Clem and a co-worker named Aud Wheeler rounded up the cattle and headed out to sell them "on the hoof." He returned with 40 head of horses. The Kansas City Star reported that his was the biggest single cattle sale to occur up to that time.

Virginia started school at nearby Briartown, but soon her father got a job building roads around the various oil fields of the state. She went to grade school for a time at Skiatook. She never really knew what grade she was in, and none of the other kids did either. At one school, Virginia and a teacher were the only ones in the room, and they sat huddled around a wood stove studying books. Later she went to a nicely painted white clapboard school owned by an oil company.

Both Clem and Hazel were members of the Cherokee Nation. At the time of land allotment, Indians who registered as 1/4 or more Cherokee were assigned a white person to help oversee their land. Clem's father was educated at Cane Hill, Arkansas, and was a judge in the Cherokee Nation during the allotment. He enrolled his children as 1/8 Cherokee, although their actual blood quantum was considerably greater.

Virginia Vann Perry

Traveling by Train

All that remains now of the busy train depot in Tahlequah is a small pile of bricks and the appellation of

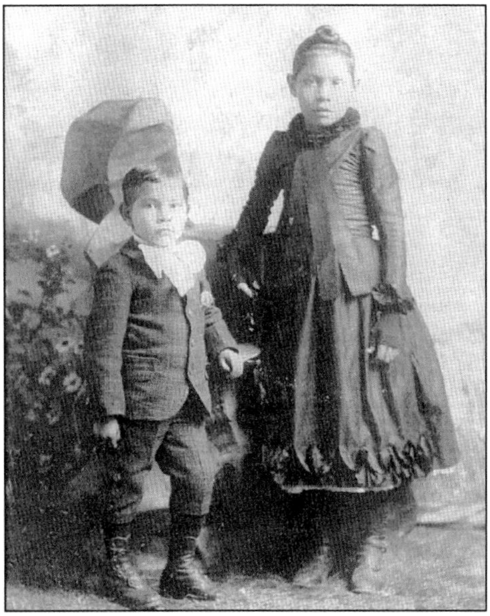

Cherokee children, Jess and Sue Ray Sevier. (Courtesy Barbara McAlister.)

"Depot Hill" for the section of West Choctaw Street leading to the old site. In the 1920s and 30s, riding the train between towns was the easy way to get around for shopping and visiting. The train made daily trips back and forth from Hulbert to Tahlequah, and Ralph Dunham remembers taking the train regularly with his mother, Ida Bailey Dunham, to shop in Tahlequah for canned milk. The trip, which cost about 25 cents, was worth the price to find the milk that was not always available at the stores in Hulbert. The stores in the bigger city also offered better prices.

The family would sometimes get off or on the train mid-way between Tahlequah and Hulbert at Mt. Zion, where Ralph's Grandpapa Bailey lived. The operators of the trains were very accommodating, and would stop for any travelers along the way who might signal them.

Ralph took a train to Sallisaw, Oklahoma, with his mother, Ida, when he was just a young boy to attend the funeral of Pretty Boy Floyd.

Ralph Dunham

Tar and Feathers

A family moved to the city of Tahlequah from Durant, in far southeastern Oklahoma in the late 1920s, and they were driving a new T Model Ford. When they pulled in to town, one of the first citizens they saw was a black man. None of the children had ever seen an African American before, but knew of a black man who came to their home town of Durant and was accused of a crime. He had actually been tarred and feathered and run out of Durant.

The elder son of the family was about 19 years old, and after seeing the black man, sat up all night in the Ford with a gun to protect his family in case the man should come along.

There have been African Americans living among Cherokees in the west since the Old Settlers arrived in the early 1800s. Many more were forced to move there with the Cherokees who came over the Trail of Tears. The person they saw was probably born right there in Tahlequah.

Memories of Her Dad

When Sally Sanders was a girl, there was a big water tower behind her house. On hot days, all the neighbor kids would head to Sally's back yard, and her dad would fire up the pump and let the water run over the sides of the tower. The kids played in the cool water for hours.

One night there was a big commotion, and several men came to the house to awaken Sally's dad. They kept saying, "The devil's coming up to get us. Come on!" Her dad grabbed his .38 and a lantern and ran to do battle with the creature. When it finally emerged from the hole in the ground, they saw that it was an oversized armadillo.

Sally's dad went to a meeting one evening very tired, and on the way back home, went to sleep driving. He ended up hitting a white mule that was standing in the road, and his newfangled car turned over in a ditch. The next thing he remembered, someone was shaking him and asking if he was all right. After that no one could talk him into driving a car again.

Sally's father was good at building things, and had a little workshop at their home. There was a couple living down the road who had a baby girl that Sally loved to play with. One day the baby became sick and could hold no food on her stomach. Although Sally's mother begged the parents to take the child to a doctor, they refused, having no trust in doctors. The baby was fed only sugar water, until she finally became too weak and died. Sally's parents didn't tell her about the baby just then, though.

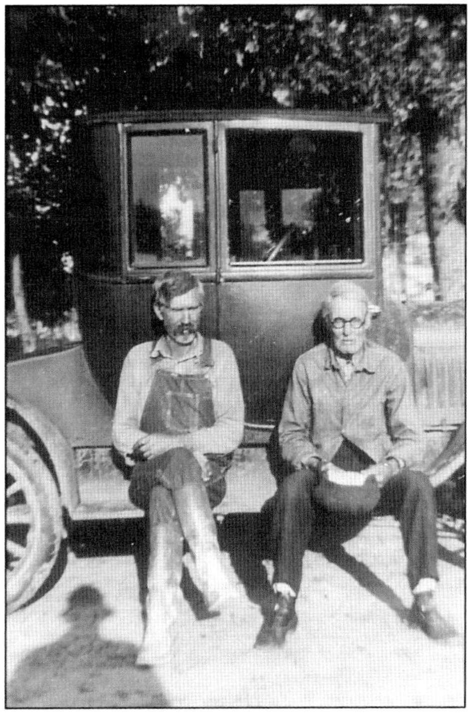

David and William Yarnell, 1926. (Courtesy Cherokee National Archives.)

Sally's father had the door to his workshop tightly shut, and her mother kept finding things for her to do. Sally knew he was making something in there and finally rushed in to find him at work on a tiny coffin. Only then did she learn about the baby. Her mother had some white satin, and she made the lining for the casket. Her father built a little slat house with a roof that was placed above the baby's grave. Sally remembers the grandmother sitting for hours beside the miniature house where the baby's spirit had gone to live.

Sally Sanders Finch

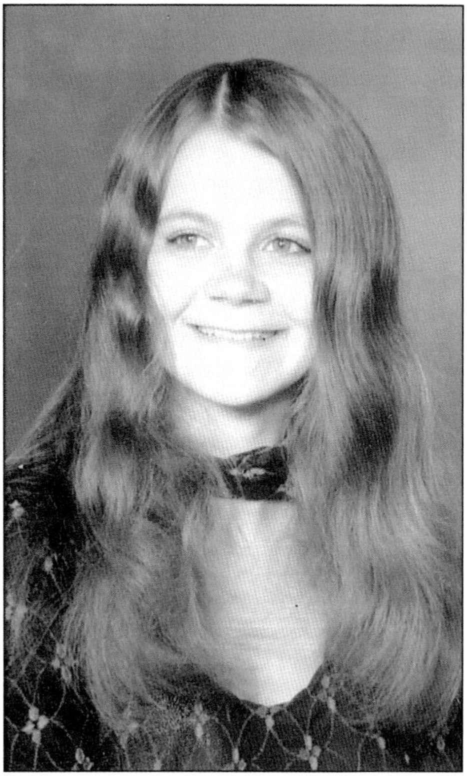

Neicey Dunham, 1972. (Courtesy Loretta Dunham.)

The Rooster, c. 1964

The house where Neicey Dunham grew up in Tahlequah was in a neighborhood known historically as Dog Town. Dog Town was the general area to the north of North Street and to the west of the football stadium. It was outside the city limits, but not really in the country, although in those days the roads were gravel. People there were not what you'd call farmers, but her family always had farm animals like chickens, turkeys, a horse, or a cow around on their four acre spread.

For a few months in about 1964 the yard fell under the reign of a big, mean Leghorn rooster. He was so hateful that no one ever bothered to give him a name, and he especially liked to torment Neicey. She was the youngest of the three children still at home and the most likely target of his attacks. He would chase her every time she walked into his line of vision. While he did not spare any child, he always left the adults alone.

Neicey and her sister Debbie came up with a couple of ideas to take vengeance on the evil white beast. They took a big piece of corn out of the chicken feed, stuck a hole in it, ran a long piece of thread through it and tied it tight. Then the girls called the chickens to eat. Naturally, the rooster always tried to eat all the feed. The kids dropped the threaded corn in front of him, let him eat it, then jerked it back out again.

Sometimes they would take a piece of rope and make a lasso in the end and wait for the old rooster to step in it. When he did, they would pull it tight and catch him by the feet, swing him round and round in the air, like a Junebug on a string, then finally let the rope go and watch where he landed.

All their efforts to tame him did not change his aggressive attitude. He continued to annoy and attack all those who ventured in the yard. One day Neicie was outside alone and the rooster caught sight of her. He ran up behind her, jumped up on her shoulders, and began pecking her head and neck. Neicey's big brother Roger heard her screaming and ran out to save her. He threw the creature to the ground and stomped on his throat, then gave him a good kick.

The rooster never bothered anyone too much after that. For a couple of weeks he walked around with his neck out of joint. Neicey and Debbie forgot about the old bird until one evening their Mom cooked him up with some dumplings. The girls skipped dinner that night.

Neicey Dunham

Biscuit Power

Before Loretta Dickenson walked all the way to Bagley School, on Tahlequah's Northeastern State College campus, she would eat about 10 homemade biscuits and wash them down with a quart of milk. Her mom was a full-fledged housewife and stay-at-home mother. The children did not eat lunch at school. Their mother began cooking about an hour before school let out, and she always had a big dinner hot and ready when her kids came in the door.

All that walking made Loretta healthy and strong. She was walking down the slope of N.S.C.'s Beta Field and looked back to see a big boy speeding right toward her on a bicycle. She knew he was going to hit her, and she moved so that he hit only her leg. The boy was thrown off the bike and injured, but Loretta's leg was not hurt one bit.

Around 1938, Loretta found herself in the direct path of an automobile. She was trying to cross the road, and the car was going much too fast. Almost without thinking, she put her left hand on the car hood and "cartwheeled" her body to the other side of the car. She walked on without even looking back then, but today Loretta thinks that must have been some kind of miracle.

Loretta Dunham

The Dutch Baby and Tall Betty

Virginia Vann Perry remembers when she was about six or seven years

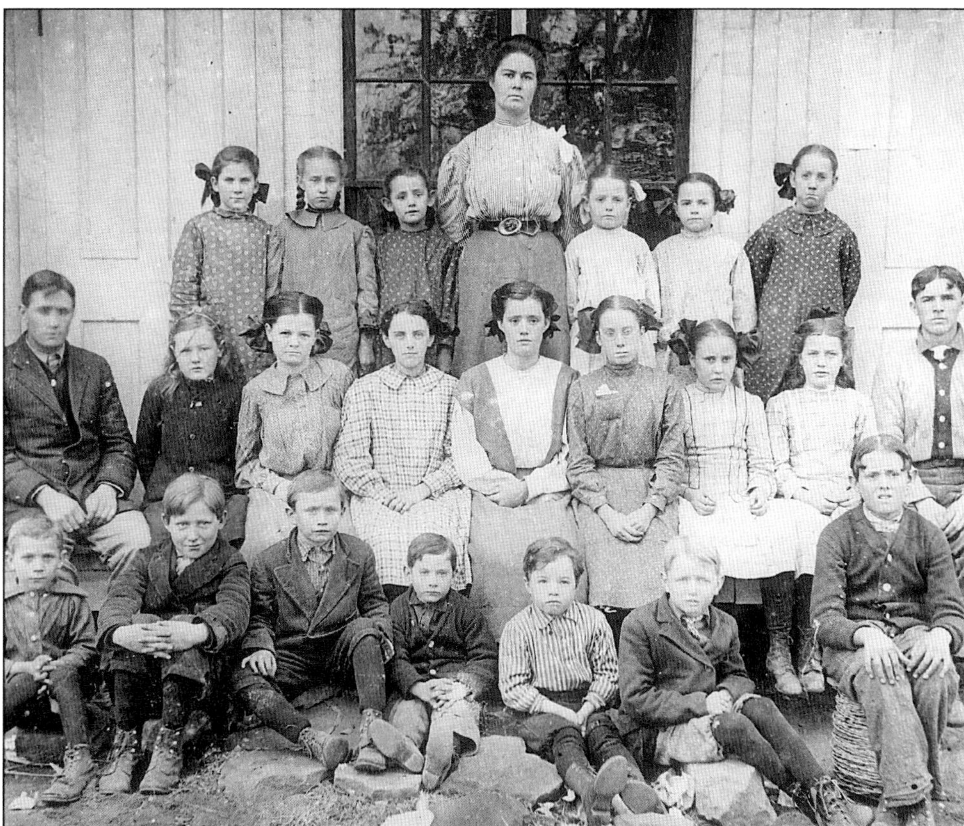

Oak Grove School Near Chelsea, 1908. (Courtesy Rogers State College.)

old, playing with her cousins at her Aunt Kate's house, and "the Dutch Baby would come see us." The children did not know then how all this came about, but the Dutch Baby was really Aunt Kate, playing a trick.

She would lie on her stomach under the bed with her elbows and forearms outside the bottom rail. Virginia's mother tied a dish cloth around Kate's wrists as she clasped her hands together above it. The cloth hung down her forearms like a long gown. A bonnet was placed over Kate's hands, and pulled down so that the kids could not see the "baby's" face. Then the Dutch Baby took on mystical powers and could answer questions with a turn of Kate's wrist, nodding its head forward for "yes" or from side-to-side for "no."

With the Dutch Baby all set, Virginia's Mom led the children, one at a time, into the bedroom. They were told to only ask the little figure questions that could be answered "yes" or "no." Of course Aunt Kate knew all about the kids, so her answers were almost always right. Virginia was amazed that the baby knew so much, and was really scared by it.

Another strange character who sometimes dropped in on the children was Tall Betty. Tall Betty was actually Virginia's Mom. She held up the bristle end of a broom over her head and Aunt Kate draped covers and cloth over the broom. This made Tall Betty about eight or nine feet high. She would chase the children around the house, bending down and dipping the broom at them.

The kids never noticed that either Mom or Aunt Kate were always missing when the Dutch Baby or Tall Betty came around. They were all having too much fun being scared.

Virginia Vann Perry

Life on the Town Branch

Donna Dickenson grew up with her large family on an 80-acre spread on the southeast edge of Tahlequah. The Town Branch, or Bear Creek, ran right through the property and near the big house where they lived. She remembers what a wonderful time they all had living on the creek. The kids cut fresh watercress and caught crawdads while their father and older brother seined the creek for minnows. Sometimes they would catch a big mess of crawdads and cook the tails in a tin can over a fire.

Donna's Dad was a big man of 6-feet, 4-inches. If he ever saw a poisonous snake, he would grab it by the tail, swing it around real fast, then crack it like a whip, sending its head flying. Sometimes, the cottonmouths who lived in the creek got caught in his minnow seine. He would just reach in and pull them out. If they ever bit him, he would suck the poison out. His hand might swell a little, but he never got sick. Once a copperhead got him on the back of the leg. He was alone and his lips would not reach the bite marks. So he took his knife and cut the bite out, filling the wound with kerosene when he got home.

Donna was close in age to her brother, Ott. One of her favorite memories is of seeing Ott running barefoot upstream in the Town Branch as fast as he could go. Right on his heels was a big blue racer, a common snake with a penchant for chasing children. Ott finally got up the courage to turn and face the snake which immediately stopped and ran from him. That is one of the little tricks you learn living in Cherokee County, but Donna could not tell Ott. She was too busy laughing.

Donna Dickenson Byrd

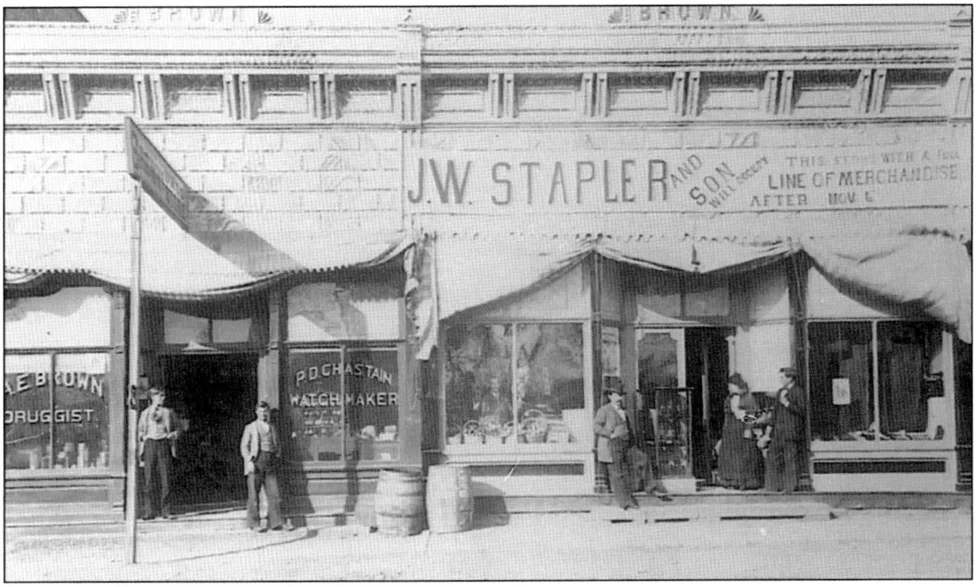

Stapler Store, Tahlequah, late 1800s. (Courtesy Cherokee Studies Institute.)

Thoughts on Aging

In the ancient days, young people were not considered adults until they reached an age of 25 to 30. The knowledge and power of Cherokee medicine people is thought to increase with their years, and 50 would be about the right age to begin the practices of healing. Traditional Cherokees do not tend to fear and dread aging as do most Americans. Instead, older people are held in high esteem as elders who have lived and learned, with knowledge to pass along.

Lazy Days in Hulbert, 1931

All the boys in Hulbert knew a secret about Alice Trapp's restaurant. There was a vent in the foundation of the building and just inside that vent you could feel around and find a string. At the end of the string was a half-gallon jug of whiskey.

Ralph Dunham and his friend Tommy Kaysinger, both age 12, decided one day they would borrow that jug. They fished it out and carried it down to the stockyards where they would not be spotted. They drank their fill of the whiskey, then went off to shoot at red-headed woodpeckers with their beanflips.

Sometimes Ralph and Tommy climbed up on the steep tin roof of Hulbert's cotton gin. Each boy would take a chaw of tobacco and spit the juice into his own rivulet on the roof. Then they would bet on whose tobacco juice could run off the edge and hit the ground first.

Ralph Dunham

School Days

When Virginia Vann was in high school no one would tell a bad joke when she was around. She had a civics teacher who would give her students an "E" in citizenship if she ever caught them in the act of chewing gum. The day came when she spied Virginia with a wad of gum in her mouth. A young man named Leo Askew implored

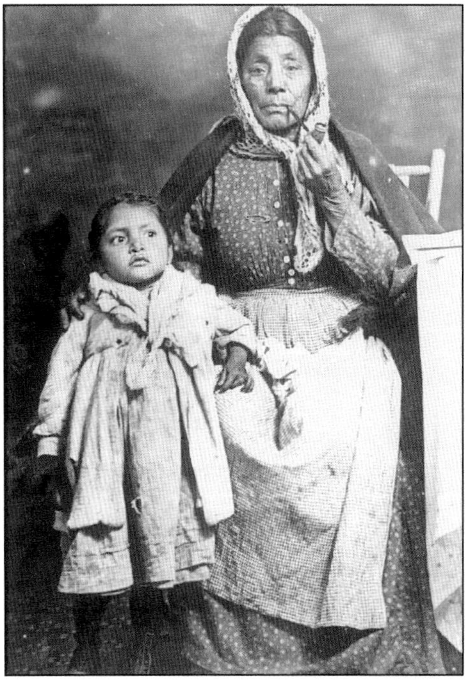

Webwee, Cherokee Grandmother. (Courtesy Cherokee National Archives.)

of the teacher, "Don't give Virginia an 'E', she always makes the honor roll. I never make it, so you can give the 'E' to me." Leo's brother became governor of Florida, and the last time Virginia saw him, he was campaigning for the nomination for president, stopping off in Muskogee.

Virginia Vann Perry

The Pearl-Handled .45

Loretta Dickenson's father Frank and her older brother, Jud, had plenty of guns. They were always taking them apart, cleaning them, and shining them up. One gun in particular, a pearl-handled .45 caliber, was especially beautiful and had a hair trigger.

The day came when Frank decided to teach his teenage daughters to shoot. Loretta chose the pearl-handled gun. She held it up real close to her face, in order to get a better aim, and the hair trigger went off. Then the gun kicked back, hard, banging the hammer into her forehead. The scar it left still remains over fifty years later.

From then on, Loretta considered it her gun. It was always going off by itself, but she didn't care. The gun was her buddy, her protection, and she packed it along with her whenever she could. When Loretta went out after dark, she would walk to and from town two miles to meet her friends. There were always hoot owls and no telling what else in those woods, but she had her gun so she was never afraid.

The Town Branch ran through the Dickenson land, and the girls were always out playing on the creek. One day they came across about 12 men hanging around on the property. The girls watched as the men went behind some tall buckbrush. The men spread out a big rug and they all sat down on it and started playing poker. Loretta ran home and came back with her pearl-handled gun.

She hid the gun behind the skirts of her dress and asked the men what they thought they were doing on her property. They laughed and said that her dad had told them it was all right to be there. She pulled out her gun and said, "Well it's me talking now, and I said get out of here." Those men scattered like chickens and never looked back.

For all her bravery, Loretta had to sneak around to get the gun out of the house. Her folks would never have allowed her to take it. The last time she had the beautiful pearl-handled gun, she was at her older brother's service station. He saw the shape of it under her coat and took it away from her right then. Her dad traded it off for a sawed-off shotgun, which now belongs to Loretta's only son.

Loretta Dunham

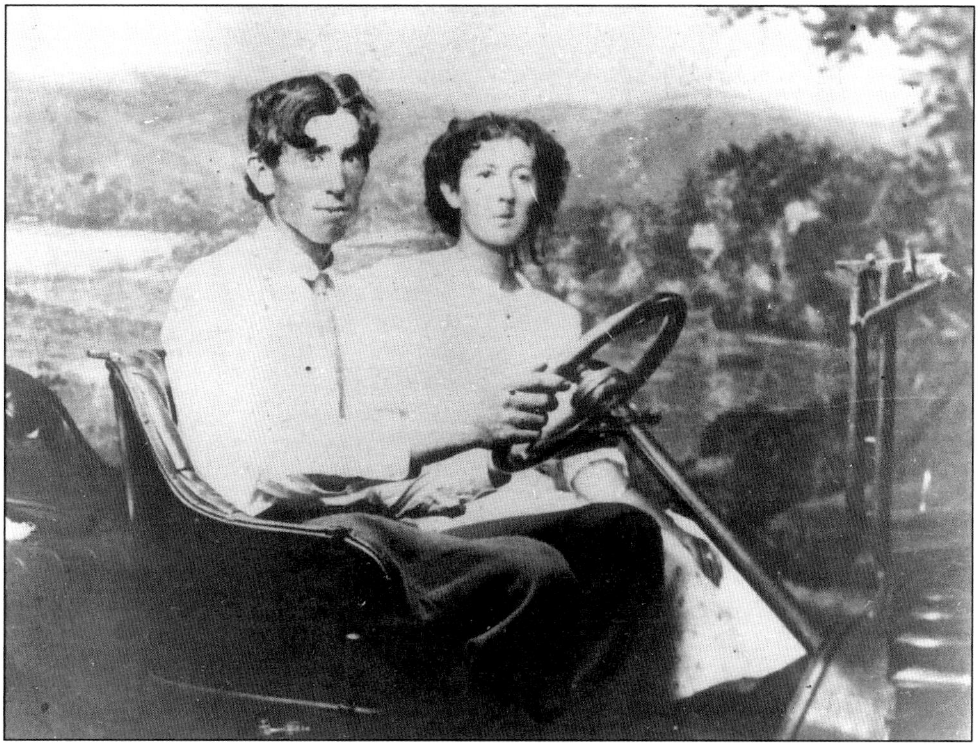

Herbert Taylor and Bessie Ledor Ballard, July 4, 1913. (Courtesy Rogers State College.)

The Town Dog of Hulbert

His name was "Little Red," and he was the town dog of Hulbert in the late 1920s. He had no owner, but the storekeepers and the townspeople made sure he was well-fed and well-loved. He was about the size of a fox terrier, and he was reddish-brown in color. He roamed freely through the town, but Little Red was no ordinary dog. In fact, he was pretty amazing. A crippling in his hips had made his back legs useless. But Little Red had overcome his infirmity. He could lift his hindquarters high into the air and walk anywhere he wanted to go on his front legs. To people living in Hulbert in those days, Little Red was an unforgettable character.

Ralph Dunham

Granny's Skirts

Sally Sanders was named after her father's mother, a Cherokee woman whose name was Sallie Clay Sanders. Clay Mountain south of Tahlequah is named for her family. The noted historian, Dr. Ballenger, once told Sally that when her father, Robert Lee Sanders, married her mother, Charlotte Mayes, the couple suddenly had more relatives than anyone else in the Nation.

Granny Sanders always wore long skirts, and Sally used to run and hide within their folds when she got into trouble. The outer skirt would be so stiffly starched it stood out around her body. Her skirts always smelled clean and fresh, with just a hint of smoke from the fireplace.

Granny Sanders smoked a little pipe, although Sally never saw her use it. She kept the tobacco in a cut glass jar on her dresser. She passed away when

Sally was only nine years old, and in all those years, Sally never heard her speak a word of English.

Sally Sanders Finch

The Lie Detector Test

When a new snack bar was opened at Northeastern State University's Wilson Hall, Loretta Dunham and Linda Mayberry were assigned to run the place. They both had keys to the snack bar, and they kept the cash hidden in the refrigerator and the doors locked at night. Someone broke in, found where the money was hidden and made off with it. N.S.U.'s policy required both Linda and Loretta to undergo a lie detector test to prove their innocence.

A campus security guard drove the two ladies to Muskogee, where the test was to be administered. Loretta knew she was innocent, but the thought of that machine made her nervous. She had heard stories about lie detector tests and feared that hers might give a false reading of guilt. Before she could calm her fears, she was strapped to the chair and told not to move. Her fingers were twitching and the test operator gave her a knowing look, thinking she was the culprit.

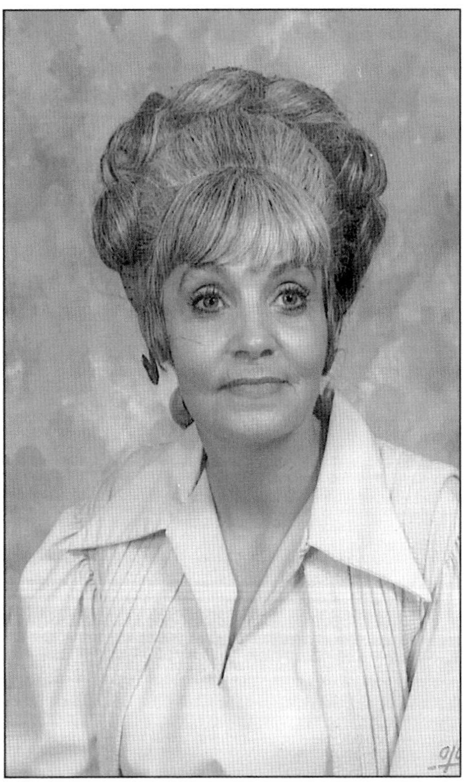

Loretta Dunham, c. 1980. (Courtesy Loretta Dunham.)

Loretta began to pray for guidance. She says God told her to let her mind go back to a time when she was happy and relaxed. She traveled mentally back to when she first began working at N.S.U., almost 20 years in the past. She could see herself exactly as she looked then. She could feel the surfaces of the kitchen in which she stood and hear the sounds of students laughing. Loretta believes that a part of her actually did leave her body and cross the years to that earlier time. Meanwhile, another part of her answered the operator's questions.

Both Loretta and Linda passed their tests. While driving them back to Tahlequah, the security guard told Loretta that the man who administered her test was one of the most experienced operators in the area. He had spoken to the guard about the sudden change in Loretta's demeanor when he began to question her. He said that, had there been time, he would have found out what she did to become so calm.

Loretta Dunham

Down to Briartown

There were times when Virginia Vann went to school 11 months out of the year. During summer break, she would go down to Briartown and attend summer session at the school where her Aunt Kate taught. Virginia visited Briartown many times, especially at Christmas. She attended the Christmas parties at Kate's school, where there was always a great big tree covered with presents.

Back at Kate's house, they decorated a fresh tree cut down in the woods around Briartown. The adults would find red berries for the kids to string and place on the tree. These were not holly berries, but something else that grew wild, maybe buckbrush. The kids cut and glued strips of colored paper to make the ever-popular Christmas chain.

If it ever snowed, the kids would go out in it with no shoes. The locals said that those who walked barefoot in the first snow of the season would be protected from frostbite the rest of the year.

Virginia always believed sincerely that Santa Claus came on Christmas Eve and put presents under the tree. One year, the children happened to look behind a tall piece of furniture in Aunt Kate's living room, and there were all the presents, hidden away. Even this did not shake Virginia's faith in old Saint Nick.

Sometimes the whole family would go over to Virginia's grandfather's house. It was built in 1879, and still sits on a prairie between Porum and Webbers Falls. There was a pond for fishing, and the house had a big screened-in area where they ate supper on warm evenings. Sometimes the family would drive to Webbers Falls and the kids would get a cool treat at the drugstore soda fountain. Grandpa's place had a windmill that kept a cement block tank filled with well water. Virginia and her sister and cousins spent lots of happy hours in that "swimming pool."

Virginia Vann Perry

Simple Pleasures

Donna Dickenson went to school in the early 1940s at Sequoyah Grade School. Her favorite thing about the school was the fire escape which made a long, round tunnel that ran down to the ground from the upper story. The school kids took turns climbing up in it and sliding down. She walked two miles to the school every day from home. When there was snow on the ground, her Dad would wrap her shoes with tow sacks to help keep her feet warm and dry.

Tahlequah had a working fish hatchery that was located between Donna's house and town. The sides of the big ponds were steep and covered with grass, and the kids from town would drag flattened cardboard boxes

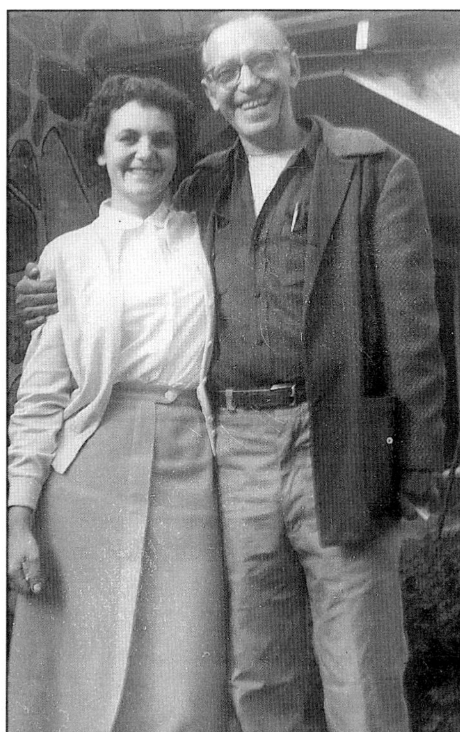

Siblings Donna and Tom Dickenson, c. 1950. (Courtesy Donna Byrd.)

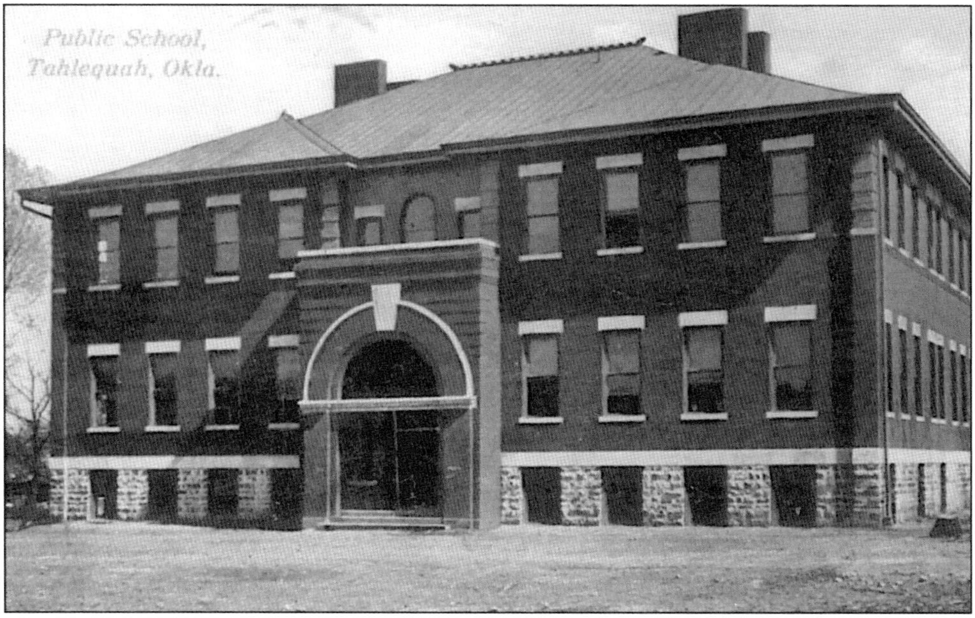

Public School, Tahlequah, 1908. (Courtesy Cherokee Studies Institute.)

to the top, then slide back down the grassy banks.

Donna's next closest neighbors were a family of Cherokees whom she would visit regularly. They spoke to her in English, but all could speak fluent Cherokee. In their yard was a hollowed out stump, where they pounded hickory nuts to make kanuche. Donna was often invited to eat some of the delicious soup they made.

Donna Dickenson Byrd

The Train at Addielee

The Addielee community was once a busy area southwest of Westville, Oklahoma, with two general stores, a blacksmith shop, and a post office. A boxcar served as the railway station. Four passenger trains a day traveled through the little town, delivering mail as they came. During and after the Depression, people would walk from farms and neighboring communities down the railroad tracks to collect their mail.

Leon Corntassel remembers a day when the conductor threw a colorful bundle off the train just before an elderly black man stepped off at the Addielee station. The man was an ex-slave, whose former masters had come to Indian Territory from Georgia. Their family name was Whitmire, and he had traced that name to Adair County. In his old age, he had hoped to visit them again. Only one woman from the Whitmire clan still lived in the area, and she knew nothing of the folks he was searching for. Townspeople drove him around looking for a few day, with no success. The old gentlemen then boarded the train back to Georgia.

Leon Corntassel

Light from Above

It was a cool autumn night, and Ralph Dunham hopped aboard an open rail car. Inside were a couple of hobos he had seen before on trains. Ralph had just left the Muskogee State Fair and was on his way, courtesy of the railroad, to Wagoner. From there he planned to catch another empty car to his home town of Hulbert. The other two men wanted to get off at Wagoner, too, but when the train got there, it never even slowed down. It finally did stop, and the three travelers found themselves in Parsons, Kansas.

So there Ralph sat at the freight yard waiting for the next train back to Wagoner, due in another hour. The two hobos had taken off already, riding on the outside of a train of oil cars. He declined their invitation to join them. Ralph had hopped lots of trains, but he always preferred the relative comfort to be found on the inside of the car.

Finally his train arrived, and Ralph picked out a suitable car. It was lined with paper, and had some loose paper stacked around inside. He made himself a nice paper pallet and rolled himself up in paper covers and went to sleep. When he awoke the train had stopped and he felt lonely, so he thought he would jump down and see if any other cars were occupied.

Ralph's legs were out the side of the door and he was just lifting the weight of his body with his arms, ready to jump down to the ground, when lightning flashed all around him. In that instant, he saw that the freight car had stopped on a trestle over a river. Had he jumped down, he could easily have been killed. Ralph rolled back up in his papers, and stayed there.

Ralph Dunham

Christmas Treasures

Pine trees can be found on the high ridges of the Cookson Hills in Cherokee County, and every December, Frank Dickenson took his children into the hills to find the perfect Christmas pine. Getting the tree and decorating it was great fun and everyone took part. The family had no need of glass decorations or tinsel, for they cut out shapes from lined notebook paper and colored them with crayons. They hung mistletoe and long garlands of strung popcorn on the tree.

Frank's daughter Loretta remembers

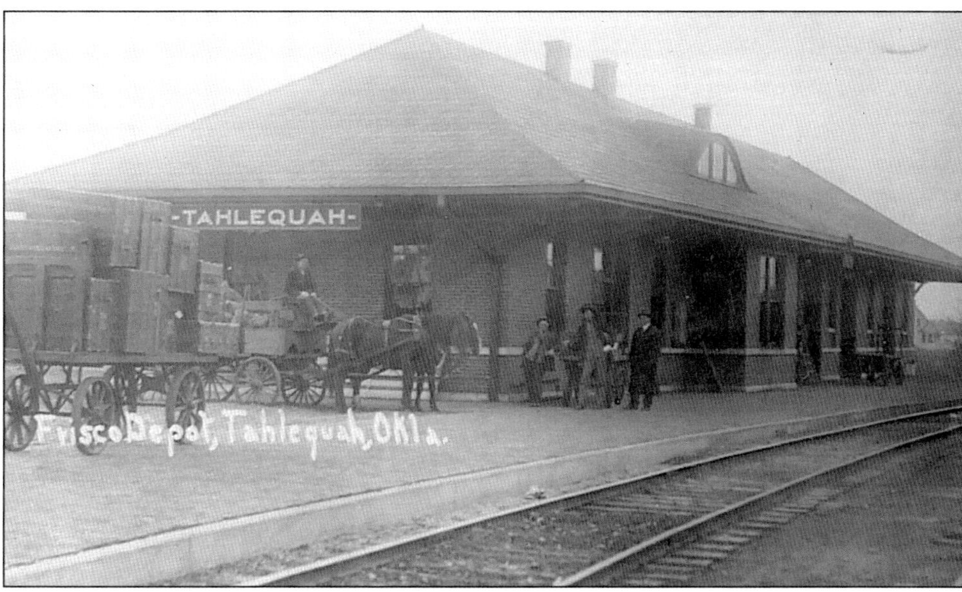

Tahlequah Depot, 1913. (Courtesy Cherokee Studies Institute.)

how her dad always made sure each of his children got a gift for Christmas. One that she recalls was a pretty dish, picked out especially for her. The children put out their stockings at night to find them filled with candy and fruit on Christmas morning. Their mother cooked up a feast to last the entire day. It was a tradition for Frank to bring home a big coconut, give each child a little drink of the milk, then crack it open for all to enjoy. The family had little money, but the holidays they spent together were the sweetest Loretta ever knew.

Loretta Dunham

Ernie's C.D.I.B.

Bob Thomas was a Cherokee scholar who moved back and forth from the Cherokee Nation. He once wrote a dissertation on the Redbird Smith movement, but it remains unpublished. His friends recall how he always wanted people to call him "Guag," the old Cherokee pronunciation of "Bob." Bob also lived in Arizona, and married a woman there.

While Thomas was in his 70s, he stayed for a while with a family in Hulbert, Oklahoma. When it was time to go home, he caught a ride to Arizona with a young acquaintance named Ernie Frost.

Ernie was driving happily along across country with Bob. About halfway through the trip, Bob Thomas died, right in Ernie's van. Ernie was determined to take Bob on home, so he laid his body down in the back of the van and continued on to Arizona.

Indian people who can document their heritage are sometimes identified by a card issued by the federal government. The card is a Certificate of Degree of Indian Blood, commonly known as a C.D.I.B. It states the persons name, tribal affiliation and amount of blood quantum, such as one-half or one-quarter.

Well as you might expect, Ernie got pulled over by the Highway Patrol. The patrolman looked over Ernie's drivers license and was checking out the van when he noticed Bob in the back. The officer said, "Is that man dead?" Ernie thought fast about how to handle this delicate situation. He opened his wallet and pulled out his C.D.I.B. Then he said, "This is my Department of the Interior identification. I am taking this man back to his tribe for burial." The patrolman accepted his credentials and sent him on his way.

Robert J. Conley

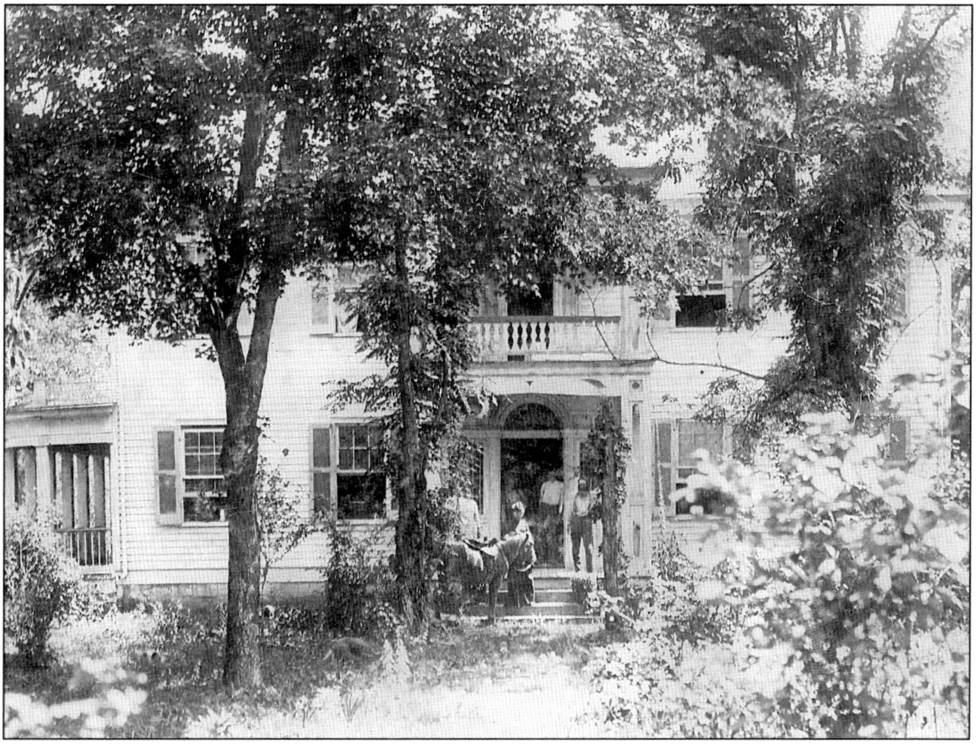

The Murrell Home, c. 1870. (Courtesy Cherokee National Archives.)

CHAPTER 7
MAGIC

Cherokees are great believers and tellers of tales as old and mysterious as their own beginnings. Their wonder stories explain the unusual occurrences of the natural world, like how the flying squirrel and the bat, who are mammals physically, can take to the air like birds. These ancient teaching tools endowed the creatures of the Earth with personalities in keeping with their behavior in the wild. The Cherokee trickster was Rabbit, who lost his beautiful tail while trying to impress his friends with the shiny coat he stole from Otter. Many believe that the Uncle Remus tales of the deep south were taken from the ancient Cherokee animal stories.

The Cherokee Nation abounds with ghosts, spirits, and other mischievous beings that haunt the woods and old home sites. The Murrell Home is a restored antebellum mansion in the Park Hill community. The house has a balcony on the second story facing the road. One evening very late, I was driving in the area alone, and my eyes were drawn toward the Murrell Home. Standing with her hands on the balcony rail, and looking wistfully ahead as if waiting for someone, was the purely white figure of a woman dressed 19th century style. I named her "Park Hill Mary," but I am told she is a member of the Ross family, now deceased.

Little People Town

Kathy VanBuskirk tells this story about her uncle and his stepson. The two men were out hunting in the daytime near Keys, a community south of Tahlequah. They came upon the entrance to a cave and decided to take a look inside. They walked in a few steps, and suddenly they were in darkness. Having no light, they rolled up a dollar bill and burned it to try and find the way out. The entrance to the cave had disappeared.

Every little while, they would burn another dollar. In the meager light, the men glimpsed something way down a corridor of the cave that looked like a little town. They worked their way in closer and closer. But when they got there, the little town was just a pile of rocks. They turned then, and could see light in the distance. It was coming through the entrance of the cave. The two got out of there in a hurry.

When the men got back home, they could not figure out why everyone was so happy to see them. As far as they could remember, they had been in the cave for a total of about thirty minutes. But their family and the entire sheriff's department had been looking for them for three days! The sheriff had even searched the cave where they were lost, finding nothing. The family believes that the men were tricked by the Little People.

Kathy VanBuskirk

The Ball

The ball used in the traditional game of stickball is made from a small piece of wood or a rock, depending upon the amount of weight desired, that is wrapped with layers of leather. A rawhide cover is stitched around this in the manner of a baseball. In the past, the cover was allowed to dry and harden in the sun or hot ashes.

Chad Smith's father told him this story about a stickball game from long ago. Both ball teams had gathered at the playing field for an important match when it was discovered that no one had brought a ball. An old medicine man told the players not to worry. He went to the edge of the field. From a hole in a tree, a baby flying squirrel sailed down into his hand. The medicine man blew smoke into his hand, closed it, and when his hand opened, it contained a stickball which he tossed to the waiting players. When the game was finished, the old man carried the ball back to the tree, talked to it, and set the baby flying squirrel up on a tree branch.

Murv Jacob

Snakebite Cures

Since ancient days, Cherokees have used herbs to treat snakebite victims. One remedy goes as follows. Immediately after the bite, use suction and apply chewed tobacco. Later an infusion is made consisting of four herbs to combat the poison. These might include lion's foot, wild lettuce, bark of the yellow poplar (tulip tree), and the sunflower. The sunflower is a sacred herb used to call upon the Great Spirit.

It is helpful to induce vomiting with such plants as lobelia and spirea. The bark of the tulip tree is made into a strong tea, used bathe the wound. Another remedy is to immediately apply tobacco soaked in vinegar, followed by frequent washings in the tulip tree bark solution.

Tulip tree bark tea can also help a person who has dreamed of being bitten. It has been recommended that a dreamed snakebite be treated to ensure total health.

Dub West recorded this cure from the memoirs of Narcissa Owen. Take the leaves of a cockleburr to make a poultice. Simmer the leaves in water until they soften, then apply to the bite wound. Have the victim drink one-half cup of the cooking water. Narcissa had a sister who had been bitten by a diamondback, a ground rattler, and a poisonous spider. All three times she was completely cured with this remedy.

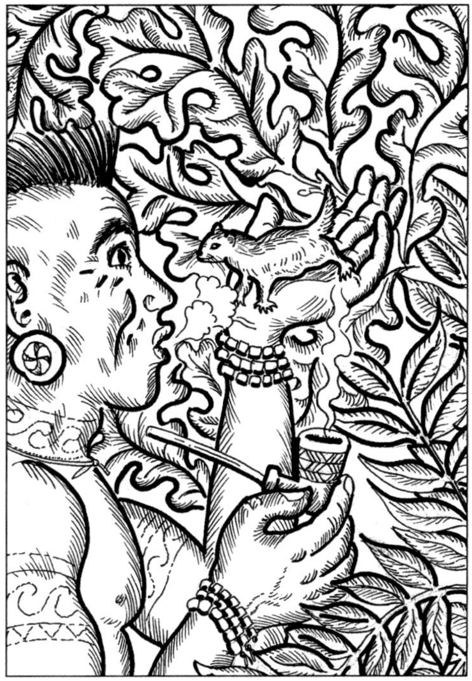

"The Ball." (Artwork by Murv Jacob.)

Magic Touch

When Julius Smith was just 11 years old, he contracted rheumatic fever and was extremely ill. In the early 1900s, antibiotic treatments were rare in remote rural areas, and hospitals were unheard of. The child's fever ran high and he was in such pain that night he just wanted to walk outside in the dark where it was cool. Julius said he saw one of the Little People standing by the gate, motioning for him to follow.

The little person took Julius by one finger of his right hand, then led him past the barn and through the pasture to a small hill at the back of the property. They came upon an entrance to a tiny cave. The passageway was hardly bigger than the size of the boy's hand. The little person told him to go into the cave, but Julius said he could never fit through such a tiny crevice. The little person took his hand again, and in an instant they were inside the cave.

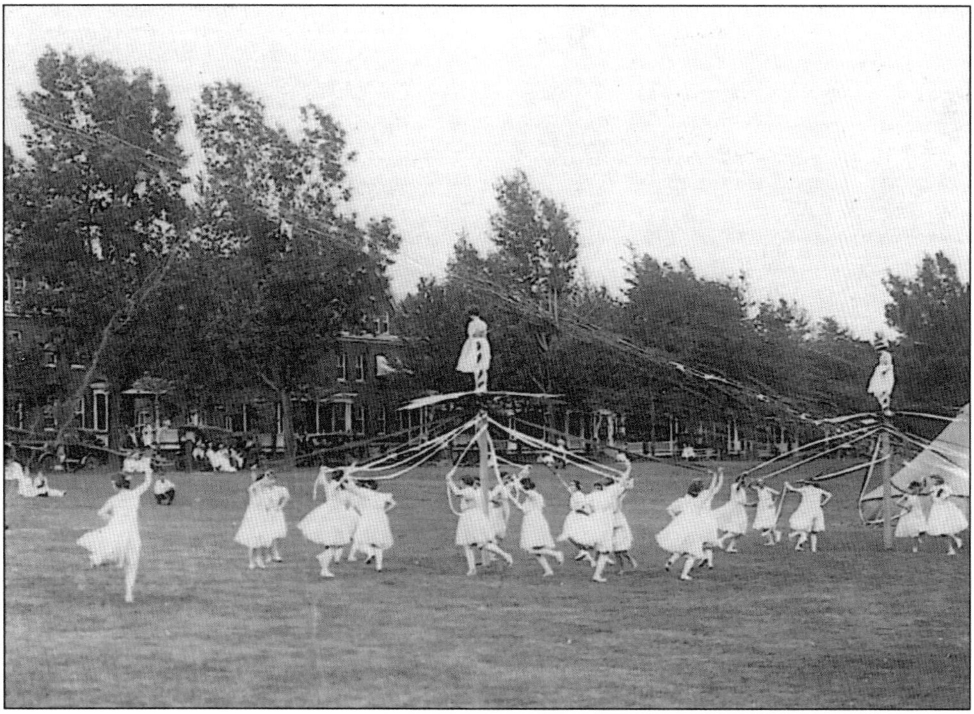

Maypole Celebration, Tahlequah, early 1900s. (Courtesy Cherokee National Archives.)

Julius was told to lie down on a bed of cedar branches. Then a tiny little Medicine Woman came to his side. She laid her hand on his forehead, looked into his eyes and smiled. Julius said he woke up later in his own bed at home. The fever had broken, but Julius had lost the hearing in his left ear.

Sioux Nell Smith Vann

The Chickasaw Dead Line

Cherokees Robert Lee and Charlotte Sanders worked for a time in a Chickasaw community near Ada, Oklahoma, called Kalihoma. Robert taught at the Indian day school. Although Charlotte was not officially a social worker, she took up those duties voluntarily, helping out whenever she was needed in the community.

Kalihoma was a settlement of traditional Indians. Charlotte's daughter Sally and her best friend Lydie Walker used to sneak off at night to watch the bonfires and the stomp dances. One ceremony that Sally remembers well was called the Dead Line.

Whenever a person was near death or critically ill, their family would build a "dead line" in the front of the person's home. Sticks about waist-high were pushed into the ground a few feet apart forming a fence. The fence would encompass the entire front yard. String was attached around this structure to create a barrier. At the base of the sticks, a groove was drawn about an inch deep into the ground around the temporary fence. The purpose of these barriers was to keep people outside the area where bad spirits had brought sickness to the family member.

Inside the fence and near the front door was a big barrel filled with water steeped with numerous healing herbs, some fragrant, some smelly. In the center of the front yard, the family would build a huge fire. They danced around the fire, accompanied by constant drumming, until the sick person either got through the crisis or died. If the ordeal ended in death, the drumming would continue for another three days.

While this ceremony went on, all outsiders other than immediate family members were supposed to stay outside the dead line, or risk becoming ill. Should a person accidentally step across that line, they were immediately taken to the barrel of healing herbs and totally immersed in the water.

Well, Sally's friend Lydie was a wild child who thought the dunking was great fun. Whenever she came upon a dead line, she would always accidentally set a foot or an arm into the danger zone, then kick and squeal with delight as she was dragged to the waiting barrel.

Sally Sanders Finch

Ghosts at Rocky Ford

The VanBuskirk family home at Rocky Ford sat near an old wagon route. Parts of the road can still be seen near their property. When Perry VanBuskirk was growing up, a number of unusual "guests" made frequent appearances at his home.

One such visitation always happened at night. It began with the sound of horses, coming from a distance toward the house. The horses circled around the building, running hard, with loud whinnies and stomping hooves. Perry's mother always told the children not to look outside, but they would "take a peek" anyway. The kids could hear that the horses were right outside, but they could see nothing. After what seemed a long time, they could hear the horses leaving their yard.

One of Perry's cousins spent the night with him and was awakened about 3 a.m. by the figure of a woman standing in the bedroom doorway. He tried to wake Perry who said, "Just don't look at it." The figure approached the bed, laid a cover over the boys, and then disappeared. The next morning, the boys decided that it must have been Perry's mother, but she had not gotten out of bed all night.

The first time Perry took his wife Kathy home to visit, they spent the night in his old bedroom. Perry had told her all about the spooks in the house saying, "If you hear anything, don't let it scare you." In one corner of the room stood a guitar that had belonged to Perry. After the lights were out for a while, and the house was quiet, Kathy heard a chilling sound. Someone struck a perfect chord on Perry's guitar.

Perry and Kathy VanBuskirk

The Monkey People

The Boy Scout Hole is a swimming area on Baron Fork Creek, deep in the woods southeast of Tahlequah near the community of Welling. It's a great place to visit in the daytime, but not a place you would want your kids to be at night. A few years ago, my husband and I took a trip to Mexico, leaving our oldest children in charge of the younger ones. My son Nick was 15 at the time, and told me this story when we returned.

It was March and the weather in Oklahoma was nice, so Nick and Jana decided it would be a good time to go camping in the family van. They took along a few of their friends and drove down the lonely dirt road to the Scout Hole. There isn't an electric light anywhere near the place, so they parked the van in the dark. Nick and his friend Mickey climbed up on top of the van,

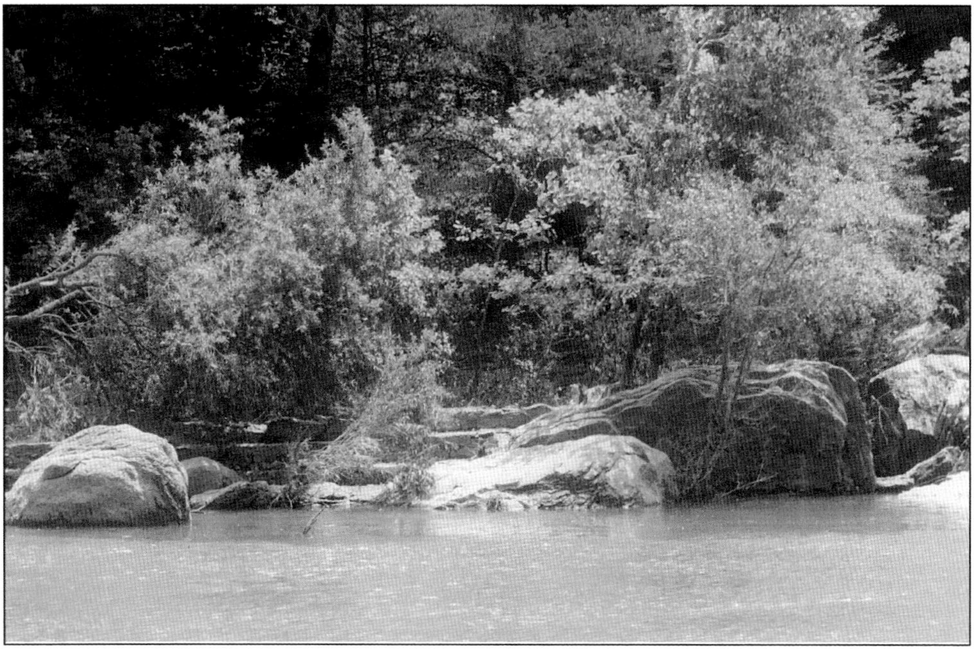

The Boy Scout Hole. (Photo by Nick Duvall.)

planning to sleep there for the night, while the other kids stayed inside.

After everyone got quiet, Nick and Mickey began to hear strange sounds coming out of the trees overhead. In the darkness, they could suddenly make out figures with human-looking faces sitting on the branches of the trees and looking right at them. Nick and Mickey leaped right off the roof of the van and jumped inside with the other kids, trying to lock the doors and shut the windows. Then, about 10 of the creatures were on the ground. Nick said they looked like the characters from Planet of the Apes, but with more human facial features.

One of the "monkey people" approached the van and put its hand on the window glass. The next thing any of the kids can remember is waking up in the daylight. At first Nick thought it must have been a dream. But then the other kids woke up. Each one remembered being terrified by those things and then somehow going to sleep until morning. Nick also remembers seeing lights off in the distance while the creatures were outside the van.

Hearing that story brought back my own memories of the time when I was at the Scout Hole at night with a group of friends. We saw a circular object surrounded by lights come down from the sky and land back in the woods across the creek, but we didn't stick around to find out who or what it was!

Nick Duvall

Hawkeye's Mane

One of the most distinctive characters to be found at Tahlequah's Cherokee Heritage Center is Hawkeye, a beautiful white horse. The traditional Cherokees who work at the Center say that Hawkeye has the "mark of the Little People". Everyone at the Center knows that Hawkeye allows only one or two people to get very close to him. These are the employees who handle him and keep him well-fed. When they arrive at work in the morning, Hawkeye's caretakers often find that his mane has been braided during the night. Sometimes he has a single braid. Sometimes there may be three or four braids. Sometimes the mane is twisted and tied into knots. One thing is for sure, though. Hawkeye would not let an ordinary person take such liberties with his glorious white mane. His handlers believe the Little People like to spend time with Hawkeye, too.

Perry and Kathy VanBuskirk

Why We Use Lightning Struck Cedar

Because of its beauty and strength, the cedar tree is held sacred by the Cherokees. It is never burned as firewood, but sometimes its branches are burned green on a fire. This keeps away ghosts who can not remain near the fragrant smoke. If a cedar tree survives a lightning strike, its branches, bark, and wood contain powerful medicine. Pat Moss is a respected Cherokee traditionalist and herbalist who tells how the medicine originated.

When people first came into the World, all was new to them and they were as yet unfamiliar with the other creations. Among them was a young man who seemed especially intelligent and who had a good heart. He said that he would go out and find something for the others to eat and something to cover their bodies for warmth. He would look for a safe place for them to sleep, as they had seen rain and storms in the distance.

The young man had traveled for some time toward the east, when he came upon a high hill where he could see flashes of brilliant light and hear the sound of big things being moved over the earth. He quickly climbed to the top to see what was happening on the other side of the hill.

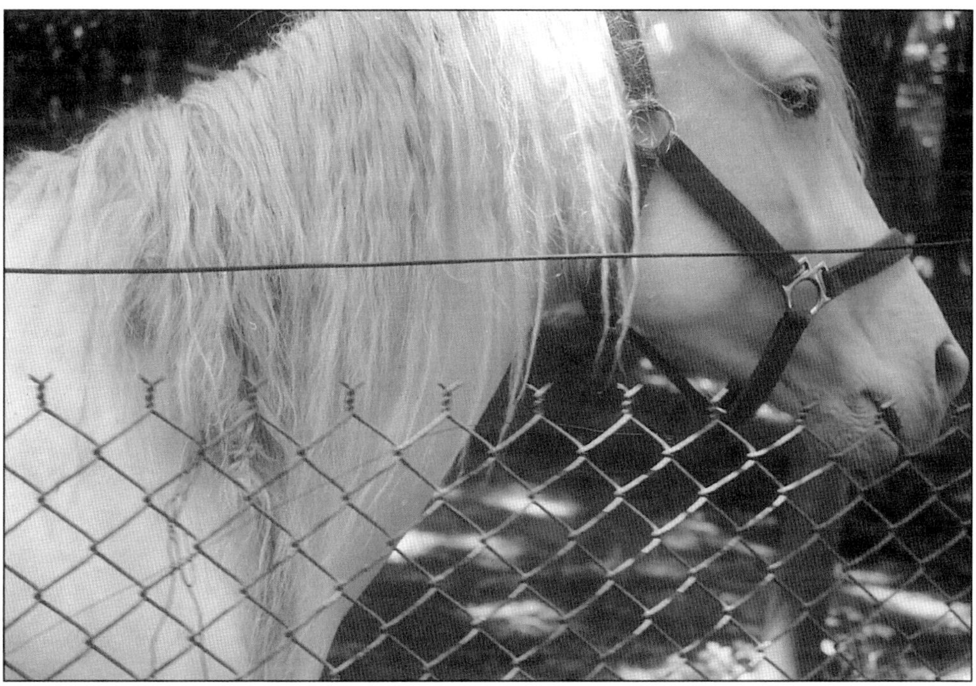

Hawkeye. (Photo by Murv Jacob.)

In the valley, he saw that a little brown man and a huge snake were having a fight. The little man had wind and thunder in his voice, and lightning flashed in his eyes and face. The snake had great strength. It could roll up the trees from the earth's surface with its powerful tail, then hurl them through the air. When the two noticed the young man, they stopped fighting, and both spoke to him. He heard their voices in his heart, not in his ears.

The snake said, "If you help me defeat the little brown man, I will make you the leader of all your people. All the women will be your women. All the animals in the woods will be yours to eat."

The little brown man said, "If you will help me to win, I will make sure that your people always have food to eat, something to keep their bodies warm, and a place to sleep that is safe and dry. I will give you herbs to make your life sweet and clean." This was exactly what the young man had been searching for, so he agreed to help the little brown man and not the snake.

The strength of the young man's commitment gave the little man the edge, and he defeated the snake, driving it away into the west. Then the little brown man spoke and said, "When the snake comes back, do not fear him because I will leave medicine for you everywhere I go." Then he made lightning go into a tree that left a mark straight down its side. This did not kill the tree, but simply marked it. Then he told the brave young man how to use the wood for protection against evil.

From then on, the Cherokees always looked for lightning struck trees, especially cedar. Before they would stay in any place, they made sure there was such a tree nearby. Pat says that this concept is the keystone of Cherokee ideology.

Pat Moss

A Tale of a Witch, c. 1930.

This story is about a witch, born before the Civil War, who lived in the southeast part of the Cherokee Nation. Among their powers, witches can change form at will, often going out in the world in the shape of an animal or bird.

Around 1930 this witch was a healthy woman of 75 who lived in a cabin with her grown daughter. It was among her neighbors that trouble came in the form of a black wolf. Nearly every night the wolf attacked livestock on surrounding farms, killing horses, cattle, sheep, pigs, goats, and chickens.

After several of these attacks, the men of the community formed a posse to try and track down the wolf. Within a few days, the men noticed a pattern in the wolf's attacks, and one moonlit night they were lucky enough to predict where the wolf would strike next.

The men went to that farm and hid in the barn with their weapons ready. The scent of the new foal inside must have lured the wolf to enter the barn. Shots rang out and the wolf was struck in the right hip.

Escaping quickly, the wolf left a trail of blood, followed immediately by the group of men. The blood trail ended abruptly at the door of a cabin. It was the witch's cabin.

The men knocked and the witch's daughter opened the door. She said her mother was in bed sick. Brushing past her, the men stormed into the bedroom, but there was no wolf in sight. There was only the old woman, looking very ill indeed and drenched in sweat, lying beneath the covers. Having proved nothing, the men left. The wolf was never seen again after that night. But before long, the witch was up and around. Ever since that time, she favored her right hip and walked with a limp on that side.

It is said that a witch can only die by fire. One day in the 1970s, the woman's

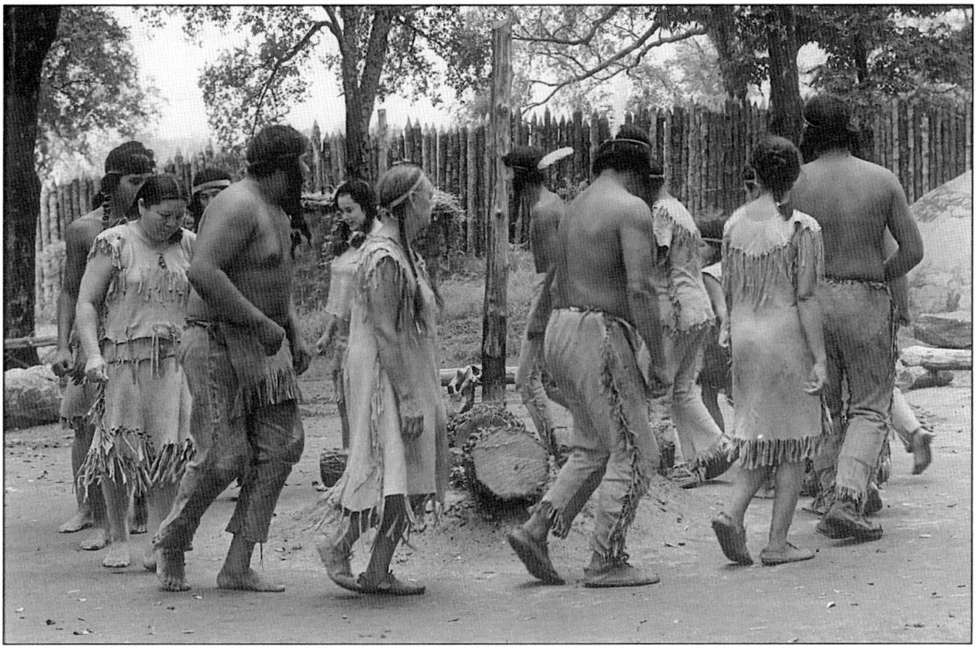

Cherokee Stomp Dance Demonstration, c. 1970. (Courtesy Cherokee National Archives.)

home did catch fire and she died within. She was over 110 years old. This story was told to my friend by his grandfather, who was among the hunting party that shot the wolf.

Nick

Nick Duvall has lived in Tahlequah since he was six months old. Until he was 15 years old, Nick had the same strange experience every Christmas Eve. He would see Indian people in the back yard, who seemed to be from a time long ago. They would peer at him from the corners of the house, showing only their faces. Sometimes Nick would be inside and could see them looking in the back door or windows.

Once Nick took his younger sister, Roxanne, riding on his motorcycle. They rode down to a secluded part of the Illinois River where they had gone fishing years before. It was the middle of the week, and it appeared that the place was deserted. A tall dark figure walking along the edge of the woods near the river caught their attention. When the thing turned to look at them, they saw that it was like a big man covered with long hair. They got out of there in a hurry. There have been several such sightings reported from various locations in Cherokee County.

At the point where First Street crosses the Bertha Parker Bypass in Tahlequah is a field where horses are pastured. Nick was riding past there on his bicycle and noticed an old man in the field, sitting on a saddled horse. Nick turned his head for a moment and looked back, but the old man had vanished. It was not the first time Nick had seen this same old man disappear from view. Nick and his friends had seen him around town lots of times and knew where he lived. But every time Nick saw the old man in or near that field, he always disappeared.

One night Nick and his friend Hub Haney were driving back to Tahlequah from Tulsa in a severe thunderstorm. They took the northern route from I-244 to the Cherokee Turnpike to Highway 82. When they were about five minutes away from Tulsa, a bolt of lightning hit Nick's car. They drove on about another six or seven miles, and lightning struck the car again. When their vision cleared from the brilliant light, they saw that the four-lane road was gone. Suddenly Nick and Hub were driving through Peggs, Oklahoma on Highway 82. They had missed about 45 minutes of the trip, and the car's gas gauge had not moved a bit. The last few miles of the trip passed without incident, but the two friends never did figure out what happened.

Nick Duvall

Fire Bringer

The creatures of the Earth were cold. Across the river from their home an old dead tree was struck by lightning and began to blaze. The creatures knew that such a blaze could warm their camp and homes. But how could they get at it? The water was deep and the flames were hot.

The first attempt was made by Raven, who flew across the water and near the tree, but the heat singed his feathers, turning them black, and they have remained that way. The owl flew into the ashes and returned with rings around her eyes that are still there, but without a speck of an ember. Snake slid beneath the water, coming up near the smoking tree. He bravely entered a hole near its base. But when he came out his scales were burned so dark he became known as the Black Snake.

The creatures of the Earth were disheartened and about to give up when a small voice said "Let me try." The tiny Water Spider set to work weaving a little bowl which she placed upon her back. She skated quickly across the river on her eight legs, keeping her bowl above water and totally dry. She managed to scoop up a coal from the burning tree which she placed in her bowl, bringing it quickly across the water where her friends waited. Soon there was a blaze in the village to equal that of the burning tree, and all the creatures of the Earth honored the little Water Spider for bringing Fire to their world.

The Fault Line

In ancient times, Uktena, the winged serpent, had a battle in the air with the great Eagle. As they fought, scales fell to the ground from the Uktena's sides. These scales went into the Earth and changed into crystals.

Perry and Kathy VanBuskirk were taken by their Eastern Cherokee friend Bill to see a special place in the mountains. The Indians call it "the Gap," the place where the great Uktena was slain. When the Uktena fell down the mountain, it took out everything in its way, clearing a swatch 100 feet across. The gap it created can still be seen. When the Uktena came to rest in the valley, the people took the prized crystal from the beast's forehead. It is said that all the true powers and medicine of the people come from that crystal.

The old people say that the Uktena lies quietly now, but one day it will rise again. When it does, a crack in the earth will split this country between the east and the west. Most Indian tribes know about similar predictions. Perry believes that those stories refer to the New Madrid Fault that runs north and south on the eastern side of the Mississippi River. The granite rocks have shifted at least once before, causing the huge earthquake that rocked mid-America in 1811.

Perry and Kathy VanBuskirk

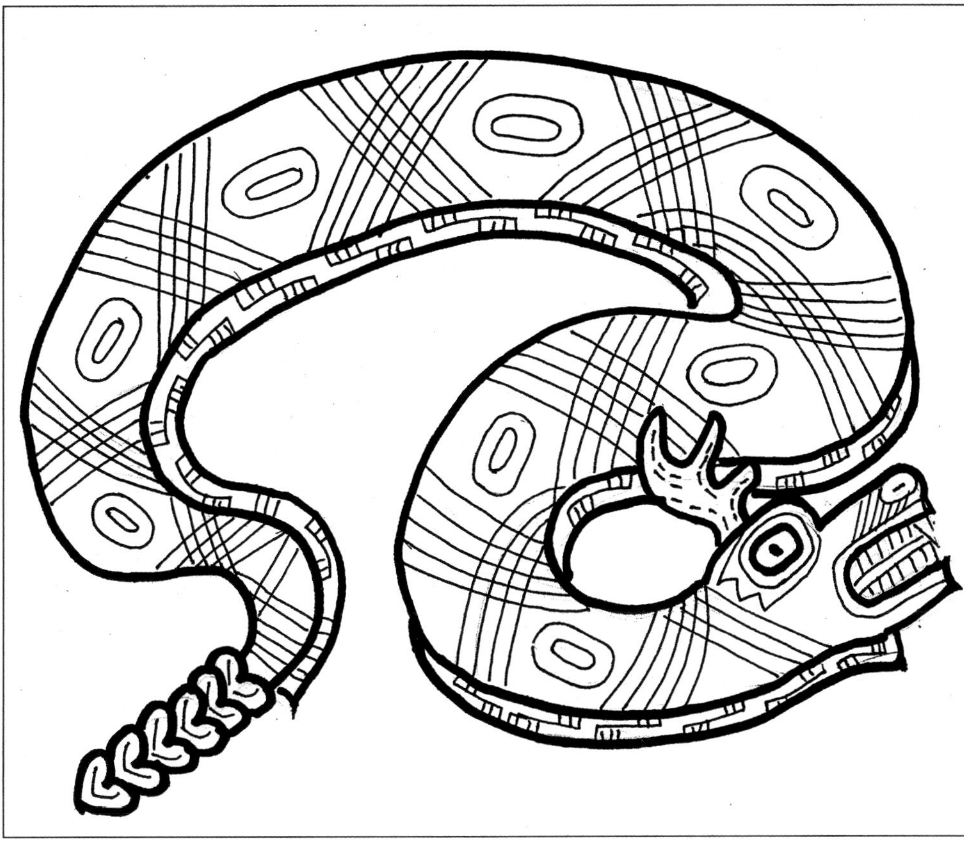

"Uktena." (Artwork by Murv Jacob, 2000.)

Charlynn

My niece Charlynn Neet was born on December 9, 1973, at the Tahlequah City Hospital. I named her myself, with the "Char" for her father, Charlie, and the "Lynn" from my middle name. I will never forget going to the hospital to look at her for the first time. All the other little babies in the nursery were lying peacefully in their cribs. But Charlynn was lying on her tummy, holding up her chest with her baby arms. Her head was straight up and she was looking from side to side all around the room.

I had left Tahlequah to join the Air Force, and Charlynn came down to Texas to visit me when she was about nine months old. She had never been to my apartment before, but within a few hours she had inspected everything in the house.

That evening I was watching her as she crawled around, occasionally pulling up to stand by the furniture. She went into the kitchen and pulled herself up on the leg of the dining table. The floor wasn't level there, and the table was unsteady when she held to its edge. I couldn't believe what she did next. She crawled over to the cabinet and opened the door. There were a few dry pinto beans lying on the shelf where they had spilled from an open bag. Charlynn took two of the beans and crawled back to the table. She pushed the two beans under the short leg of the table, then pulled herself up and tested the table top. Satisfied that it was now level and steady, she got down and crawled away.

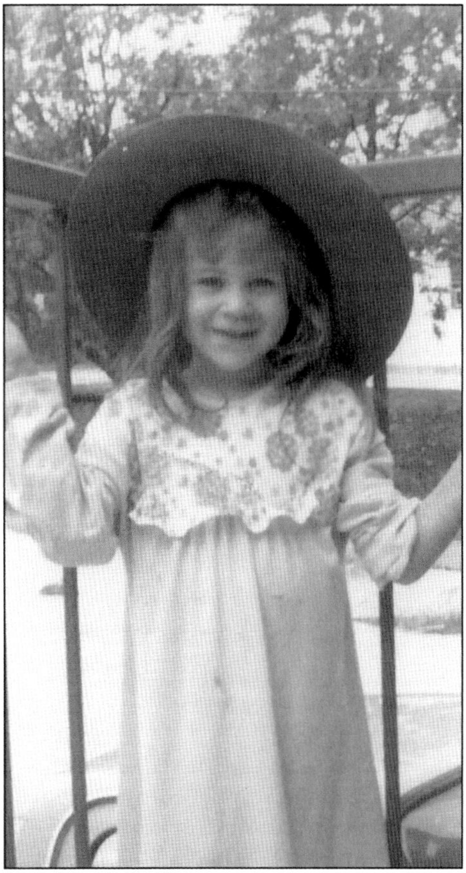

Charlynn Neet, 1978. (Courtesy Neicey Dunham.)

As Charlynn got older she began to talk about her friend "George" all the time. George lived in the broom closet of her Mom's kitchen, and he was Charlynn's constant companion. Everyone knew that George was invisible, but none of us were too sure he was imaginary.

When Charlynn was about five years old, she came to my place to spend a week with me. One night we were about to go to bed and I asked, "Charlynn, who taught you all this stuff you know?" Her answer raised the hair on the back of my neck. She looked at me for a minute, pointed her right index finger straight up and said, "Up there."

The Four Stages of Death

Many Cherokee traditionalists believe that the death of an individual involves the leaving of the human body of four separate souls. The time of death is a time of great vulnerability when the services of a medicine man are required to protect the life forces of the person. The dead person is to be mourned for one year, and the grave is tended and cared for during that time.

The first soul lives in the head and contains the consciousness and personality of the deceased. It is the first to leave the body at the moment of death. Sometimes the soul stays nearby and may be seen as ghost that is continuing on with its personal life before its eventual journey to the Western Land of the dead. This ghost may try to communicate with the living.

The second soul resides in the liver. This soul can remain for a few days after death. It contains the life force and vitality of the person, that gradually weakens and disappears. Witches may attempt to consume the liver soul in order to prolong their own lives. A powerful witch will come for the liver on the first night of the death, while the life force is still strong. The witch may appear as a Ravenmocker and may have accomplices. This is a time when the medicine man must be prepared to defend the body and prevent intrusion of the witch.

The third soul lives in the heart and controls the blood of the individual. This soul will remain with the body for about a month before it, too, disappears. It is said that the blood soul sometimes attacks living people by stealing their blood. They then become anemic.

The last soul lives in the bones. Its essence goes into the ground and causes crystals to form. By the time a year has passed, there is nothing left to protect or mourn, and the grave of the individual can be left to Nature.

Buzzard Wing

Buzzard Wing was a Cherokee doctor who could cure almost anything. One day a little boy was off playing near some tall weeds when he was bitten by a snake. By the time he got back to his house, the poison was making him deathly ill. The women of the house sent a messenger to get help from Buzzard Wing.

Before Buzzard Wing left his home, he sent a message through the air to the little boy, telling him that he would get well. Back at him home, it was said the little boy had stopped crying then. Buzzard Wing also sent a message directly to the snake, telling it to die at that moment.

Then Buzzard Wing went to the boy's home. He gave the child a round ball of herbs to chew, and told him to swallow the juice. Then he blew his breath on the bite marks and the boy was totally cured of the snake venom. Buzzard Wing told the men of the family to go and find the snake, then burn it in a fire. When the men arrived near where the snake had bitten the boy, they found the lifeless body of a copperhead.

Legend of the Strawberries

The first man and woman who lived on the Earth were happy for a while, but then they began to argue. In her anger, the woman decided to leave the man's side, and began walking toward the east. The man was deeply troubled and followed her trail unhappily until the Sun took pity on him and offered to help bring the woman back.

The Sun made huckleberries to grow in the woman's path, but she hardly noticed them. Then the Sun made blackberries and many more inviting fruits to grow before her. But the woman ignored them, refusing to stop. Finally the Sun made a special fruit and it grew in tempting patches on the woman's path. The luscious red berries were strawberries, the first ever known.

This time the woman could not refuse the gift. She began to eat the red berries, and as she did, memories came to her of her husband. Her desire for him grew until she lost her resolve to escape him. She picked a handful of the fruit and carried it back down the path to where he waited. The woman gave the strawberries to her partner, and they walked home together.

Magic Words

When Ralph Dunham was a boy growing up in Hulbert, he would often attend meetings at the Hulbert Holiness Church. Among the church members was a righteous woman who never missed a service. The meetings would reach such intensity that this woman would become "filled with the Spirit" and speak in unknown tongues. Each time this happened, she uttered the same words over and over again, and Ralph, being an attentive child, memorized them.

Like a character from one of Mark Twain's stories, Ralph was always getting into activities of interest that were sometimes illegal. He truly loved to shoot "craps" or dice, and like everything he tried, he shot craps well. If the game ever started to go bad, Ralph would recite the magic words he had learned from the woman in the church. With their help, he could not miss.

As an older man, Ralph was a heavy equipment operator who worked all over Cherokee county. He was clearing

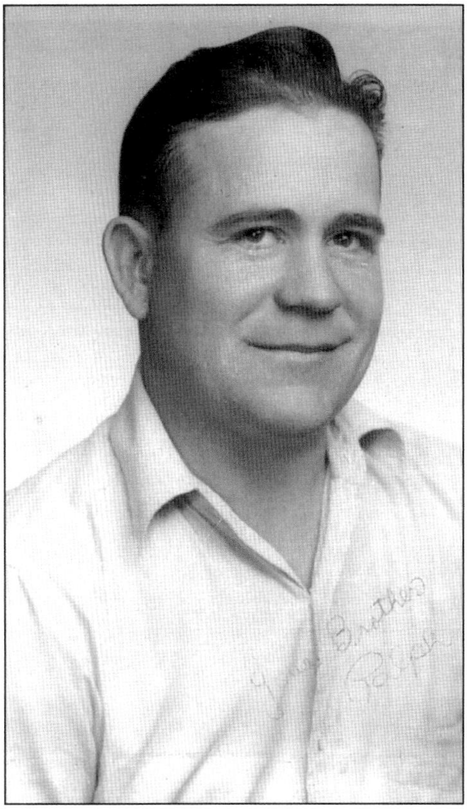

Ralph Dunham, 1949. (Courtesy Loretta Dunham.)

out a creek bed with a dozer one day when he noticed something strange in a patch of dried mud. The patch was several feet across and was totally smooth except for a word that appeared in its very center. The word looked as if it had recently been drawn in with a stick, but there were no footprints or tracks in any of the mud surrounding it. The word was "Whence."

Ralph Dunham

Bald Hill

Bald Hill is situated close by the Cherokee Ceremonial Grounds near Sequoyah High School where the students from Sequoyah make frequent hikes. One young man named Johnny Hawk found an old Spanish conquistador's helmet on the hill. Dan Robbins, a former professional baseball player, likes to tell the story of how his brother once saw a ghostly group of ancient Spaniards riding their horses down Bald Hill.

Robert Conley

Down at Rocky Ford

All around the Cookson Hills, you can run across raised mounds of earth that look like graves. Almost everyone who lives in the Cherokee Nation has seen them. There are five such mounds on the VanBuskirk homeplace at Rocky Ford, and Perry VanBuskirk remembers digging up the mounds to see if something was inside. He and his brother hoped to find buried guns from the Civil War days, but the mounds contained nothing but dirt and rocks. Two of the mounds sat in a field that was used for planting, while the other three were close together in the woods. There were many strange things about these mounds. For example, no matter if they were plowed up, dozed down, or taken apart, they formed themselves back into the same grave-like shape. Perry said this has occurred over and over again with those five mounds. Also, at one end of a mound, two little trees grow up and twist together. If the trees are ever removed, another set will grow and twist together.

Down in the woods at Rocky Ford is a cave where years ago the Indians kept a whiskey still. People are afraid to go around that area much because of the bears and the Little People. Where the creek runs through, pine trees and cedar trees are often pushed down to the ground, the likely work of bears.

There is a spot where the ground is solid rock, with holes that contain water. Many believe that the Little People live around there. Whenever traditional Cherokees walk through the area, they leave a gift of tobacco for the Little People.

Little People love to play tricks, especially on children. When overheard talking, they sound like children themselves. Sometimes a person can make out a word or two of what they are saying. Parents who believe in them keep their children indoors after dark. A child might follow the voices, or actually see the Little People, and be drawn away from home.

Perry VanBuskirk

The Beginning of Conjuring

Many years ago, the Creator gave a special gift to the people. The purpose of the gift was to allow the people to kill game animals for meat, and to reach them from a great distance. The hunter would take thin strips of wood from a tree struck by lightning. These splinters were then sharpened at one end. When the hunter spotted a game animal, he would point the wooden strip in its direction and blow on it. The splinter would then fly through the air and into the heart of the animal, killing it. Its work complete, the sliver of wood would return to rest on the hunter's hand.

One day two hunters were out together, using the magic splinters. One was able to locate and kill a large deer, but the other could only find small deer. He grew jealous, and then angry. Finally he was so angry he decided to blow a wooden splinter into the heart of his hunting companion, who immediately died. This misuse of the Creator's gift is how the practice of conjuring got started.

Vicie

It is estimated that Vicie Walker was 118 to 120 years old when she passed away. She lived in a cabin up in the woods, and was one of the most colorful characters around the Chickasaw settlement of Kalihoma. When health department officials went there to vaccinate the children, Vicie would round up as many of them as she could find and hide them in the woods. She thought the shots were the work of the Devil.

Almost all the people in the community had scars between their shoulder blades where they had been doctored as children by Vicie. If a child became ill, Vicie would go out and find a broken piece of glass. She could not break the glass herself, nor could anyone else. When the glass was obtained she would use it to make three little cuts on the child's upper back. She would then suck out the blood and spit it out. This removed the poison that was causing the sickness.

Most of Vicie's family continued to live with her after they were grown. One of her daughters passed away, leaving a five year old boy, Jimmy, behind. She was buried in a red satin dress. The woman had always loved flowers, and had several planters in the yard made of old tires.

About two weeks later, little Jimmy was pointing toward one of the flower planters, crying and screaming for his mama. He said he could see her standing there, wearing her red dress, then she went away.

Vicie's cabin sat upon stacks of rocks. She hired a house mover to take the entire cabin about fifty yards down the hill to separate it from the garden where her daughter's spirit was seen.

Sally Sanders Finch

The Stone

When Perry VanBuskirk and his family make their annual trip to North Carolina, they avoid the commercialization of the city of Cherokee. You are more likely to find them in the traditional communities like Big Cove, seven miles to the north. On one of his first visits there, Perry attended a stomp dance. He was sitting quietly, watching the proceedings, when the medicine man of the grounds sat down beside him.

Pretty soon the older man turned to Perry and gave him a glass of water to drink. The elder said it came from a magic healing spring. He told how the spring comes out at the very top of a mountain, runs above ground for about 100 feet, then goes under again. All the animals know about it, and have left trails from every direction to the spring. When they are injured, they lie down in the water and are healed.

The old Cherokee man went on to explain that only certain people could find the spring, but he believed that Perry could. Perry's grandfather had been a medicine man, and this one guessed accurately that he had "come down from medicine." He left Perry with a quart of the precious water to take with him the next day on his journey back to Oklahoma.

When Perry awoke in the morning, he walked down to the Oconoluftee River to wash his face in the cold water. He was looking down at the rounded rocks through the clear stream when something caught his eye. He saw a long cylindrical rock that had obviously been used in ancient times as a tool. He lifted the stone into the air to examine it. Its handle end fit perfectly in Perry's hand. Thinking that it could have been used as a grinding stone for corn, Perry took it to Walker Calhoun, a respected traditionalist of the Eastern Band. Calhoun said that such a grinding stone would not have been used for corn. This was an old stone used by a healer to grind medicinal herbs. He went on to say that Perry was meant to have it, and that it was sent to him by the "Old People." Walker told Perry that someday, maybe even in another state, the stone bowl that goes with the grinding stone will come into his hands.

Perry VanBuskirk

The Twins

This story took place in the Rocky Ford community, back in the 1920s. A Cherokee family lived there near a spring where they got drinking water. Two of their children were twin girls about six or seven years old. One night in midwinter, the family was hosting a gospel singing at their house and needed some fresh water. The twins were sent to the spring with a bucket.

The family began to worry when the girls did not come back. They were just about to go out searching when the two little ones returned with the water bucket. Although it was the middle of winter, their bucket was filled with beautiful, fresh-cut flowers. An old woman who came for the singing warned the family, "Don't let them talk for four days."

But the girls would not keep quiet. They began to talk at once about how they had played that night with the Little People. They told what the Little People had showed them, and where they had taken them. On the fourth day, both twin girls died.

A lot of people believe that if you see one of the Little People, you must not say anything about it for four days.

Pat Moss

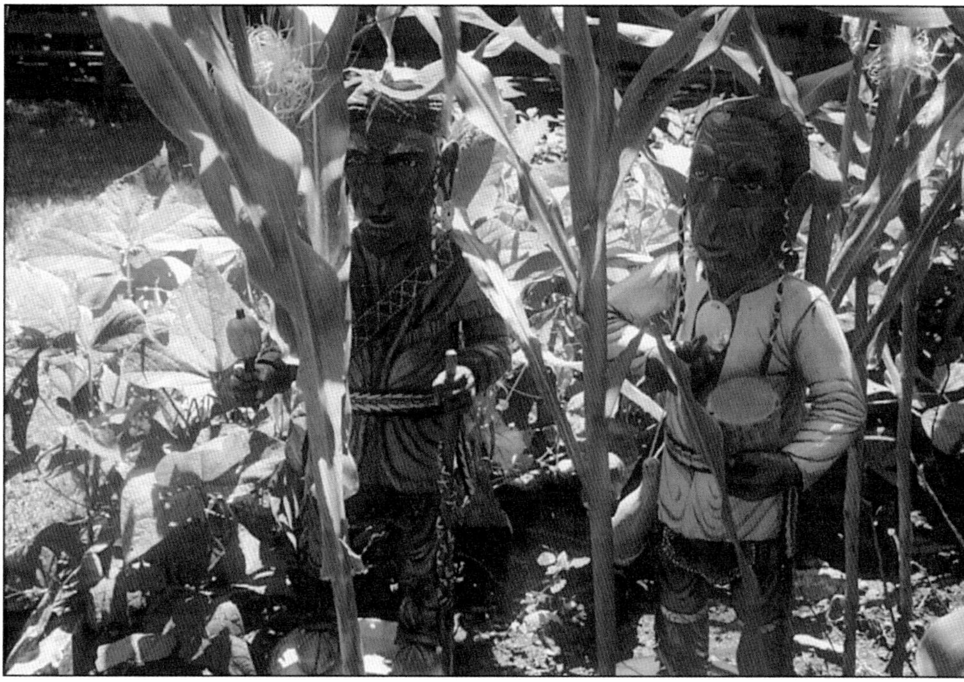

Little People. (Carvings by Dean Cheek, Photo by Murv Jacob.)

Julius and the Little People

Julius Smith was originally enrolled during the Dawes Commission. His daughter Sioux remembers him as "the most connected eighth-blood Cherokee you would ever want to meet. His demeanor was so unassuming and he thought things out before he spoke. He always had good things to say or he said nothing at all. He was a big man, 6-foot, 2-inches, and weighed 210 pounds. He had large hands that were so stern when we disobeyed, yet so tender, especially when we were ill or needed the sashes tied on our dresses."

Julius used to tell his children stories about the old times when he lived on his family's allotted land near Porum, Oklahoma. He, along with his siblings and parents, worked at the Vann Ranch during the day and at their own farm in the evenings, feeding and milking the cows. Julius said he sometimes resented having so much work to do when he really wanted to play.

On one occasion, Julius' mother asked him to go out and pick some apples. He grudging took the two baskets from her and walked slowly toward the orchard, kicking at clods of dirt on the way. He remembers sitting down beneath a tree and thinking about playing games and fishing, anything except picking apples. Then Julius began to hear voices nearby snickering and giggling. He expected to find that his brothers and sisters had followed and caught him daydreaming. But the voices came from above. Julius looked up to see two or three "little people" sitting on a limb. He said then that he guessed he dozed off for a while, because when he woke up he was still sitting beneath the tree. All around Julius were little piles of apples waiting to go into his baskets. He never told his family the story until he and his brothers and sisters were grown.

Sioux Nell Vann Smith

Bob and the Hummingbird.

Robert Rucker, a member of the Milam family of Cherokees, enjoys feeding the wildlife in his back yard. Numerous species visit the large feeders he keeps filled for both birds and squirrels. Bob relayed this story of his encounter with a tiny hummingbird.

One day Bob stepped onto his back covered porch and noticed a hummingbird caught in a thick cobweb near the roof. Very carefully, he pulled the little creature free and held it in his hand. He saw that the bird was weak and had probably been caught in the web all night. He held it close to the hummingbird feeder while it drank its fill.

Bob could see that the bird was still struggling with sticky webs caught in its wings. He brushed the strands away, opening his palm out flat so that the bird could fly. Bob watched as the hummingbird rose slightly, hovering just above his palm. Its wings were beating so quickly they were invisible. Then it landed back on his hand. It tested its wings in this manner a couple more times.

Then a wonderful thing happened. The hummingbird used its long beak to pull out a feather from beneath its wing. This the bird laid in Bob's hand. According to Cherokee traditionalist Pat Moss, that is how you get a hummingbird feather...it has to be given to you. If a person happens to receive one, he or she can be assured that the bird itself allowed it.

Strong again, the little hummingbird flew away, leaving Bob with its gift. This story is a treasure he shares with his many friends, who, knowing Bob, believe every word.

Bob Rucker

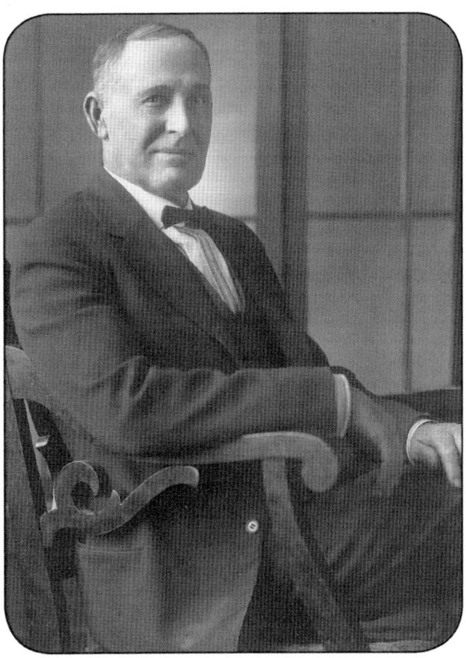

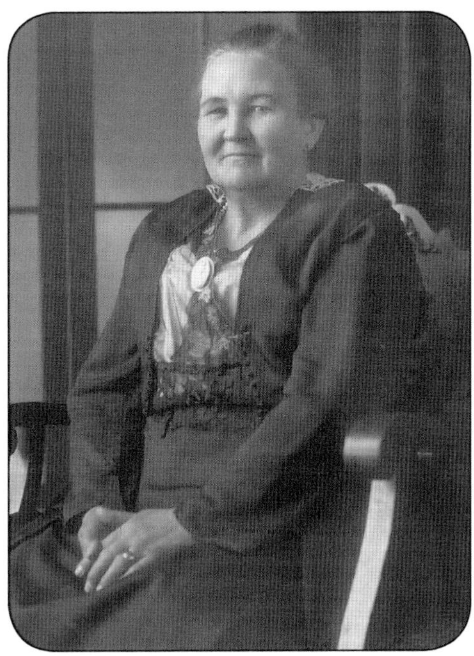

William Guinn Milam and Sarah Ellen Couch Milan, Robert Rucker's Grandparents. Their Son, Jesse Bartley Milam, Served as Principal Chief.